Popular Science

LEISURE HOMES

by Alfred W. Lees
with Ernest V. Heyn

POPULAR SCIENCE BOOKS

 VAN NOSTRAND REINHOLD COMPANY
New York Cincinnati Toronto London Melbourne

Library of Congress Catalog Card Number: 79-4709
ISBN: 0-442-21263-1

Manufactured in the United States of America

Contents

Preface   v
Introduction   vii

Part One: Choosing Your House Plan

1. **Sleek Custom Homes   3**
   Biosphere   4
   Underground Solar House   8
   Sun Trap   12

2. **Unusual Design Concepts   17**
   Atrium House Built in Stages   18
   Four-Module Pinwheel   22
   High-Security Weekend
      Retreat   26
   Two-Phase Contemporary   30
   One-Room Leisure Home Sleeps
      Ten   34

3. **Homes for Family Comfort   39**
   Suncrest: Passive Solar Plus   40
   Skewed-Prow Two-Story   44
   Multi-Level Lodge   48
   Sky Vista with Stacked
      Bedrooms   52
   Modified Saltbox   56
   Expandable Retreat   60
   Two-Phase Split Pavilions   64
   Fireproof Retreat   68

4. **Energy-Efficient Homes for the Do-it-
   Yourselfer   71**
   Six-Way House   72
   Energy-Saver   74
   Gambrel Frame   78
   Sun Cottage with Garage   82
   Gambrel with a Solar Wall   84
   Vertical House with Sun Deck   88
   Hexagon House that Grows   90
   Peak House on Stilts   94
   King-Post Pagoda   96
   Upside-Down Retreat   98
   The Sun-Seeker   100

5. **Far-Out Shapes   103**
   Holiday Hill for Entertaining   104
   Engelframe Towable   108
   Cruciform House   110
   Stilt House (Apache)   112
   Twin Prow Split Level   114
   Two-Phase Twin Ridge   116
   Arrowhead Retreat   120

Octagon House for Tight
    Perch   122
Bridge House for Small
    Stream   124
Stretched Hex (Omaha)   126
Lean-to House   128
Round House on a Pedestal   130
Split Gable with Privacy
    Offset   132
Stacked Shack   134
Double-Decker Salt Marsh   136
Bunk Tower: Rooms with a
    View   138

Arrowhead Lodge (Akanu)   140
Stilt House Stacks Two Ways   142
Two-Story Sleep Wing   144

6. **Potpourri of Special Shelters   147**
    All-Metal Solar Wedge   148
    Tent Cabin   152
    Frame-Hung Dome   156
    RV Chalet   164
    Cool House for a Hot Climate   168
    Leisure Homes from Catalog
        Components   178

7. **Ordering Information for All House
    Plans   188**

Part Two: **The Popular Science Lockbox House**

1. Erecting the Pole-and-Beam Skeleton (with complete plans)   194
2. The Lockbox Spreads Its Wings   220
3. Two Unique Roofing Systems   227
4. Closing the Lockbox   238
5. Shutter Deck and Entry Door Complete the Closure   253
6. Tie a Spiral Stair to Exposed-Joist Flooring   264
7. Ceilings Float in Invisible Grids   270
8. How We Laid the Vinyl Floor Coverings   275
9. A Fireplace for the Lockbox   278
10. Action Built-ins for the Bedrooms   284
11. The Open Kitchen: Ideal for a Leisure Home   295
12. Build a Dining Divider for the Open Kitchen   302
13. Radiant Panel: Versatile Install-Yourself Heat   308
14. Freeze-Proof Waterline You Don't
    Have to Bury Below Frost   313
15. Aerobics: The Waste System for Leisure Homes   320
16. Security Electronics for Leisure Homes   325
17. Beefing Up Your Burglary Protection   331
    Bibliography   341
    Information Sources   342

Preface

The leisure home has changed the lives of hundreds of thousands of American families by offering a practical and economical escape from the bustling world, which, as the poet warned, "is too much with us." This book is dedicated to that escape. It offers a wide variety of houses you can build—or have built—at reasonable cost, thereby opening new vistas of greater enjoyment and relaxation for you and your family.

Alfred W. Lees, my collaborator on this book, developed the idea of a leisure-home series with the editor-in-chief of *Popular Science* magazine, Hubert Luckett. In their May 1972 issue they introduced the Lockbox House, which was designed by architect Lester Walker and built by Al Lees himself. (Al has more to tell you about the birth of this project in the introduction that follows.) The many features and innovations of the Lockbox appeared in seventeen subsequent issues; all this material has been updated and included in this book. The series was so successful (the build-it-yourself plans offered in those articles quickly sold out) that Hugh Luckett and Al Lees have continued to present in their pages superb renderings by fine artists of other leisure-home designs, together with floorplans, descriptions of the houses, and instructions for buying complete construction plans from the master architects who created the homes. We've now gathered this wealth of material into a single volume.

A note on the structure of this book: We've put the chicken before the egg by presenting our portfolio of leisure-home designs in Part One, followed by the Lockbox saga in Part Two. The logic to this sequence? Once you've chosen the house that's right for you (and your site), you'll want to trace the progress of someone who's *been* the whole route of do-it-yourself construction, and has lived to tell of the joys (many) and sorrows (a few) of leisure-home ownership. This way, you can evaluate exactly which of Al Lees' experiences apply to the house you've selected. If you've already decided you want to build the Lockbox itself, treat Part Two as your complete instruction kit:

it contains every article the magazine ever printed on this project, updated and expanded, plus all the working drawings originally sold as a plan set.

The fifty-plus houses reproduced in Part One were designed for Al Lees by these architects: Alfredo De Vido, Robert Martin Engelbrecht, Marc Harrison, Jeff Milstein, Samuel Paul, Ralph Rittenour (and associates), Lester Walker, and William Ward. And there are special projects here by George Bunzer and Robert Gannon. Thanks to all these sources, you are able to secure reasonably priced plans for the home of your choice. Complete ordering instructions—including addresses and prices—will be found beginning on page 188. (Remember, the publisher of this book does not fill orders for building plans. You order direct from the architect.) A bibliography of helpful books on house building begins on page 341, followed by a list of information sources.

I am indebted to Robert H. Dougherty for his wise advice, which appeared in the first "Vacation Homes—Plans and Products Guide" published by the V-Pac Council. "The design you select," he writes, "must be of ample size to suit your present family—plus having provisions for expansion or additions, if required . . . your site should be kept in mind when considering designs . . . plan to retain the natural qualities of the land and create a setting that can be easily cared for . . . the chosen house design should blend into that setting . . . orient the house for the best view and protection from the elements." He also advises that all your building plans should be checked with a local builder where your house is to be, or by the building department of the local government.

Needless to say you should be informed about local codes and regulations and obtain the necessary permits. Financial details about a mortgage and/or loan should be checked carefully with a trusted officer of the bank where you live or in the area where you plan to build your leisure home.

I cannot close this brief preface without

sharing my thoughts on the economic conditions which exist as I write this and which may continue a long time in the future. I refer especially to the problems of gas prices and availability. *Popular Science* magazine devotes many pages, besides those on leisure homes, to current developments in energy and transportation. I would advise any reader who plans a leisure home to consider carefully its distance from his permanent residence. I suggest he estimate that distance in relation to gasoline or other fuel required to make a round trip without a refill, perhaps 100 to 150 miles.

And a word about buying your plans. Once you have selected your favorite house, I suggest you decide whether you are "shopping around" or whether you have settled definitely on this specific design. It's more economical to take advantage of the reduced price for several sets of plans rather than one. Eventually, if you go ahead with building, you will probably need one set of plans for yourself, another for your contractor or subcontractor, one for your bank or other source of financing, one to secure your building permit, and one that can be shared by your electrician and plumber. If you are still at the dreaming stage, however, a single set will suffice.

You may be surprised at the broad range of prices from the various sources. Our sources don't necessarily offer comparable plan packages, and we asked them to price accordingly. That old merchandising truism applies in most cases here: You get what you pay for. The more expensive packages tend to be more complete, with more detailed information on the specific house you're ordering. The less costly packages often contain less (and more generalized) data. All packages, however, will contain all the basic dimensions and information required to build the house.

One way to save money is to build your house yourself. Generally the restrictions on leisure-home construction are less stringent than those for primary housing; and your source of financing may well give you the benefit of "sweat equity," since you are backing your commitment with the special no-cost value that accrues from hard work—the sweat of your brow!

Before my retirement as editor-in-chief of *Popular Science* magazine, I paid close attention to our regular monthly surveys which report readers' preferences and reactions to all the features in each issue of the magazine. So I was especially delighted to learn that the highest readership score of any feature in a recent issue of the magazine (December, 1978) was won by Alfredo De Vido's Underground Solar House, which you'll find on page 8 of this book.

When I first proposed the idea of a book on leisure homes to Lees, Luckett and our publisher, I knew we had a mighty popular feature of the magazine to transpose into book form, and that vote of the readers confirms my faith beyond my fondest expectations. I hope you will give the houses offered in this book a similarly favorable vote, and will be able to select a dream house for yourself and your family.

And now, I turn you over to the man who not only planned and built his own Lockbox House but also masterminded and wrote the whole series of leisure-home articles which followed it. Here's *Popular Science's* group editor, in charge of reader activities, Alfred W. Lees, to fill you in on all the nitty-gritty details of his adventure in house building.

ERNEST V. HEYN
Westport, Connecticut

Introduction

Until you've sunk your heart in a plot of wilderness . . . Until you've tramped each square yard of it to choose the perfect site for the home you'll erect on it . . . Until you've watched that structure grow out of ground you've chosen to plant it in, reaching up and out like a sturdy, sheltering tree . . . Until you've circled the completed house in slow awe, not able to accept, quite yet, that this is all your doing (*your* choice of house on *your* choice of site) . . . Until you've rewarded yourself with a hot shower in that house and a good meal from its kitchen, and have settled into a night's noiseless rest with the special peace that comes from being under a roof you put there . . . you haven't relished one of America's great adventures.

I've spent virtually every weekend of the past seven years at the Lockbox House you'll find me erecting on a Pennsylvania mountainside, in Part Two of this book. I've known all the pleasures (plus a few of the griefs) of leisure-home living, and if you're contemplating a similar venture—as your purchase of this book suggests—I can't recommend it highly enough.

And now's the time to confirm your intention—while there's still choice property within feasible distance of your primary home; and before building materials spiral right up out of reach. This book is designed to help you make decisions you can spend the rest of your life with, mellowing along with a house that's ideal for your site and your lifestyle.

I didn't have the luxury of either contemplative time nor much helpful literature when I—almost inadvertently—propelled myself into this life-time commitment, back in the early 1970s. My collaborator on this book, Ernie Heyn, was instrumental in launching the Lockbox project. I had been searching for wild country property for some months—not an easy task when your commuting base is Manhattan. When I at last found my ideal plot in Pennsylvania, I proposed to the editorial executives of *Popular Science* that I work with an imaginative young architect to develop a truly unique leisure retreat for an "unbuildable

site." Ernie Heyn, at that time about to retire as editor-in-chief, endorsed the project, and the planning began.

It is no easy task to design a house that a novice—without prior carpentry experience—can build, and at the same time create a house with universal appeal; a house that can be adapted to virtually any type of site, yet has clean, contemporary lines, and is demonstrably practical for its special purpose. But after many design revisions and several scale models, architect Lester Walker, co-builder Ron Nelson and I were satisfied that we'd packed a dramatic statement into our snug cube, and were ready to start building.

Architect Walker (who had no more experience with pole construction than I) underestimated the problems of securing delivery of properly treated poles, and of getting them erected and tied together with the basic beam skeleton. He predicted our modest crew of non-professionals could have this done in a week. Alas, it was two months before this cage stood on our forested mountainside.

It was then that H. P. Luckett (who had just succeeded Heyn as editor-in-chief) dropped the bomb.

"Al," this tall Texan said to me in a *Popular Science* corridor one late autumn day in 1971, "we need your leisure home for our 100th Anniversary issue next May. Everything about this issue has to be special—including the projects."

"But, Lucky," I stammered, "it's just not possible! Snow's about due at the site, and we're not even under cover. When I proposed this project for future publication, I meant it as a long-term thing. We're only working weekends, you know, to demonstrate the feasibility of 'spare-time' construction. It'll take a *year* to have a house to photograph."

"Editorial deadline for the Centennial issue is February 15," Luckett replied loftily. "I know you'll do the best you can." Subject closed.

And thus did the Lockbox greet a waiting world in the now-legendary 100th Anniversary issue of May 1972. We had to present it in artist's renderings, since the lead photo was only able to show our pole-and-beam cage rising from a snowy mountainside. That first article is reproduced in a revised version as the first chapter of this book's Part Two.

The Lockbox story was snugged between a Hexa-Pent Dome we'd commissioned from Bucky Fuller, and articles by Barry Commoner, Wernher von Braun, Edward Teller and Nobel-prize inventors Charles Townes, Dennis Gabor and William Shockley. My project was auspiciously launched.

At that time, none of us suspected it would grow into so major an editorial project that nineteen feature articles on it would spread over the next seven years. Nor did we yet anticipate that the popularity of the project (at its peak of publication throughout 1974, the Lockbox was the widest-known owner-built home in America; articles on it also appeared in hundreds of newspapers, coast-to-coast) would spawn the *Popular Science* Leisure Home Series—the collection of unique vacation houses from top designers that fills the first section of this book.

The enthusiastic reception of the initial Lockbox series led me to lend a sympathetic ear to architect Robert Martin Engelbrecht when, late in 1972, he proposed to create a series of homes for us on behalf of his V-PAC Council, an informal group (mostly building materials manufacturers) formed to promote quality leisure-home designs. Editor-in-chief Luckett and I discussed the proposal with Bob Engelbrecht at some length, stressing that these houses should be out-of-the-ordinary. We didn't want commonplace vacation-home styles—A-frames and Tyrolean chalets—that were readily available from other sources. Each house in the *Popular Science* Leisure Home Series should be characterized by at least one novel, unexpected element—something that justified its appearance in the What's New Magazine.

Popular Science had never before ventured into house design—the Lockbox was the first set of construction plans it had sold to readers. We never considered that it was our role to offer plans for primary housing. The design of such houses is restricted by the necessity to conform to neighborhood cohesion. It's only when a home is relatively isolated that it is truly free to assert itself—not without due regard for its setting, of course, since any retreat should be at home with nature—but without conventional restraints. Most owner-builders of leisure homes look for novel, innovative design—and that's what we set out to bring them.

Those initial policies have shaped my selection to this day. Our philosophy remains that, of all single-family structures, leisure homes provide the best opportunities for individual expression, unfettered by restrictive codes and the more subtle controls of "appropriateness." Most of us wouldn't be comfortable imposing a geodesic dome on a neighborhood of conventional houses, even if local codes and financing would permit it. We tend to trot with the herd in wanting our "home in town" to look pretty much like our neighbors'. But set us loose in the country and the shackles fall away.

As other architects and plans sources sought us out, we set the same goal: Give us your most original designs. And that is why the collection in this book is unique. Every house we present here sports at least one unusual feature—an octagonal floorplan, perhaps, or an offset roof ridge. There's not a commonplace house in the batch, and you'll find no such collection elsewhere.

A few of these houses may have appeared in other publications or catalogs, although at the time *Popular Science* first presented them, each house was exclusive with us. That has always been our understanding with the architects who bring us their work: Once the design has appeared in *Popular Science*, they are free to promote it elsewhere. Any architect has a heavy investment in any set of plans he or his staff prepares, and we encourage our sources to find the widest possible market for their homes after we've introduced them.

Since our designs aren't standard and may call for unusual construction techniques (as many homes in this book do), you can't count on local contractors knowing what to do without detailed instructions—in case you don't want to tackle construction yourself, or need help if you do. So from the start we've insisted that plans be available for every house we published, and we've adhered to that policy in this book. I urge you not to try a shortcut by launching out on your own in hopes of building from the limited information given in this book. Nor is it wise to take this scant data to a local builder; these are unusual houses and only their architects can tell you how they go together. (Exceptions to all this are the five Jersey Devil homes in Chapter 6, for which no plans exist, and the Lockbox, for which complete construction details are given in Part Two's opening chapter.)

It's been a particular joy collecting these designs over the past few years. Though the Leisure Home Series is only one of my many editorial responsibilities at *Popular Science*, I suppose it has become my favorite "chore." This is partly because it has corresponded with my own leisure-home adventure at the Lockbox, which has given me a deep personal identification with the impulse toward and pleasure in this very special leisure activity. But, also, the series has brought me into close association with a group of notably creative men—the architects whose homes form our collection.

Hearing their proposals, exploring their design philosophies, offering suggestions, learning how past plans sold—these considerations have occupied many pleasurable lunches over the years, and I'm glad to have this opportunity to pay tribute to these men, each of whom I count as friend. Let me salute them, individually and collectively, with a lift of my inevitable bourbon-manhattan-on-the-rocks. Surprisingly, they have not met each other, and might not find too much in common if they did, for each has his own style and approach to leisure-home design. It has been my privilege to be the common point toward which their talents flow.

Architects are independent types; you just don't expect them to conform to a basic set of procedures. (That's one reason there's such diversity and creative range to the houses in this book.) Why, you'll even find some of their terms spelled inconsistently: "clerestory" and "clearstory" both mean the same thing: windows above an adjacent roof, for high-level light and ventilation. We've made no attempt to banish individuality, herein.

Since this is largely a picture book, I think a nod is due to the architectural renderers whose work is cataloged here. Though their styles vary widely, these artists share the unique talent of being able to bring flat floorplans and elevations to three-dimensional life—both outdoors (in an enticing setting) and indoors (with appropriate furnishings). If you've ever attempted to visualize a house from a set of plans—or better still, tried to roughsketch, from the working drawings, how it would look—you can appreciate the skill with which the men represented here have done their jobs. Since renderings are most accurate when the artist works closely with the architect, I've always encouraged each architect to select his own renderer. Note how consistently each has worked with his chosen artist, within the various chapter groupings of Part One. (These artists are identified in the chapter introductions.)

A word of appreciation, too, for that finest of how-to draftsmen, Carl De Groote, who did all the original drawings and plans for the Lockbox series, and who has adapted them so skillfully for this book.

My collaborator has noted in his Preface that I'm the author of what follows—but there are several exceptions: In Part One, two of the house descriptions are separately credited. You'll see why when you read them: These texts are personal experiences by the builder (or—in the exotic case of the Cool House—the not-*yet* builder). For the record, I should also mention that in two cases where I was out of the office when inexorable copy deadlines rolled around, staff colleagues Elaine Smay and Rich Stepler provided the original text adapted here. Finally, my collaborator has relieved me of some of the editorial burden by augmenting my original texts for a number of the houses that originally appeared with too scant a description for presentation here.

The house that started all this—the Lockbox—is the only design in this book that I'm qualified to tell you how to build. Since *Popular Science* collaborated in this design, and constructed the house for publication, we did, in this instance, prepare and sell complete construction plans. And since these plans have never been available from another source (our original printing quickly sold out), it was essential that we include them here, assuring any reader of this book access to plans for every house featured herein. You'll find them in the first chapter of Part Two.

We simply took the original sheets of construction plans and converted them into book-page-sized elements, altering and updating them to conform to our actual construction procedures. The plans were unique to start with, since we never took the conventional blueprint approach. We were assuming that the Lockbox would be the first—and doubtless only—house the plans purchaser would ever build, so we treated it as a *project* and developed the plans in the same way we would for a piece of furniture. We've been told by many builders that our original plans sheets were the easiest-to-follow house plans they'd ever worked with—and we've now restudied and improved them for this book. Nothing has been excluded: You can duplicate our Lockbox from the working drawings in this book; no additional instructions are available or necessary.

To my partner in my own leisure-home adventure—co-builder Ronald Nelson—this book is gratefully dedicated. He is living (if aching) proof that you need no prior construction skills to erect a successful and original house; and neither the Lockbox nor this book would exist without his invaluable help.

ALFRED WM. LEES
The Lockbox,
Shadowglen, Pennsylvania

PART ONE

CHOOSING YOUR HOUSE PLAN

1. SLEEK CUSTOM HOMES

Alfredo De Vido (AIA) brought us his first proposal for our series in 1976. He was already widely known for several sleek custom homes for well-to-do clients commuting to New York City. His work had been heralded in the *New York Times* and *House & Garden*, and by various architectural awards. His first home for *Popular Science*—the Sun Trap—won two government grants in HUD's Passive Solar Residential Design Competition, conducted in co-operation with the Dept. of Energy and Solar Energy Research Institute.

De Vido's renderer is Bill Phillips, whose Architectural Illustrations office is in Wisconsin; all of their communication is by mail. Since De Vido's designs are complex and unexpected, it's always a joyous surprise to see how expertly the floorplans, elevations and section sketches are brought to three-dimensional life by Phillips, who works in ink line and watercolor.

For ordering information on this group of plans, see page 188.

Biosphere

It's a live-in greenhouse with an indoor solar pond complete with waterfall. Dream stuff? No: There's not an element of this stunning house that you can't duplicate with today's materials and technology. When award-winning architect Alfredo De Vido first proposed the idea to us, we specified that construction should be kept within the skills of our advanced do-it-yourselfers. De Vido confirms that he's met this stipulation by offering low-cost building plans for the project (see page 196), though you'd be wise to seek professional help with erection of the supporting tubular steel frame and installation of those large, unmullioned expanses of glass.

To name the house, De Vido uses the term Biosphere in its newly expanded sense of a self-supportive living unit—a microcosmic ecosystem where a family can live as independent of external supports as is comfortably feasible.

The entire south face of the house is a solar membrane that capitalizes on the "greenhouse effect" to trap the sun's radiation. This section can be closed from the rest of the house (by means of internal glass walls) to avoid excessive temperature swings. Within the enclosed space are thermal masses to retain heat: brick-floor terraces and masonry retaining walls (over which the solar pond spills its recirculating waterfall).

Heated air from the greenhouse can be moved through the house or directed to a

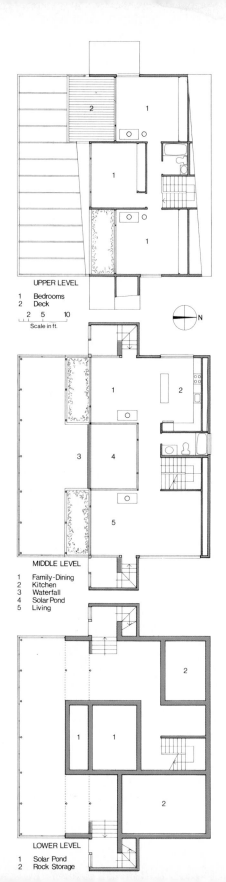

UPPER LEVEL

1 Bedrooms
2 Deck

2 5 10
Scale in ft.

N

MIDDLE LEVEL

1 Family-Dining
2 Kitchen
3 Waterfall
4 Solar Pond
5 Living

LOWER LEVEL

1 Solar Pond
2 Rock Storage

Bill Phillips

rock storage bin. "The entire enclosure," De Vido points out, "serves as an inhabitable active collector."

The same duct system that circulates air through the storage rocks provides summer venting by siphoning off heat at the top of the house. By isolating the greenhouse in hot summer weather, you can cool the rock storage at night so the house can draw on this cooling capacity during the day. In most climate zones where leisure homes are built, this would let you omit standard air conditioning.

As for the live-in greenhouse—planting areas are scattered. The main vegetable plots are at three levels: ground for cool-loving plants such as salad greens and radishes, middle for peas and beans, high for heat-loving tomatoes, cucumbers, and peppers. (Our artist took the liberty of planting some tomatoes at the livingroom level.) The terrace-wall planters are ideal for spinach and strawberries; the north wall can be used for climbing plants. And there's a heat chamber under the lowest

level, for starting seedlings. The pond—which might be a rainwater cistern—can be used for irrigation or fish culture.

Four strategically placed, high-efficiency wood stoves let you heat each space individually. Collectors for domestic hot water are placed at each end of the roof ridge so they can't be shaded by the housings for chimneys and air vents.

The western bedroom has its own private terrace for sunbathing. The other two overlook the greenhouse—and any view beyond the dual glazing. For improved traffic flow between ground floor and living level, there are boxed stairways at both ends of the house, as well as the

three-level stair in the center. These stairway sheds are large enough to double as storage enclosures for outdoor gear. They also serve as the main entries to the house; if the site doesn't lend itself to the double entry, one of the sheds can be omitted.

Ideally, the windowless north wall would be dug into a hillside, but on a flat site like the one in our rendering, earth is bermed against that wall and along the sidewalls up to the entry sheds. The north slope should be densely planted with evergreens, to serve as a windbreak. This berm is pierced vertically by an outside vent with a weather cap. It's represented

Dampers and fans direct air flow six ways for heating and cooling

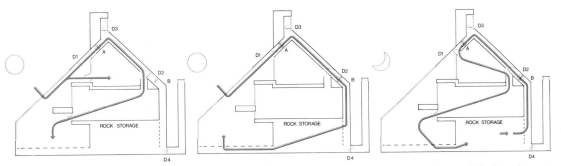

1. Greenhouse to House Heat: Fan A operates, damper D1 open to greenhouse, D2 closed to storage, D3 & D4 closed. Fan A operates. Air circulates from greenhouse through house. **2. Greenhouse to Storage:** D1 & D2 open to storage duct, closed to house. D3 & D4 closed. Fans A & B operate. **3. Storage to House Heating:** D1 closes greenhouse side; opens house side. D2 in neutral position, leaving both inter-level & storage chases open. Dampers D3 and D4 closed, fans A & B operate. Stored air supply to house, return air from house to greenhouse.

in the airflow diagrams, connected directly to the rock bin.

The two bathrooms are stacked for economical plumbing runs. The kitchen (adjacent to the lower bath) is the open type that permits anyone involved in food preparation to maintain direct social contact. This can be an area of real shared activity, with dinner guests harvesting peas or beans from the "hanging garden," then passing the produce across

the island counter for cooking. You can't serve vegetables fresher than that!

The architect has omitted all furniture from his floorplans to encourage truly personal arrangements.

The solar pond is compartmented for two depths—the major eight-foot-deep section and the half-depth basin into which the waterfall overflows. The rock storage is also split into two areas (see ground-level plan).

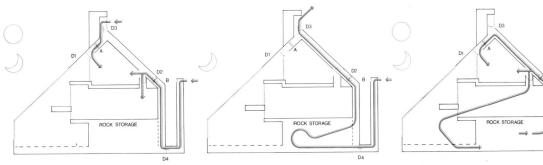

4. Outdoor-Air House Cooling
D3 & D4 open, D1 closed to greenhouse, D2 completely open, fans A & B operating.

5. Storage Purge-Cooling
D2 & D3 open to storage area. D4 open to let cool night air into rock storage. Fan B on, night air cools rocks.

6. Storage to House Cooling
D3 & D4 closed, D1 closed to greenhouse, D2 open completely. House air to storage & back.

7

Underground Solar House

Bill Phillips

The many advantages of an underground house can be especially pertinent if you're building a leisure home. First, you can be sure your house won't substantially alter the appearance of your site.

Then you have the practical advantages: In winter, your fuel bill will be dramatically reduced because the surrounding earth minimizes heat loss. In summer, the cool earth will keep you comfortable with little or no air conditioning.

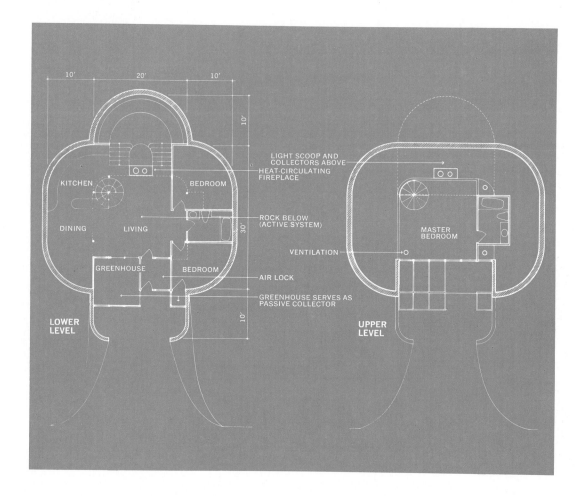

Outside maintenance is minimized. And if your site is a bit too close to a railroad or highway, you'll appreciate the quiet and privacy afforded.

Our solar-heated underground leisure home has some of the same features as the Sun Trap house which follows, and the Biosphere just discussed, but in most ways it is unique. Its brick shell, curved for strength against the massive earth pressure, is shown nestled into a steep hillside. But on flatter terrain, the house could be built on the surface and bermed

with earth after completion. The vaulted walls are of corbeled masonry, which should be within the skills of an experienced mason.

Three tiers of south-facing windows—about 300 square feet in all—bring light and solar heat into the house. The first tier shelters a greenhouse (actually two; the space to the right of the air-lock entry is also a small greenhouse). The second tier rims the south edge of the loft-style master bedroom. These windows can be double glazed or made of Beadwall for heat conservation. (For an explanation of Beadwall, see final paragraph of the Sun Trap text.) The third tier of windows caps a snorkle-shape light scoop, which directs light into the back of the house. Its curving surface can be lined with Mylar to amplify the effect. Automatic aluminum-clad louvers called Skylids insulate these windows.

Above the house is a hot-air solar collector, which provides the domestic hot water and additional space heat. It is ducted to a rock storage bed beneath the floor of the house. Both should be designed to suit your family and climate. A free-standing high-efficiency fireplace supplements the solar heat.

The house is carefully waterproofed, ringed with drain tiles, and backfilled with gravel. Wind-driven ventilators and a dehumidifier keep the interior comfortable even in humid summer weather. The walls are insulated on the *outside* with 2-inch Styrofoam. Thus the thermal mass of the masonry can be used for heat storage.

This house is engineered to withstand considerable earth pressures, so it may cost more to build than a conventional house, depending upon your building site. But with fuel and maintenance savings, you should recover a higher initial cost in a reasonable number of years.

An interesting aspect of the Underground Solar House is that in the monthly readership survey of *Popular Science* magazine it ranked first of all the features which appeared in the same issue.

Sun Trap

Bill Phillips

"How come," runs a typical letter about the plans that initially appeared as a leisure-home series in *Popular Science* magazine, "you don't incorporate major energy-conscious systems?" Or: "Why not ask an architect to design a solar vacation home from the ground up?"

"Plan a passive solar house for us," we said to architect Al De Vido, "with elements that serve as their *own* collectors, so you don't need elaborate systems."

The house that meets all these requirements turns out to be as delightful inside as outside. It's a tight 900-square-foot

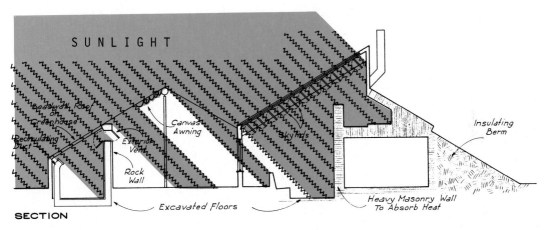

Each element soaks up sun a different way. Glass-roof house has pivoting louvers that let rays strike central masonry wall; at night, louvers close to prevent heat loss. Greenhouse section (left) does much the same with Beadwall roof.

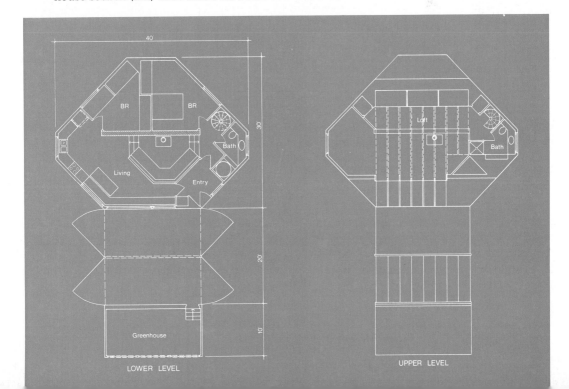

structure to be sited as near due south as possible to expose maximum wall and roof surface to the sun. Its windowless north wall prows into an insulating berm formed with earth excavated from the sunken seating area around the fireplace. This brick-paved recess traps radiant heat from the fireplace, which is a circulating type with its metal liner left exposed.

The glass roof over this living area focuses the sun on a masonry wall (stuccoed concrete block in our rendering but it could be native stone) that retains the heat and reradiates it during the night. An automatic louver system (the commercial name: Skylids) closes off this glass at night to conserve the stored energy. (The louvers can also be closed to block unwanted heat gain in summer.) An airlock entry prevents drafts and heat loss.

Adjacent to the entry wall is a versatile patio area with corral-type gates that swing open to summer breezes but close to trap the sun the rest of the year. They double as privacy screens for sunbathing or patio entertaining. Supported by the gateposts is an adjustable canvas awning.

Closing this area to the south is a greenhouse with an insulating fiberglass roof operating on the Beadwall principle: Opaque plastic-foam beads are sucked in and out between the double glazing (they store in a tank inside the greenhouse). The sun heats a pebble wall during the day, and this heat is recirculated at night by means of an underground duct and a small fan.

2. UNUSUAL DESIGN CONCEPTS

William J. Ward, Jr. (AIA) was for many years one of two partners heading the prestigious architectural graphics firm, Sigman-Ward, whose technical and construction drawings appeared regularly in *Popular Science* and many other national magazines. When the partnership was dissolved, Ward found the prospect of retirement irksome and remains actively involved with such publications as *Colonial Homes*. Ward lives in a north New Jersey suburb. As an architect, he publishes exclusively with *Popular Science*, and also designs for private clients. His renderer is a robustly independent fellow-Jerseyite, Carl R. Kinscherf, who is a master of opaque wash technique.

For ordering information on this group of house plans, see chart on page 188. A mail-order office called Idea Enterprises handles the sale of all Ward plans except the first house he did for us—the One-Room Sleeps Ten; for this home, order through V-PAC (address in same chart).

Atrium House Built in Stages

The Atrium house can be built in stages, as budget and time allows. We wanted an initial stage that—for a modest investment—would offer all amenities, but would lend itself to expansion as family size (and income) increases. The architect devised stages that wrap themselves around a central atrium—an approach we find intriguing enough to recommend for primary housing as well.

But it could prove particularly appropriate for a leisure-home site. Just suppose: When you buy your plot, nobody's yet built on lots to your left or behind, so you face the first-stage L that way and

enjoy a sheltered patio in the corner. Then, as your development grows and neighbors press in, your house additions solve both your space and your privacy problems: Add two bedrooms and you've created a U that screens the patio from three sides. If someone then builds on your open side, you simply complete the atrium with an arcade and a shingled wall that can later become a structural part of the final cabin wing. And you end up with a gracious privacy core.

The *utility* core remains the same from the start, so if you plan to go the full distance, you may want to overscale the washer/drier, furnace, and water heater to accommodate the maximum number of occupants these appliances will eventually serve. An exception: That cabin wing would have its own heat.

Note that the second bath is private to the master bedroom. The original bathroom then serves the house itself and any later bedrooms.

The atrium has been part of domestic architecture from early Roman times. At first it was the central room, with a hearth and a smoke hole in the roof. As the floorplan got more sophisticated, a more formal kitchen appeared and the hearth was moved there. The atrium took on aspects of an unroofed court, often with a surrounding colonnade. It became the center of family life—as ours will.

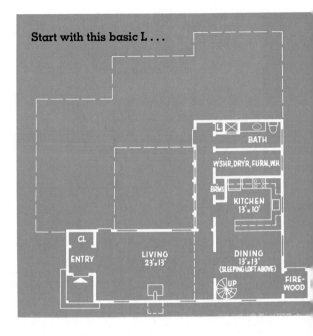

Start with this basic L . . .

BATH

W.SHR, DRYR, FURN, W.H.

BRMS

KITCHEN
13' x 10'

CL

ENTRY

LIVING
23' x 13'

DINING
13' x 13'
(SLEEPING LOFT ABOVE)

UP

FIRE-
WOOD

It's a two-story house where basic L turns corner: This sleeping loft is tucked in peak over dining area, and becomes a study or hobby space when bedrooms are added. Exposed rafters and tie beams add to rustic charm of living room.

. . . add a master bedroom and bath

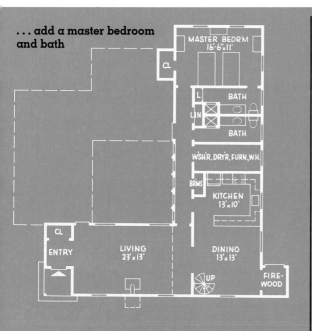

. . . tack on a second bedroom

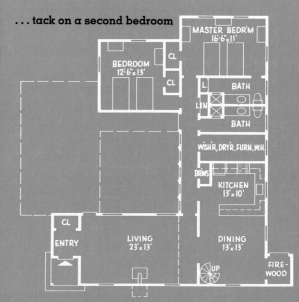

. . . erect a privacy wall to close the atrium

. . . and complete the circle with guest cabins.

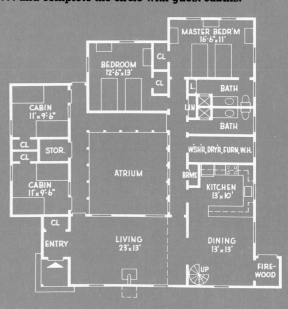

Four-Module Pinwheel

This isn't a phase-built design like two other Ward houses in this chapter: You don't add shed units one at a time. Instead, you frame up the complete four-module pinwheel (with or without the storage extensions shown in the floor and roof plans at right).

But Ward shows in his floorplan where you can append later shelters for car and boat—or even a hot-tub alcove (or attached workshop, if you prefer). These options aren't included in the roof plan, which helps clarify how the basic modules spin around that skylighted planter at the core. No two modules are identical, but they're all based on a shrewdly scaled framing module that assures simple, fast and inexpensive construction

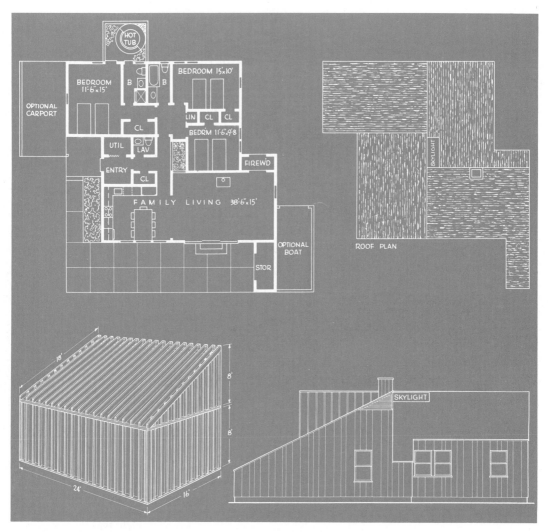

Shed framing is similar for all four modules, except for placement of windows, doors, mating interior walls (floorplan at top, left).

from basic-length studs and joists. "At today's lumber costs," says architect Ward, "any owner-built home should feature efficient, economical use of framing members (which come in two-foot-multiple lengths) and four-by-eight sheets of plywood siding and interior drywall.

"Designing a shed-roof box with this in mind and nesting four of these as shown results in an architecturally interesting, well-planned home."

The design has another important advantage for the amateur builder: It breaks a house down into non-intimi-

dating components. Have another look at
that basic framing module on page 23:
There's not a reader of this book who'd
hesitate to nail such a unit together. Think
of this house one shed-unit at a time and
you see how simple the construction
really is. And since this module calls for
standard lumberyard lengths, your cutting is minimal—and so is your waste.

Yet you end up with a handsome house
that boasts a spacious living/dining room
(it's over 38 feet long!), three bedrooms of
varying sizes, two full plus one half baths,
and ample storage space.

You'd site the patio entrance toward
your view, of course. This means your
waterfront or mountain vista will be
framed in both the three-panel patio door
(the center section slides for entry) and
the windows of the dining area. And
when your outdoor furniture must be put
away for the season, the storage shed is
handy at the right end of the patio.

That planter core, bathed in light from
above, provides a striking visual accent
for the living room (above) and for the
passage to the back hall, off which all
three bedrooms open. Twin beds are

shown in all bedrooms, but you'd create greater space in the smallest one by using a standard double bed. Directly opposite the planter core is a shorter entry hall, so this sunny welcome greets each arrival. This hall also gives onto the guest lavatory—a facility that's central to the whole house, so it can also relieve morning congestion when all bedrooms are occupied.

Accessible from both master bedroom and bathroom is an optional hot tub, set within its own enclosing privacy fence, but open to the sky.

As shown, the house is erected on an insulated concrete slab. With proper insu-lation in the floors, walls and ceilings—and an adequate supply of firewood for an efficient woodstove in the living room—and with storm sash and doors through-out, any backup furnace should operate with minimal energy expenditure, should you decide to use the house as a week-end retreat during the winter. Having roofs pitched in four different directions also gives you the option of installing solar collectors for domestic hot water, since one of the roof planes will be ideally sited for maximum solar exposure.

The house can be sided with random-grooved or Texture 1–11 plywood—rough-sawn or smooth.

High-Security Weekend Retreat

An important feature of this weekend retreat designed by William Ward is in the phrase "high-security"—not a window is exposed when you're not there (see opposite page). Every time you leave—whether for the week or over the winter months—you lock all shutters and pull in the colonial latch string on the entry door. While you're gone the house waits undisturbed, with all glass (so vulnerable to vandals, thieves, storms) boarded up. On your return shutters slide or swing aside.

This design was inspired by my Lockbox house detailed in Part Two of this book. But the house shown here is larger, with three bedrooms, and for a more conventional site. My many years' experience of weekending at the Lockbox has demonstrated the practicality of those self-

Open loft has its own self-storing shutters: When house is in use, large front one just hinges down (it's same height as railing); those at sides swing back.

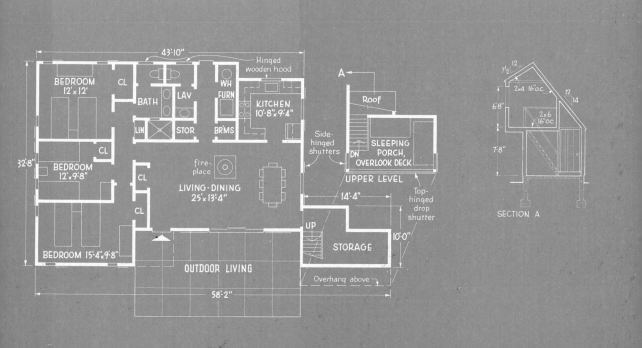

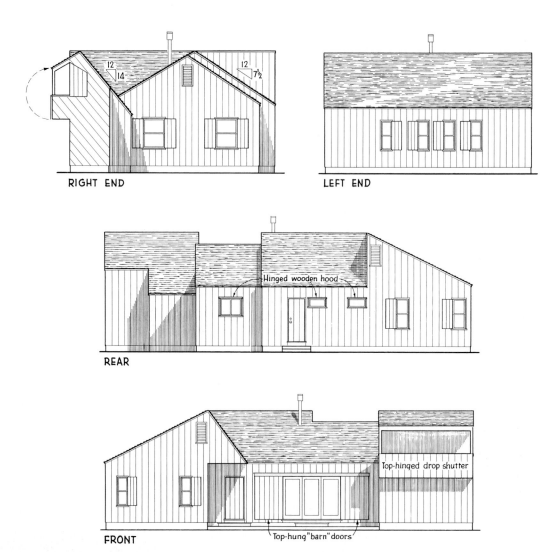

RIGHT END

LEFT END

Hinged wooden hood

REAR

Top-hinged drop shutter

FRONT

Top-hung "barn" doors

storing shutters. Where shuttering is readily at hand, you use it; if you had to wrestle awkward panels out of storage each time, you'd tend to skip the job, except for extended absences. And a security system is only good when it's used.

By comparing the two renderings you can see that the narrow double-hung

windows are equipped with side-hinged panels made of two sheets of a Texture 1-11 plywood glued back-to-back so either face will match the siding. The two shutters that cover the broad three-panel patio door (only the center panel slides for access) are hung from a track on "barn-door" hardware. When not in use, they flank—inconspicuously—a window-wall that bathes the living-dining area with light. The other window in this area is one of two wider double-hungs in the right-end wall that are secured with a *pair* of shutters, hinged to the frames at each side. Note that at least one window in each room is large enough to provide an emergency fire exit—except, of course, for the bath and half-bath. These windows on the rear wall have top-hinged shutters that must be provided with a prop. All other shutters are held open with hooks-and-eyes or turnblocks.

For effective security, all shutters must be latched or bolted from the inside, through the open window; so the bath windows should be awning types that open inward.

Since all shutters are kept readily available, the house is a quick one to secure. You could "batten down the hatches" at the first storm warning.

Ready shutters are especially valuable for the open loft section. Whether or not those broad openings are screened (depending on local insect problems), this section is normally open to the weather, and a driving rain could send enough water in to wet the stairs. If you can dash up there when a storm hits, you'll be able to shutter the loft in no time. Architect Ward has built in another precaution to assure that any flooding of this rustic wing can't affect the house proper: He's set this wing one step below the main floor—directly on its own slab.

Those eight skinny double-hungs shrewdly spaced along three walls offer a bonus: They meet today's stringent needs for energy efficiency. By reducing glass area (any wall's major area of heat loss in winter and heat gain in summer) the house becomes easier to heat and cool. If

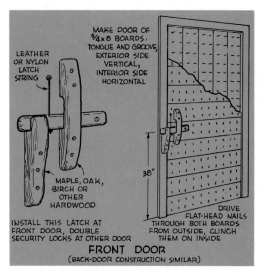

MAKE DOOR OF ⁵⁄₄ x 8 BOARDS, TONGUE AND GROOVE, EXTERIOR SIDE VERTICAL, INTERIOR SIDE HORIZONTAL

LEATHER OR NYLON LATCH STRING

MAPLE, OAK, BIRCH OR OTHER HARDWOOD

38"

DRIVE FLAT-HEAD NAILS THROUGH BOTH BOARDS FROM OUTSIDE, CLINCH THEM ON INSIDE

INSTALL THIS LATCH AT FRONT DOOR, DOUBLE SECURITY LOCKS AT OTHER DOOR

FRONT DOOR
(BACK-DOOR CONSTRUCTION SIMILAR)

Here are more security tips:
Homemade door of "cross-banded" t&g boards studded with clinched nails offers greater impact resistance than usual entry panel. Rugged latch can be augmented by surface-mounted steel bolt, 16" higher on door. Also: Avoid plantings that could hide intruders. Store ladders indoors—or chained and locked. Enclose outside utility meters. Recess exterior lights behind unbreakable windows, or cover with wire baskets. Remove handle from outside water spigot. Store all summer furniture, garden tools, small boats inside. Keep list of valuable contents at your home in town.

possible, orient the window-wall to the south or southwest; if you plan to use the house in winter, install double-glazing.

The procedure for closing the house is quickly established. From the patio, you slide the "barn-door" panels across the window-wall, then close the entry door behind you and tug the latch-string in. After you latch each shutter, lock the window. Exit through the back door, which should be equipped with two security locks, one high and one low.

Two-Phase Contemporary

In the color rendering above, Phase I version (single bedroom plus sleep loft) dominates; at right is completed house (with two-bedroom addition in right-front notch).

This home's unique appearance stems from a floorplan that cleverly skews the two-story living room for the broadest possible vista through its glass prow. The exterior remains a novel but honest statement of this plan, whether you settle for the Phase I mode shown in the main sketch left, or go on—as your family grows—to add one or two more bedrooms. You can fill in that right corner in stages, or all at once as in the rendering below. In the final version, you lose the alternate entry (toward which that dripping sailor is dashing, left; it leads directly to the rear bath, sparing your living/dining-room floors those wet footprints).

But even the final phase retains the easy traffic flow of the main floor. To the left of the main entry, the patio doors have central sections that slide—not only for walk-through access, but to turn the prow into a summer breezeway. (There's also a direct entry from the carport—especially welcome on rainy days.) The prow area would be equally inviting in the winter, since a fireplace—and the stairway to the loft—is tucked into the return corner that shelters the carport entry. (The construction plans provide for an optional double garage, to be added later; our artist omitted it from both versions.) Should you not need any provision for a car, you can leave off the carport without affecting the architectural unity. But with carport *and* garage you've got shelter for two cars and a boat.

The upstairs bath and closet corridor will doubtless come with the final phase—at which point the sleep-loft can be finished as the master bedroom, leaving the two or three downstairs bedrooms for children or guests. The loft balustrade can then be fitted with accordion doors for full privacy from activities below. Until such time, the loft provides a fine play area in inclement weather or work space for spread-out projects, as well as casual sleeping on bunks or air mattresses.

Second-floor plan (bottom) is in final phase mode; in Phase I, corridor to right of loft would run along exterior wall.

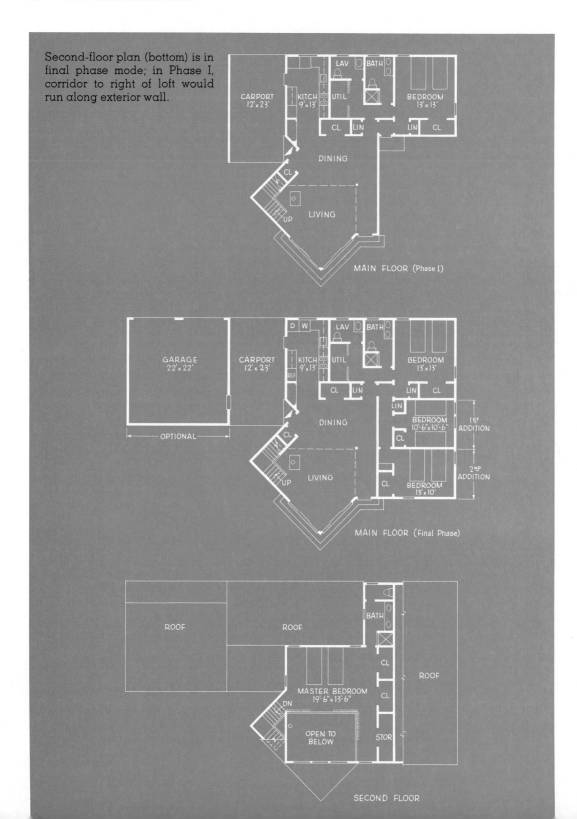

MAIN FLOOR (Phase I)

MAIN FLOOR (Final Phase)

SECOND FLOOR

One 6x6 post is only support needed for second-story loft that projects over dining area, entry hall. Clerestory windows and underside of roof deck add architectural interest above prow window-walls.

Whether you put in the upstairs bath as part of Phase I, or wait for the house to grow up to that need, you may want to rough in the plumbing for it—an easy extension, since its floorplan duplicates the one below. There's a half-bath tucked behind the utility alcove—a handy dressing room for summer bathers.

One-Room Leisure Home Sleeps Ten

One motivation for building a second home in a remote recreational area may be antisocial: to provide an escape from the people-pressures of daily life. But it seldom works out that way. The more fun your site offers, the more it's likely to draw guests (both invited and un-) so "putting people up" becomes a way of life at a country place. Your children compete for the right to include their friends for the weekend, and relatives plan their own trips with your place as a stop-over.

We've heard so many people claim (with a sigh) that leisure homes should be all bedrooms that we began to ponder better solutions. Bill Ward came up with this one: a modest (though high-style) house *designed* for a sleep-in. It's basically one-room with various append-ages for storage (indoor and out). You build as many of those separately-roofed units as you want. Don't need a boat house? Leave that section off. Does a detached garage provide enough stor-age for bulky items like deck furniture? Omit that outdoor-access shed behind the boathouse.

The major feature of the house is at its core—the big living-dining room that's open to a loft above. Accordion doors, hung along a beam that supports this loft, meet at a post to close off the left side of this space at night—for the hosts' bed-room. Two couches (by day) convert to comfortable bunks. Upstairs, guests fend for themselves. If there's another adult couple to accommodate, a folding panel screen can be set up beside the stair well to create snug privacy for the pair of beds

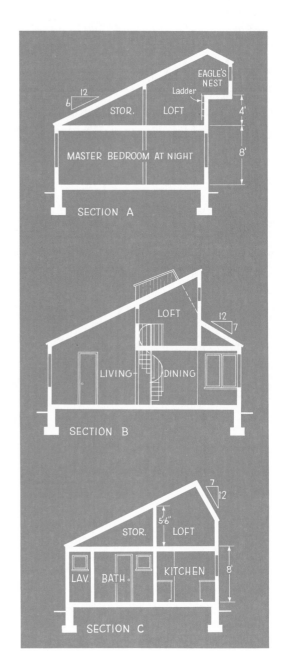

(see loft plan). Wee-hour raids on the kitchen can then be accomplished without disturbing any adults. And if one guest is more shy (or more adventurous) than the rest, tuck this one in the Eagle's Nest—a Pullman-berth niche, floating in space and offering a truly unique wake-up experience.

Note other amenities on the downstairs floorplan: There's a separate entry for "activists" (it's at the right end of this house, but you could reverse the plan right for left if that's better for your site). Designed especially for swimmers fresh from lake, pond or pool, this entry gives them direct access to a shower without dripping through the house. Or, if they just want to duck in for a cold drink, the same entry opens into the kitchen.

In exterior styling, the home is dead-center-Today, with multiple shed roofs at varied pitches (the three major ones are diagrammed in our sections). Paradoxically, the framing complexity these roof-planes present makes this even more of a do-it-yourself project: You can contribute the time and patience required to customize all those different rafter cuts, which professional carpenters might consider an expensive nuisance.

This design avoids needless decorative elements, attains pleasant mass and form, eschews pretense. The exterior and interior wall finish is plywood, which is at

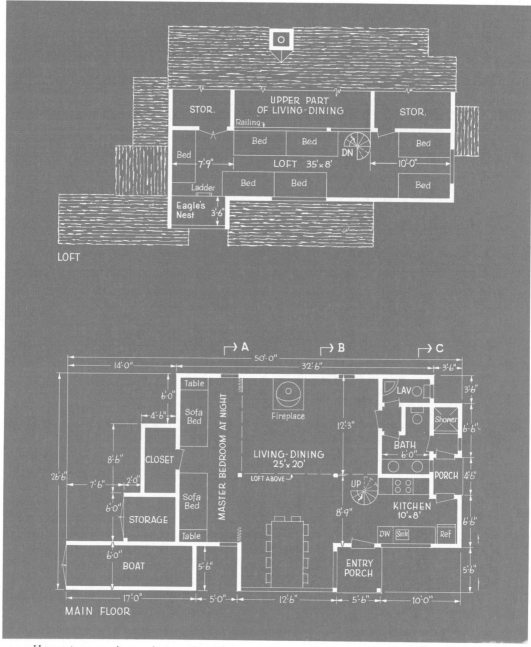

House is many-faceted gem of overlapped space with unusual facilities for putting up visitors. Tucked under the highest roof ridge is an open loft with space for seven single beds, plus (for that guest who craves privacy) a climb-up sleep perch.

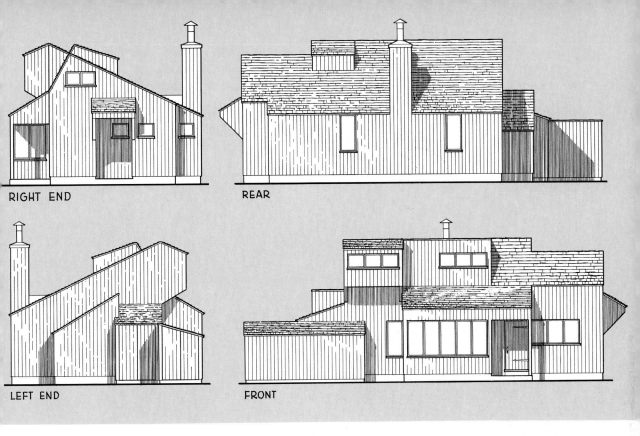

RIGHT END

REAR

LEFT END

FRONT

once structural and attractive and—as a domestic building material—is probably the greatest advance since the log.

This plan is well-integrated in more respects than its solution to sleeping problems. All plumbing is concentrated at one end of the house to avoid wasteful runs. Bathroom facilities are split up to accommodate several people at once.

The dining area is light and airy, facing the view (the ideal orientation for this window side of the house would be south).

The understructure of the house will depend on many local conditions, including code requirements, terrain, soil type, water table, climate. It can be a concrete block foundation on a poured footing below frost; it can be masonry piers bridged with joists, or an insulated slab on grade. Unless you have building expe-

rience, it's usually best to have a contractor familiar with local conditions put in your foundation. From then on, framing and cladding are fairly routine, and even insulating the house for year-round use is a do-it-yourself job.

In our artist's rendering, a deck (or patio) has been added at the front entry, but this could as easily be positioned at the right side.

As an extra design feature (see elevations), we boxed our fireplace chimney in plywood. To prevent back-up of snowmelt or rain in the valley thus formed, we provided a drainage cricket, as shown in the loft plan. You could, instead, erect a standard chimney of stacked metal units and use a flashed rain cone where the chimney pierces the roof. Either way, you'll need to lift the cap above the ridge for best draw.

3. HOMES FOR FAMILY COMFORT

Samuel Paul (AIA) is a Long Island architect with a dual personality. His office bids on—and often wins—major public housing commissions, several of which have garnered design awards. But Paul's personal preference is designing single-family dwellings, and when we first discussed projects for our series with him, he said he'd find leisure homes particularly liberating. Paul (working with his architect son David) has now designed nine homes especially for *Popular Science;* eight of them are included in this book. Paul's renderer is Edward Kelbish, who works expertly in several media, choosing whichever best suits the house at hand.

For ordering information on this group of plans, see page 189. Paul has established a marketing arm that handles the sale of his plans under the name Homes for Living Inc.

Suncrest: Passive Solar-Plus

A weekend retreat you use all year should take care of its own heating, as far as this is practical. Here's a shrewdly-designed house that not only keeps you snug all night on stored daylight heat, but will keep itself above freezing while you're away, with minimal thermostat demand on any backup heat source.

Interior masonry walls and tiled-slab floor capture heat from the winter sun and store it for slow release during the night. Placed about 6 inches behind the side portions of the all-glass south-facing facade are thermal walls that function as low-temperature radiators. The air space between glass and masonry is heated

Butterfly roof area at center provides ideal mounting for two to four solar collectors to supply domestic hot water, as shown in exterior view (left). Interior rendering, above, shows how this roof section adds architectural interest to ceiling and provides clearstory vent windows flanking fireplace chimney (compare with floorplan). Living/dining area is bathed with light.

and, through convection, circulates heat throughout the 496-square-foot living-dining room. These Trombe walls take their name from Trombe and Michel, the French developers of this solar-heating method. The low rays of the winter sun also penetrate all the way to the masonry wall that runs nearly the full length of this big room, creating a mass for thermal storage.

All other exterior walls are cedar shingles over 6-inch studs filled with fiberglass insulation. This keeps the heat in during the winter and out during the summer. Primary heat for the kitchen and bedroom areas is provided by the centrally located prefabricated wood-burning fireplace-furnace. Heat rises through a main duct from the glass-doored firebox into a plenum over the bath and bedroom

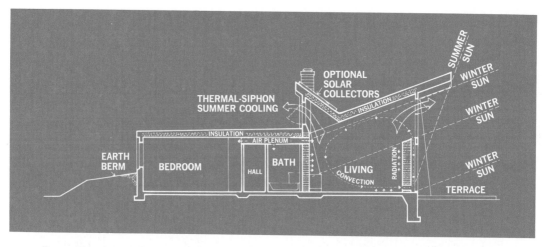

Outer Trombe wall—plus inner masonry wall and floor—give off radiant heat after being warmed by low winter sun. Trombe wall also sets up convection currents. Roof projection shades thermal masses in summer, and high windows siphon off heat.

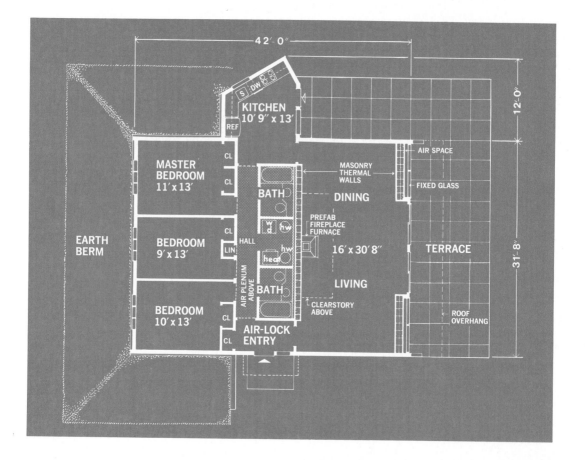

hall. Adjustable registers above the doors to the bedrooms and kitchen deliver this heat; other registers off this plenum—directed into the living-dining area—are opened only during sunless days when heat stored in the masonry has dissipated.

A second backup system consists of a regular furnace controlled by thermostats in both the bedroom wing and living-dining area, for periods when the house stands unattended. The same overhead plenum and registers serve this heating system.

Surrounding the bedroom wing, an earth berm has been heaped to about 3½ feet above the floor, minimizing heat loss or gain. (Ceiling insulation is 9 inches.)

Summer cooling is designed into the house via high windows that siphon off heat as it rises to the dual-pitch ceiling—and via the projecting awning. Though not shown in our interior rendering, you'll probably want to equip the lower glazing with insulating drapes—both to draw against the summer rays that cut under that roof overhang, and to cut down heat loss when you're using the house on cold winter nights.

Architectural design is not compromised for these heating and cooling functions. The living/dining room gains space, light and drama from that clearstory notch above the hearth—the roof of which provides mounting for solar collectors, as shown in the section, left.

Skewed-Prow Two-Story

If you've got a great view—frame it. That's the philosophy behind this cleverly skewed modification of the popular A-frame. And it applies equally to a mountain vista or a seascape.

The center of the prow is shifted toward the chimney, and the left half of the roof is raised on a wall of nearly conventional height to avoid that cramped under-eaves feeling of a full A-frame. As a result

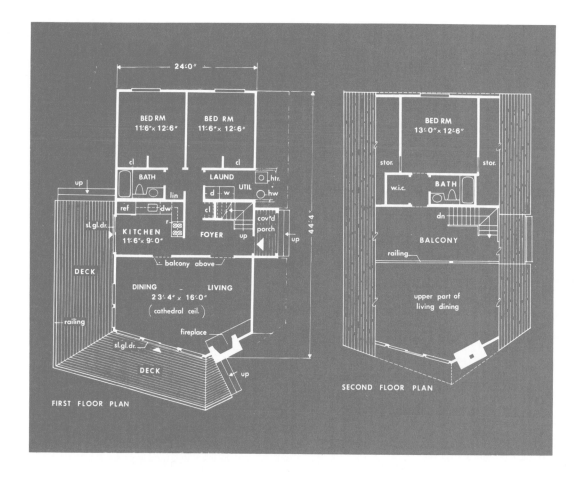

of these variations, the glazed side of the prow expands dramatically. The window even turns the corner to provide a dining area with a view no standard A-frame could offer.

Two widely separated sliding glass doors give onto the ample deck, which adds nearly 500 square feet of living area to the 1015-square-foot first floor. Nearly half of that floor space enjoys the impact of the soaring cathedral ceiling shown in our interior view. The rear portion, however, boasts a second story, with the larg-

est of the three bedrooms, a second bath, plus handy eaves storage along both sides.

The asymmetrical roof rises from the ground at a steep pitch on one side (enclosing the utilities beside the laundry room); the other side of the roof starts from the window head at a lesser slope. This aligns the ridge with the peak of the prow and adds design interest, as do the exposed rafters and tie-beams.

The central entrance foyer inside a covered porch is another unexpected touch.

Many leisure homes lack any formal, sheltered entry.

The deck access to the fully equipped kitchen invites outdoor dining. And it's easy to carry in groceries from the other direction, since the kitchen is opposite the entry.

Also directly accessible from that foyer is the broad balcony, which could easily become the favorite space in the house. Measuring about 9 feet wide by 21 feet long, it can serve as an upstairs lounge for reading, a play area for rainy days, or—equipped with a convertible sofa—could double as an extra guest room (the upstairs bath would be shared). Whatever its function, it affords the best view in the house.

Exterior finish materials can be left unpainted for a rustic effect—wood shingles on the roof, walls of natural wood siding. The same wood is carried inside to become the side-wall paneling. The exposed roof deck high above and the plank flooring underfoot complete this effect.

Multi-Level Lodge

Call it a double split level. The stepped-up living areas of this house not only offer spacial variety, they provide privacy zoning. Since each of the three bedrooms is on its own level, completely apart from the activity areas, it's easy to withdraw from family hurly-burly.

What feature could be more appropriate for a leisure home? It will be appreciated by weekend guests—who can set their own pace of participation; and it also makes the house ideal for sharing singles, for two married couples, or for a three-generation family.

Note that each bedroom has its private bath. Despite the fact they're on four different levels, the three baths (plus the laundry) are stacked against a common wall for efficient plumbing runs.

That steeply sloped roof over the living room offers a good place for mounting solar collectors to provide the home's hot-

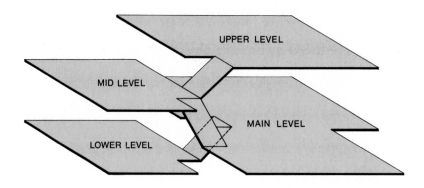

UPPER LEVEL

MID LEVEL

MAIN LEVEL

LOWER LEVEL

Four-level scheme is hard to grasp from conventional floorplan. Each plan below represents two levels, as shown in diagram above. Center stair ties all levels together in half-flights. From main-entry level, it descends to lower bedroom and ascends to mid-level room (at first platform) and on up to master bedroom. Open upper-level plan over living area creates cathedral ceiling.

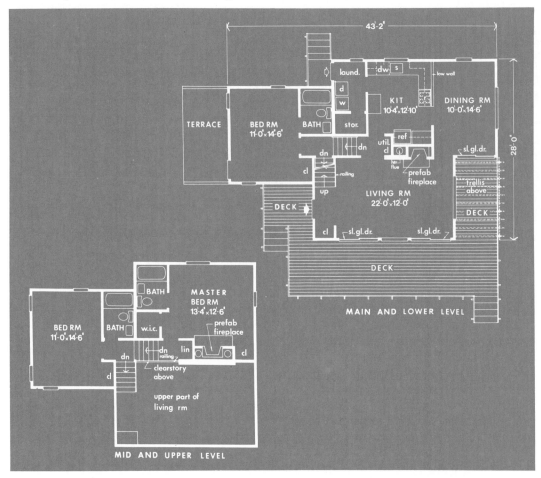

43-2'

laund.   dw s   low wall

d

w   KIT   DINING RM
      10-4'x12-10' 10-0'x14-6'

TERRACE   BED RM   BATH   stor.
          11-0'x14-6'

                    util. ref
                    cl   sl.gl.dr.
          dn   dn   htr-
                        flue prefab   trellis
          cl   railing fireplace above

          up   DECK
                         LIVING RM
DECK   22-0'x12-0'

          cl   sl.gl.dr.   sl.gl.dr.

                    DECK

                              MAIN AND LOWER LEVEL

28-0'

BATH   MASTER
          BED RM
          13-4'x12-6'
BATH w.i.c.   prefab
                fireplace
BED RM
11-0'x14-6'   dn lin
          dn railing   cl
          cl clearstory
              above

              upper part of
              living rm

MID AND UPPER LEVEL

water supply. Inside, this slope becomes a dramatic and energy-efficient ceiling that moves heat from the activity areas up into the higher bedrooms. In summer, you can open the clearstory windows and create a thermal-siphon effect for natural cooling. Those windows also flood the stairway with daylight.

The living-room ceiling starts at a normal 8-foot height along the front window-wall, then soars up two stories at the fireplace wall. There's a small second-floor balcony (an extension of the stairs) that overlooks the living room.

Seven steps above the main level (which clusters all common areas—living and dining rooms, kitchen and laundry) is the midlevel bedroom; another six steps up is the master bedroom, featuring a second heat-circulating fireplace. The third bedroom is six steps down from the main level, and boasts its own private terrace on grade. A partial basement is an option that adds a fifth level. On the blueprint, it's located below the living room.

The dining room is tucked under its own gable at the right rear. Its cozy 8-foot ceiling contrasts with the lofty living room, and the low, 4-foot wall that separates it from the country kitchen defines the space without sacrificing an informality suited to leisure-home entertaining.

A wrap-around deck contributes more space for guests and eases traffic flow with four access doors. The most delightful section is the trellised part next to the dining room—fine for intimate suppers.

The home's exterior is vertical siding of cedar or redwood, left to weather naturally. The same wood is used on feature walls inside, as shown in the color rendering on page 49.

Sky Vista with Stacked Bedrooms

This house would fit into any vacation setting, mountains or seashore. The exterior components—vertical cedar or redwood siding, stone chimney, opposing roof slopes with clearstory windows, cantilevered balcony—all relate to nature in a unique way. And contemporary technology is represented by a pair of solar collectors that supply the home's hot-water requirements.

Solar makes special sense for a weekend home, since the collectors can be storing and maintaining a hot-water supply while you're away, avoiding the heavy power drain of starting from scratch on your arrival. Because of the extra time the system has to build up the supply, you should get by with the plates shown on facing page.

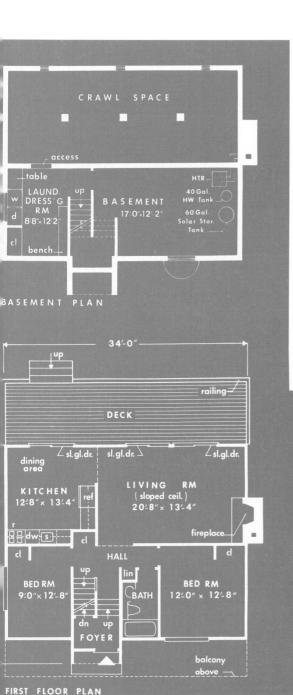

BASEMENT PLAN

FIRST FLOOR PLAN

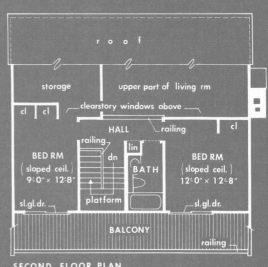

SECOND FLOOR PLAN

Viewed from kitchen, living room soars from one to two stories. On roof above sloped ceiling are solar collectors.

Chances are that the house will be steadily occupied only during the vacation period when the sun's giving its best performance.

Although the outside dimensions of this house are only 30 by 34 feet, it packs in a lot of living space by stacking one pair of bedrooms on top of the other. The two bathrooms are also stacked for efficient plumbing runs. Below the tall bedroom section is an excavated basement that offers a combined laundry-dressing room (for swimmers or skiers) and space for the solar system and an optional furnace.

The living room slopes dramatically from the single-story window-wall along the deck side to a balcony overlook along the opposite side, as shown in the sketch, left. At one end of this room is a rustic stone fireplace from floor to ceiling. The other end opens to a country-style eat-in kitchen, which has its own access to the deck to facilitate outdoor dining. This room has a conventional flat ceiling that provides storage above.

The main entry is recessed and protected with a canopy. It leads into a foyer and up four steps to the main hall, with first-floor bedrooms right and left. You continue up the turn-around stairs to the second floor; the bedrooms here duplicate those below, except for their sloped ceilings. The hall balcony overlooks the living room and is flooded with light from clearstory windows above; each upper bedroom also has a clearstory peep at the open sky.

The opposite wall of both bedrooms features a sliding glass door that gives onto a cantilevered deck. Its closed ends make it ideal for sunbathing.

Modified Saltbox

Light floods into this split-level living room; the higher front section has sliding-glass-door access to the giant deck, next to the screened "outdoor room" inset. The ceiling soars to a full two stories over this section and the adjacent dining area. Three steps down is a cozy sunken den with fireplace and perimeter seating. There's a second fireplace in the bedroom overhead.

This delightful update of that American classic, the New England saltbox, has undergone major transformations, but the basic saltbox shape comes through—here, complete with traditional entry overhang. The narrow horizontal siding (whether actual clapboards or a simulation) further asserts the ancestry of this house.

Entering from a small deck (unseen, left, midway along the cantilevered face), you step into a foyer with a generous closet for outerwear. As you continue on into the dining area, you begin to sense the great variety of spaces that have been created. The ceiling rises two stories, and the upper part of the wall facing

you is pierced with three true clearstory windows. That's the term for glazing that "clears" the story below by looking out over the lower roof—in this case, the roof of the screened "outdoor room" that thrusts itself out onto the deck. On your left hand, now, is the scene depicted in the above rendering, with the matching "false clearstory" windows in the upper wall of the living room, and the "conversation pit" with built-in seating beside a heat-circulating fireplace. Also note that, since the adjacent living-room floor is at bench height, seat cushions to the right of the fireplace can provide additional seating—ideal for big parties.

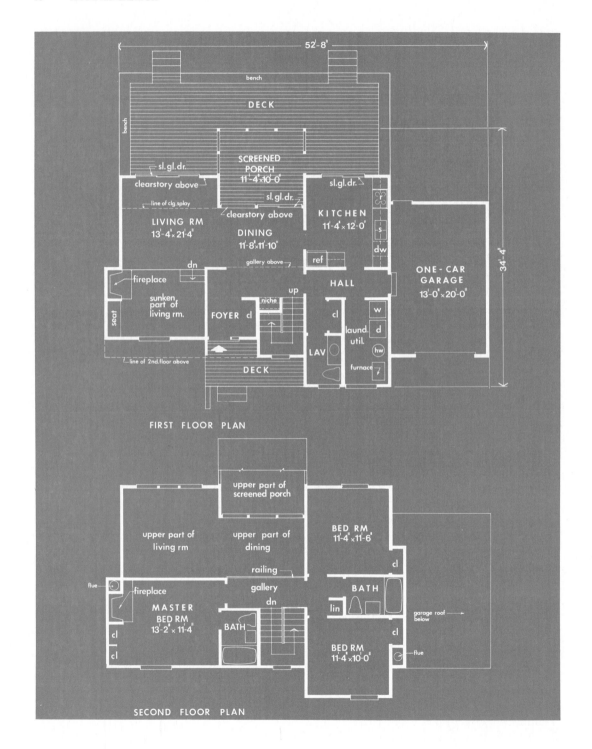

FIRST FLOOR PLAN

SECOND FLOOR PLAN

The screened area of the deck notches into the house and the sliding glass-door access is handy to the kitchen, since this "room" is designed for insect-free summer dining. You'd probably become so fond of this space you'd consider converting it to a sunroom for winter use, as well.

The kitchen is handily located near the garage (for unloading the week's supply of groceries after one of those long country shopping trips) and near the laundry-utility area (which keeps plumbing runs short).

Square footage for the first floor (excluding the screen-room's 124 square feet) is 882. Add 696 for the second floor and you have a total of 1578 square feet, plus deck and garage areas.

The stairs to the second floor have a naturally-lighted landing, and lead to an open gallery that forms a bridge between the master bedroom and the other two. From here, there's a dramatic view of the two-story dining and living spaces.

The master bedroom has its own bath and heat-circulating fireplace (the latter shares the chimney—though not, of course, the flue—of the fireplace below) and a private bath. The other two good-size bedrooms share the bathroom that separates them (avoiding a common wall that could be a source of noise pass-through). It's a house with built-in hospitality, and your main problem will doubtless be controlling "repeaters" on your guest list.

Expandable Retreat

First Stage

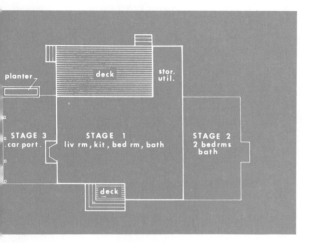

planter

deck

stor.
util.

STAGE 3
.car port.

STAGE 1
liv rm, kit, bed rm, bath

STAGE 2
2 bedrms
bath

deck

The handsome contemporary cottage shown in the large exterior rendering is only the beginning of this adventure in leisure living: It's the first stage of a clever three-phase house that you add to as family needs—and budget—grow.

Roof extensions can sprout from either end to add another pair of bedrooms plus bath, and an open carport, enclosed garage, or boathouse. The smaller rendering and the dimensioned floorplan (page 63) show the completed project.

Of course, if the first stage is all you need, stop there: You'll have a complete

Final Stage

700-square-foot, single-story dwelling with all amenities (except a spare bedroom; occasional guests could be accommodated on a convertible couch in that spacious living/dining area shown in our interior sketch).

You have the option of solar collectors for the hot-water system. The architect has placed them just below the lowest eaves, on a frame that lets you angle them for optimum exposure. Inside the low-roofed

wing is the utility/storage area, including the solar hot-water gear.

The little floor plan in blue, green and yellow offers a key to the three-stage construction. The renderings, of course, show the rear or private-deck side of the house—the side you'd site toward your sunniest exposure, whether you build at waterside or in the mountains.

Our view of the interior is from the hallway that separates the open kitchen and

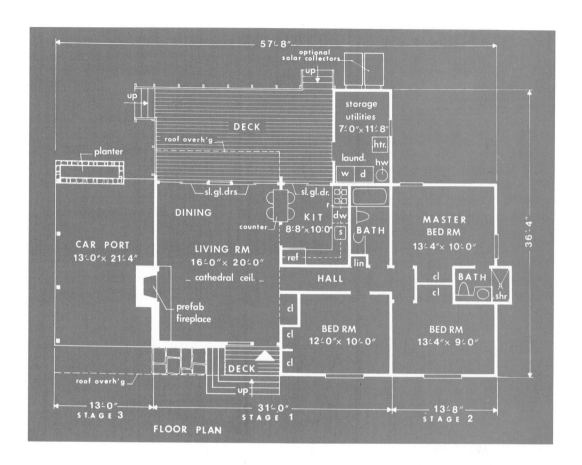

FLOOR PLAN

the original bedroom. The cathedral ceiling soars from an 8-foot wall at the left to top out at over 13 feet, just 5 feet from that dramatic 11½-foot window wall on the right.

Aside from a roof extension, the major structural change involved in splicing on the bedroom wing is cutting an entry in the weather wall to extend that hall into the two additional rooms. You can either leave the original siding in place as a

rustic feature wall in the new rooms or remove it for reuse.

Stage Two adds 342 square feet for a total space of 1042. Note that one of the added rooms has a private bath with a shower bay. This bedroom becomes the hosts' retreat-within-a-retreat.

Two-Phase Split Pavilions

Even a nuclear family can be happier in a bi-nuclear house. Two square pavilions of identical dimensions (576 square feet) are joined by a large breezeway. The nucleus of family *activity* is in the unit shown below, which features a living room open to the roofbeams, plus a kitchen-dining area with a dropped ceiling. The second nucleus—for post-activity rest—is the sleep pavilion: three cleverly devised bedrooms with ready access to a central bath. This second pavilion also contains the utilities and laundry equipment.

Although this separation is ideal for families with children or teenagers, whose noisy play can be isolated from adult activities, the split-pavilion concept really comes into its own when you're entertaining guests for a weekend. If the guests wish to retire from your activities, they simply walk across the deck to their quiet retreat. (Each bedroom has space for two beds; you can double-up kids with two pairs of bunks in one room.)

If your family is up first, next morning, you don't all have to resort to the "host

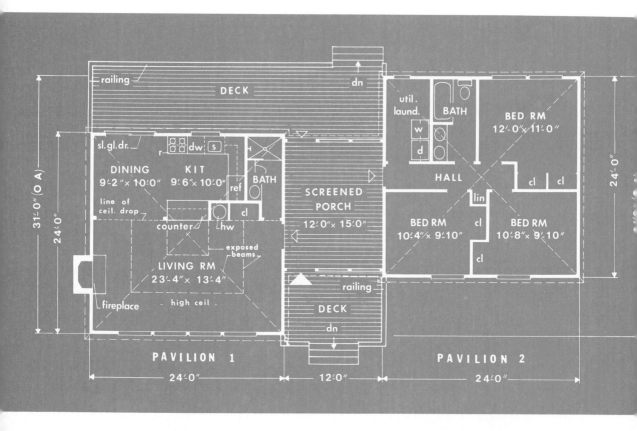

tiptoe'' for fear of disturbing the still-sleeping guests. Note that the two pavilions turn blind walls toward each other; even their entry doors are offset to avoid any pass-over of noise.

The large breezeway creates the effect of an old-fashioned screened porch. It becomes an outdoor den for evening cocktails or alfresco dining. And although our artist shows the home in a remote setting, this tucked-away deck would be even more welcome on a small plot between other homes, since it offers a breezy haven of privacy, as no patio could.

There's another boon to the split-pavilion concept: It's an ideal plan for two-phase building. As soon as you've erected the activity unit, you can move in convertible couches and live there while you work on the second pavilion and the deck areas. (That broad rear deck is optional, of course, but it's great for sunning and snacking—especially if it has a view.)

A couple without children might well find the first pavilion—plus the deck areas—sufficient for their leisure- or retirement-home needs, and skip the second unit. The furniture arrangement in our interior sketch shows convertible sofas against the right wall. The shower-stall bathroom, handy for daytime use, would be sufficient for one-unit occupancy.

One side of the U-shaped kitchen is defined by a counter for informal dining. If you installed a circulating fireplace, you'd need only minimal electric-heat backup (radiant panel or baseboard) to keep this pavilion snug during cold-weather use. The sleeping pavilion could have its own forced-air furnace.

As shown here, the pavilions are set on concrete piers, the floor floating about 2½ feet above ground. Exterior walls can be vertical siding or grooved plywood. The smooth plywood panels under the windows are painted. The pyramid roofs are shingled, with a mansard-type fascia that ties in with the shingled edging on the flat-roofed porch.

Fireproof Retreat

One concern haunts any owner of a leisure home in a remote area. When he must leave it far behind, he fears fire even more than those peculiarly American scourges of vandalism and burglary. Fire can wipe out his entire investment, and there's relatively little he can do to protect a conventional home against it. What good is the best alarm system if there's no one around to alert?

So when architect Samuel Paul offered to design us a snug retreat of non-combustible materials, my only stipulation was that the construction technology stay within reach of the determined do-it-yourselfer. Here's the result: Exterior walls are masonry block; interior facing is fire-coded plasterboard; the roof structure is steel, supporting a fire-resistant decking. The steel joists and other members can be ordered to exact length to avoid on-site cutting, and they're lightweight enough for two novice builders to install.

Concrete block can be an easier wall for an amateur to erect than conventional framing—and it sheds its gray prison-wall

identity when you use a split-rib block for a textured honeytone effect. The white aluminum edging around the roof slab sets off these walls ideally, and monotony is avoided by the indention at the entry and the set-in walls of the bedroom wing and patio.

At the heart of the interior is an open kitchen—an L within an L. An all-purpose counter serves for food preparation and dining. The plumbing backs up to the utility core to provide efficient hookups and minimize wasteful hot-water runs.

This compact (1072 square feet) house isn't hard to build: You erect your perimeter walls (on below-frost footings), apply

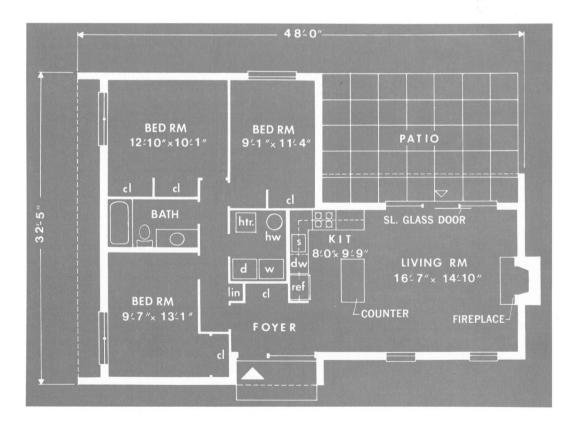

Typical Exterior Wall Section

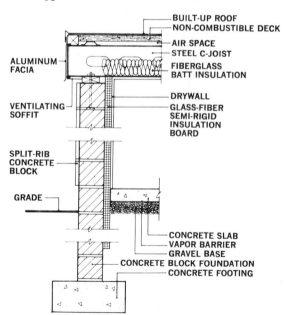

BUILT-UP ROOF
NON-COMBUSTIBLE DECK
AIR SPACE
STEEL C-JOIST
FIBERGLASS BATT INSULATION
DRYWALL
GLASS-FIBER SEMI-RIGID INSULATION BOARD
ALUMINUM FACIA
VENTILATING SOFFIT
SPLIT-RIB CONCRETE BLOCK
GRADE
CONCRETE SLAB
VAPOR BARRIER
GRAVEL BASE
CONCRETE BLOCK FOUNDATION
CONCRETE FOOTING

insulation board to the interior faces (1 or 2 inches, depending on your temperature extremes) with metal Z-strips, then pour your interior concrete slab. The rigid insulation projects about 2 feet below the slab (see section). Your interior partitions can be steel studs.

If you have no local source for the steel roof joists, you could go with lumber; but ask your yard to order joists that have been chemically treated for flame resistance—and cover them with a two-layer plasterboard ceiling. Then, if you choose your furnishings with care, the only things that'll burn in this house are the logs in the fireplace.

4. ENERGY-EFFICIENT HOMES FOR THE DO-IT-YOURSELFER

Home Building Plan Service is a design factory in Portland, Oregon. Under the soft-spoken leadership of Ralph Rittenour (just retired), the company grew to national prominence, creating plans for primary as well as recreational homes. Despite the number of new designs the group creates each year, adding to an awesome total of designs already in stock, this company's construction plans remain among the most thorough offered; this makes them especially helpful for novice builders. And since HBPS's home state has some of the most stringent housing requirements in the nation, their specifications nearly always meet or exceed local codes and standards elsewhere. They've also been leaders in developing plans for energy-efficient and solar houses. The unique relationship between HBPS and *Popular Science* has been established through the cooperation of Western Wood Products Assn., also Portland-based. The HBPS renderer is Carl Lauersen, whose settings always seem native to the cool-moist air of Pacific Northwest forests and beaches.

For ordering information on this group of plans, see pages 189–190.

Six-Way House

Your second home should be better tailored to personal needs than most *primary* homes can be. Since you're building from scratch on raw land, you can exercise many options that weren't open to you when you bought or rented your place in town.

This leisure home has a design that a prospective builder can adjust to a specific site and his family's life-style. Though its ground floor plan of 1056 square feet remains constant, this house can be built six different ways.

You choose whether the plans you buy include basement or second bath and two or four bedrooms to suit your needs.

The version shown in our color rendering is the second-floor bedroom/bath

plus daylight-basement version. It's ideal for a sloping site where driveway access is practical at the downhill foundation wall. The garage space is long enough for two cars parked end-to-end, plus a utility/workshop area and that "daylight" room at the front, which could serve as a playroom or studio.

The standard-basement plan (not shown) merely provides one big (22'8"-by-42'8") space within the foundation walls. You excavate and pave as much of this as is practical for your site and your storage needs.

Two second-floor plans offer you a choice of an open dormitory or a third bedroom with two closets, a second bath with stall shower, and a balcony hall that overlooks the vaulted living room.

There are even more options than these flexible floorplans suggest. If you'd like to simplify construction, you can trim back

on that striking double dormer: the higher one is mainly for the stacked bathrooms, and if you omit the bath upstairs you could skip the dormer as well. The lower dormer provides dramatic lighting for the stairway. The entry door, farther to the right, is tucked under standard eaves.

Whatever your version, the house boasts rustic good looks and increased insulation values gained through use of western wood framing plus red cedar for both siding (1x8 channel rustic, applied vertically) and interior cladding (1x6 V-joint). Materials and design comply with the Uniform Building Code rules for conserving heating and cooling energy. For example, although that vaulted ceiling features exposed cedar, the joist system allows for insulation batts above.

Along three sides of the living room runs some 350 square feet of fir decking with sliding glass doors.

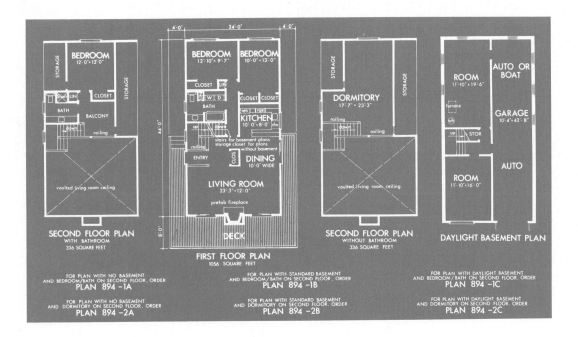

Energy-Saver

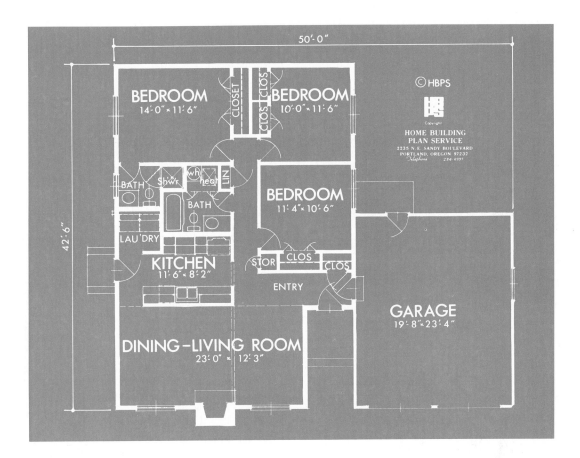

A second home (for leisure living) is certain to double your awareness of energy conservation—not just by getting you closer to nature, but by forcing you to face two sets of utility bills!

In most cases, your primary home was built before energy concerns were a dominant factor in design and construction, so the best you can do there is to upgrade and retrofit to meet today's realities. When you start from scratch, however, as in building a second home, you can make sure that construction incorporates all the latest techniques for making the structure energy efficient—including an unusual underfloor plenum system for heating. Other construction innovations include:

● The walls are framed with 2x6's, 24-inches on center to increase the depth and width of stud cavities, for thicker insulation with fewer gaps.

● The plans detail an All-Weather Wood Foundation to create the insulated crawl space and to replace cumbersome concrete walls. With this technique, foundation walls of pressure-treated lumber and plywood can be erected in rainy or freezing weather, when concrete could not be poured (and some areas of the country have periodic concrete short-

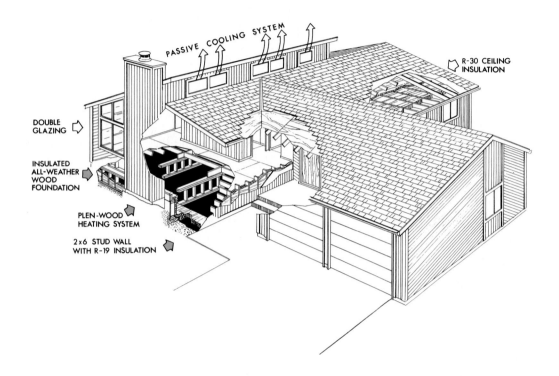

PASSIVE COOLING SYSTEM

R-30 CEILING
INSULATION

DOUBLE
GLAZING

INSULATED
ALL-WEATHER
WOOD
FOUNDATION

PLEN-WOOD
HEATING SYSTEM

2x6 STUD WALL
WITH R-19 INSULATION

ages). The new system also adapts well to panelized construction: you could get a head start on construction in your home shop, then truck the foundation components to the country site for erection.

An alternate plan offers the option of a poured masonry foundation, but you must apply special insulation in the Plen-Wood system, to create the underfloor plenum. The all-wood foundation, however, can be conventionally insulated, with fiberglass batts.

By using the space within the perimeter foundation as the air-distribution chamber, you not only save the fuss and cost of ductwork but you provide a warm floor that encourages lower thermostat readings if you use the house as a winter retreat. Beefed-up insulation (R-19 in walls, R-30 in ceilings) and double- or triple-glazed wood windows also hold down heat loss.

For summer cooling, the Plen-Wood system works well with a central air-conditioner—if you're building in an area (Gulf Coast, southwest) that requires it. For most other locations, this house should cool itself by air movement. Those clearstory windows above the center beam will move air up and out, taking along heat from solar gain and cooking.

The deeply recessed, sheltered entry is protected from summer heat and wintry blasts. For ski-chalet use, you may want to tuck a storm-doored vestibule in front of it. A door from the double garage lets you reach the same entry hall without stepping outside.

Entry traffic flows directly to the living/dining area and kitchen, or down a hall to three bedrooms and the main bath.

Board siding of cedar (or other western species) plus shingles or shakes on the roof add the natural insulating properties of wood, to contribute still further to energy efficiency.

Gambrel Frame

You're familiar with the popular A-frame, where the planes of a peaked roof are carried to the ground. This leisure home with its gambrel-frame design is endowed with some of the virtues of the A-frame while avoiding some of its faults. And the materials used in its construction are specified to meet stricter energy-saving building codes spreading from state to state.

This design borrows much of the excitement and drama of the A-frame, but makes more practical use of interior spaces. Steeper walls, for example, allow

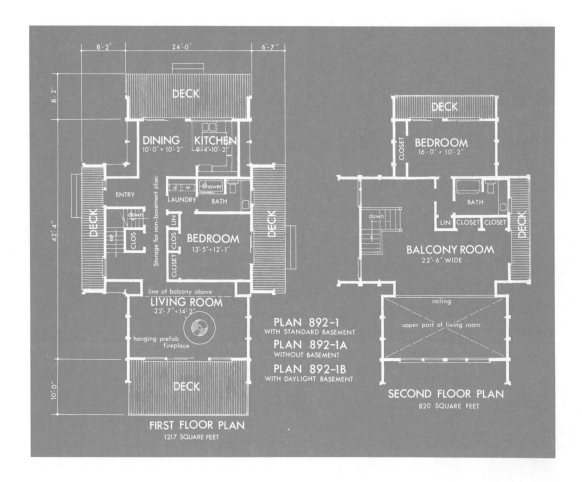

PLAN 892-1
WITH STANDARD BASEMENT

PLAN 892-1A
WITHOUT BASEMENT

PLAN 892-1B
WITH DAYLIGHT BASEMENT

FIRST FLOOR PLAN
1217 SQUARE FEET

SECOND FLOOR PLAN
820 SQUARE FEET

greater use of floor space, and headroom is no problem. Also, heating is more efficient, and there's greater latitude for window placement.

The gambrel design provides more possible furniture arrangements as well. The interior drawing shows how a grouping can be arranged around the metal fireplace to enjoy the view—and the heat.

Extensive use of western woods, notably cedar, is the key to the home's rustic interior. The soaring, two-story-high living room with its glass wall and cedar decking provides a suitable frame for the view.

The floor plan is also efficient. From the entry, served by its own covered side deck, it's only a few steps to any area of the house. The kitchen and dining area are at the rear of the house, and look onto a house-spanning deck. Also on the main floor, the master bedroom, with two closets and bath, fronts on its own side deck reached through sliding glass doors. And don't overlook the laundry facilities tucked into an alcove off the entry hall.

A stairway leads from the main floor's central hallway to a large second-floor balcony room, a second bedroom, and a second full bath. The balcony room and bedroom each opens onto its own deck.

The main floor of the gambrel-frame design provides 1217 square feet of living space; the second floor adds 820 square feet. The greatest width of the house is 40 feet 9 inches, and the overall depth is 62 feet 7 inches.

Three different plans are offered for this design. One has a standard basement (plan no. 892–1), the second no basement (no. 892–1A), and the third (no. 892–1B) provides a daylight basement (shown in the rendering, page 79). The latter plan also includes a garage under the first floor.

Sun Cottage with Garage

A vacation-time retreat that fits any setting, the Sun Cottage also offers full-time
livability and a perfect retirement-haven,
all with the easy upkeep of any apart-
ment.

You enter this snug house down a dramatic corridor that starts as a canopied
deck between house and garage. The
corridor narrows to a low-ceilinged entry
hall, then bursts into a sun-filled living

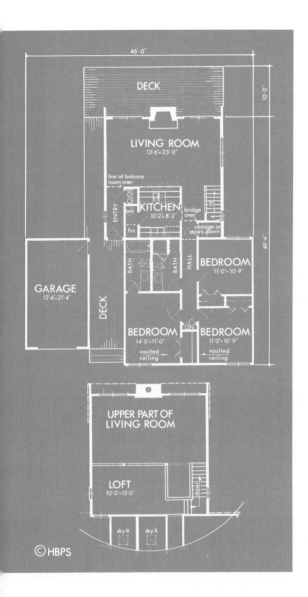

of the house and back around to the entry.

The living room also has a dramatic cathedral ceiling and an upper-level bridge leading to a 10-by-15-foot sleeping loft along the back wall.

The modest first-floor area of only 1229 square feet also includes the kitchen, three bedrooms and two baths.

The kitchen, below the loft, opens across its service counter to the living area. It has been left open to the living room so that persons working in the kitchen may visit and converse with others in the living area. For economy, kitchen plumbing centers on the wall that's common to the bathrooms; the water heater and central furnace unit are in an adjacent utility room. The two skylights (see them on the roof of the rendering) bring sunlight to the bathrooms.

The sleeping areas are grouped to the right of the entry tunnel and include a master bedroom with a cathedral ceiling and two 10-foot 9-inch-by-11-foot rooms, with ceilings tipped toward a raised ridge. The master bath has a tub/shower, the second bath has a stall shower.

All the bedrooms have generous closet space.

To add to the convenience and function of the house, an attached garage is accessible under covered deck entry, and also serves as storage for boat or trailer while the owners are away.

The exterior is finished with western wood board siding applied in an attractive combination of vertical and diagonal.

Overall width of the house and garage is 46 feet, the greatest depth 49 feet 4 inches, plus 10 feet for the projection of the rear garden deck.

room, with the view—whether lake front or mountain vista—framed across the full width of the opposite wall. Flanking a massive fireplace, sliding glass doors lead onto a big deck that runs the width

Gambrel with a Solar Wall

Here's a gambrel roof with a difference. Both sides drop all the way to the foundation, so that the only vertical walls are at the ends and within the window recesses. But the rear roof *isn't* a gambrel, since it plunges in a single plane, like an A-frame. The reason? This provides an ideal surface for mounting solar collectors, and the extra headroom you get with a gambrel's secondary ridge isn't needed over the upstairs floorplan.

This two-story, three-bedroom house is compactly designed around a central circular staircase. A large fireplace is centered on the end wall of the living room; its chimney housing also carries the flue for a fireplace in the master bedroom. Both are vented for outside combustion air.

The house is an energy saver, winter and summer. The recessed glazing is shielded from both wind chill and sun

On solar wall at rear, four collector banks of varying sizes would provide major portion of home's heat, if wall is sited for south exposure and storage is efficient. Fifth pane of top-left bank is not another collector, but a window over central stairwell.

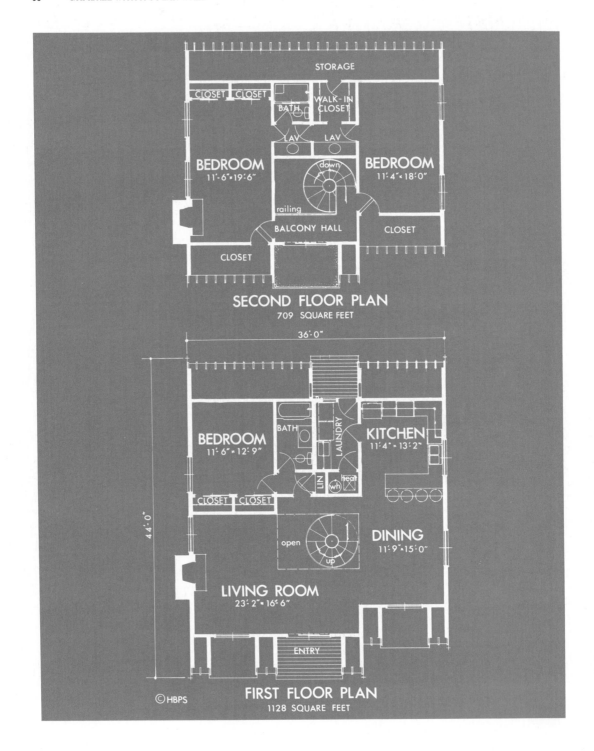

SECOND FLOOR PLAN
709 SQUARE FEET

FIRST FLOOR PLAN
1128 SQUARE FEET

glare, and the construction plans allow for R-30 insulation in that huge roof area (R-19 in walls).

Plumbing runs are kept efficiently short by grouping the first-floor bath and laundry/utility along a common wall and stacking the upstairs bath directly above. Note the clever floor plan for the latter, with four doors giving access to both bedrooms while assuring privacy for simultaneous use.

The broad front entry leads into a living room that spans the whole 24-foot main section of the house and flows past the open stairway and into the kitchen/dining section. Adding to the expansive feel of this floor is the balconied stairwell and the open kitchen, defined only by a breakfast bar with four stools.

Horizontal board siding clads the exterior walls.

See the Sun-Seeker, page 102, for a description of the Solar Schematic—data sheets for planning the solar system for this house.

Vertical House with Sun Deck

As land costs climb, so do houses. The sprawling ranch style is no longer viable if you're building on a small plot in a vacation-home development. And a stacked house is cheaper to build and heat. You've less foundation and less roof area to worry about.

And if you top the stack with a sun deck, as here, you've provided an elevated platform for solar collectors—for your hot-water supply, space heating on cool days, or both.

Covered deck areas and novel windows give special character to this house as does the three-story stairway tower. Angular windows follow the flights. The portholes to the right of them light the

bathrooms on two levels. The stairs continue to the roof, where three skylights help illuminate the step-down living room far below. Wood-framed sliding doors give access from the living-dining area and master bedroom to the wraparound deck.

Clad in western-cedar board siding, the geometric structure is a blend of curves and jutting angles. Glazed areas are balanced by windowless walls that can be sited for privacy or energy saving. The compact kitchen is tucked handily by the entry, and the interior spaces offer constant surprise, with great open light wells dropped through at two opposite corners.

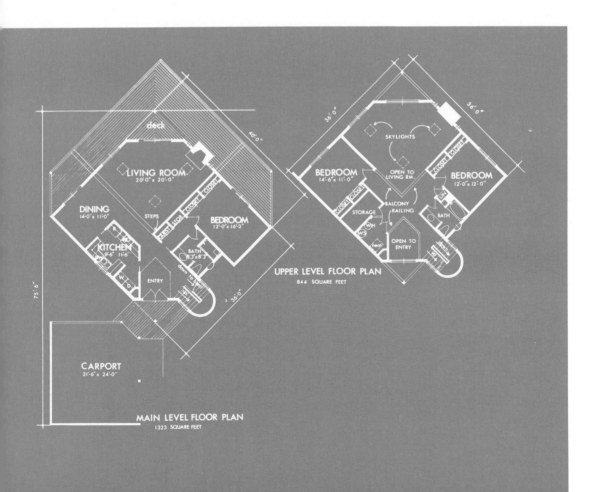

Hexagon House that Grows

View above relates directly to floorplan. Rear view (right) shows decks at two levels.

Hex-shaped pavilions, fitted together like rock crystals, form this unique home. It's designed to serve equally well for vacation or year-round living, and it offers the option of building in stages. The kitchen/bath hex (far right in floor plan) can serve as an independent cottage until time and finances permit you to expand.

At first glance, the angular floorplan and dramatic roof shapes appear more expensive to build than a conventional structure, but we estimate the square-foot

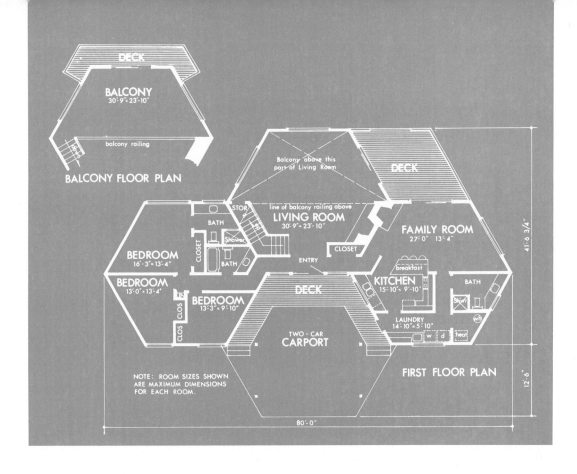

BALCONY FLOOR PLAN

DECK

BALCONY
30'-9" x 23'-10"

balcony railing

Balcony above this
part of Living Room

DECK

line of balcony railing above

LIVING ROOM
30'-9" x 23'-10"

STOR.

BATH

Shower

BATH

CLOSET

FAMILY ROOM
27'-0" x 13'-4"

BEDROOM
16'-3" x 13'-4"

BEDROOM
13'-0" x 13'-4"

ENTRY

CLOSET

breakfast

KITCHEN
15'-10" x 9'-10"

BATH

Show'r

wh

CLOS

BEDROOM
13'-3" x 9'-10"

CLOS

DECK

LAUNDRY
14'-10" x 5'-10"

w   d   heat

TWO - CAR
CARPORT

FIRST FLOOR PLAN

41'-6 3/4"

12'-6'

NOTE: ROOM SIZES SHOWN
ARE MAXIMUM DIMENSIONS
FOR EACH ROOM.

80'-0"

cost will be close to average, since the plans call for a standard joist and beam structure. It is 1995 square feet for the main floor, plus 333 for the balcony, for a total of 2328.

Our interior sketch is of the central, two-story hex. Note that the balcony that projects over more than half of the living room is tucked at the far side, out of traffic lanes. This makes it a visual feature as one enters the house from the carport deck, and also provides it with spacious windows that will doubtless frame the home's best views. (The central one is actually a sliding glass door for access to the cantilevered deck.) This balcony is a fine retreat for painting, piano practice, sewing—even playing pool. It's also an overflow sleeping loft.

The third hex, if added as a last stage, provides the house with three bedrooms and two baths, to relieve the temporary congestion in the other two units. The fourth hex is the open carport, whose roof bridges the entry and projects 12½ feet to shelter the parking area. Two skylights above the entry illuminate this cave-like space. There's a side door from the deck to the laundry/kitchen area.

Siding and interior paneling of western woods add to the warmly informal aspect of this home.

Peak House on Stilts

By lifting itself on seven poles (plus a utility pedestal), this clever house provides sheltered storage for cars and a trailered boat. And on a waterside plot, this off-the-ground stance means good ventilation and less dampness. Elevating the living level enhances the vistas from all windows—and from the deck that's notched into the dining/living corner. The height also improves privacy if neighboring houses crowd in on all sides. Since side yards aren't needed, you can put more house on a small lot: A frontage of 50 feet would be adequate for this 40-foot-wide house.

Part of the 183-square-foot sheltered ground area could be paved or decked for outdoor dining, or as an inclement-weather play area for children. An elevator of the dumbwaiter type provides a convenient means of transporting groceries and other bundles from the carport. You enter the house from either side of the utility pedestal, which encloses a spiral staircase that arrives at the center of the 1235-square-foot main floor. The skylight peak is directly above, dramatizing the entry and illuminating the stair. (The pedestal also houses laundry and furnace equipment.)

The broad living/dining areas flow together without partitions to benefit from that central skylight and give a sense of spaciousness. A sliding glass door in the

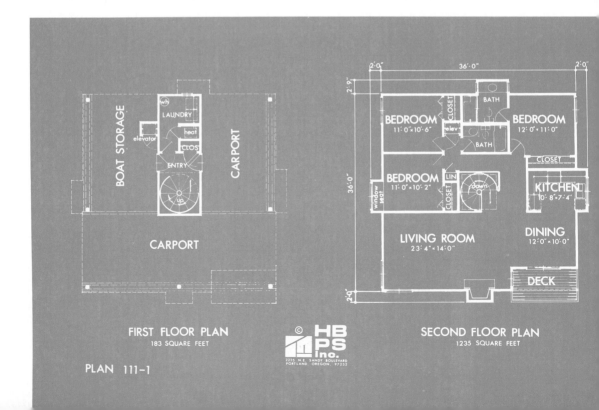

FIRST FLOOR PLAN
183 SQUARE FEET

SECOND FLOOR PLAN
1235 SQUARE FEET

PLAN 111-1

dining area, plus a pair of fixed picture windows at a corner of the living room, also help flood this activity area with light. The kitchen projects from the house into a windowed bay for its own light source. A wide access to the dining area provides a semi-open plan, yet a wall masks kitchen clutter from the living room.

A component-built fireplace snugs into its own cantilevered chase near the deck. The framed-siding treatment of this chase extends above the roof to enclose the chimney stack as well. Lightweight metal fireplace components permit this sort of installation, since no masonry footing is involved.

Three bedrooms are grouped in the opposite half of the house. The master bedroom boasts a bath bay, and one of the others has its own window-seat bay, giving a similar architectural feature to each of the four exterior walls.

A crisp, contemporary look is achieved outside with a low-pitched hip roof terminating in wide overhanging cornices. They're functional, too, since they screen the high, hot rays of the summer sun. Horizontal western-wood board siding and this heavy shadow effect help the house keep a low profile.

King-Post Pagoda

A vaulted ceiling, bowing down from a central king post to cap all rooms, produces the spacious interior in this open-plan cottage.

A massive fireplace (faced in stone or brick) dominates the living room, which also features accent walls of western wood board paneling sloping to the high center point.

Wide vistas are afforded through broad windows and sliding glass doors, both here and in the adjoining dining area. This glazing is shaded from the hot summer sun by deep roof overhangs.

The sliding doors also offer access to the enclosed deck of the dining alcove and to a large wood deck with a bench-railing that wraps around the living room.

The novel but highly functional kitchen is located at the heart of family activity. There's an eating bar along the window wall of the kitchen, and an L-shaped

counter provides more than 16 feet of
work space. The gap between the counter
top and the cable-hung overhead cabinets gives a view into the dining room.
(The flue rising from this floating unit
vents a built-in range hood.)

The master bedroom has a walk-in
closet that also provides access to a private dressing room and bath. Two other
bedrooms, with generous closet bays,
share the second bathroom.

The laundry and furnace room is the
core of the house, contributing to heating

and hot-water economy. The laundry
area is brightened by a skylight. The traffic plan from the front entry eliminates
cross-room traffic and circumvents this
core.

Outside, the attractive styling features
cedar shakes on the pagoda roof, and
diagonal wood siding. The scoop of the
roof peak is echoed in the chimney cap
for the siding-faced fireplace chase.

If you send for the basic plan you'll find
it includes a detached 22-by-24-foot two-
car garage in matching style.

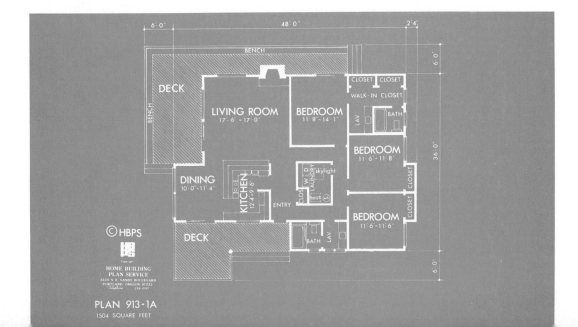

PLAN 913-1A
1504 SQUARE FEET

Upside-Down Retreat

This two-story house which fits any site puts daylight activities up where the views are—and tucks the bedrooms downstairs. On the sloping site depicted below, you reach the house across a catwalk that thrusts out to a wraparound deck at the second-floor level. For a flat site (see alternate floorplan below right) this bridge is eliminated and the left arm of the deck terminates at the entry. Otherwise, the upper-level floorplan is identical, so we didn't repeat it. On the lower level, though, a second entry is provided at the back, recessed into the house line beneath the kitchen, displacing the utilities grouped along that blank "plumbing wall" in the first version.

Whichever version you choose, the house boasts stacked side entries with a two-story slit window alongside to light the circular stair that connects them.

Upstairs action centers on a spacious living room that looks out on three sides. An optional sliding-glass door at the center of the long, front wall provides another access to the broad, cantilevered deck. Tucked behind the built-in fireplace is an ample kitchen; meal service can be on stack tables—on the deck in good weather.

The advantages of this upside-down concept aren't limited to sloping sites: The lofty deck can be a problem-solver on a flat site where another structure or obstacle stands in the way of your view. When you retire for the night (or when you're doing the laundry) the vista's not important, so these activities are relegated to the more mundane ground level.

The basic exterior dimensions (26 feet square) suggest a compact, space-efficient structure that calls for minimal site disruption, whether you erect it on masonry foundation or a poured slab. But the broad upper deck and the wide roof overhangs give the house a larger appearance; they're also practical energy savers, since they shade windows from high summer sun, saving on air-conditioning. Yet a low winter sun can beam its heat under these shaders, cutting fuel costs. The plans provide for a double-flue chimney to serve both upstairs fireplace and a downstairs furnace.

The exterior is enhanced by bevel-pattern western wood siding, applied horizontally to lengthen the appearance of the structure, and by compatible, and durable, western lumber for the decks and railings that add to architectural detail.

Though the house has an abundance of windows, it's designed to meet new energy-thrift specifications. Building codes are getting tougher each year, especially in insulation and sanitation. There are tighter electrical codes, too.

The two levels—totaling around 1300 square feet—are highly functional. There's a full bath on each level (downstairs, it has a one-piece fiberglass shower with molded-in seat). And plumbing costs are minimized by stacking the baths.

Upstairs areas have a spatial continuity that avoids wasteful hallways. This level is adaptable for overflow sleeping (on convertible couches); there's a wardrobe closet and dressing room between the living room and bath.

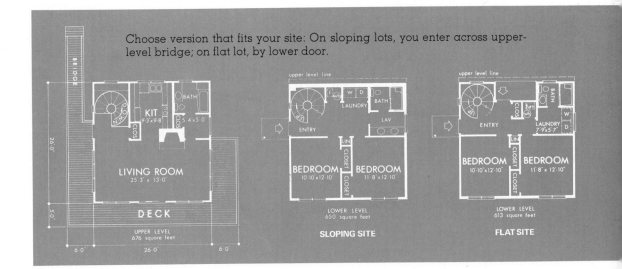

Choose version that fits your site: On sloping lots, you enter across upper-level bridge; on flat lot, by lower door.

The Sun-Seeker

As one example, we've sited the house so the living room—and longest roof plane—face due south. Plans you buy show collectors applied to each of the roof pitches; you select best application for your site, build or buy collectors to suit.

A glance at the painting of the front of the house and our sketch of the rear makes clear why this house has been called the Sun-Seeker. The entire house is designed to provide any site with an ideal roof area for applying solar collectors—whether for a water heater or for a supplemental heating system. Orientation of roof-mounted collectors is critical, since optimum winter heating occurs when they face due south, with less than 15-degree deviation to east or west. The multiple roof planes of this handsome contemporary let you face any side south, since all four sides present an optimum roof pitch for collector-mounting.

The plan further adapts itself to solar siting with its novel window treatments. If you choose to face the front wall to the south—mounting collectors on that upper roof—the summer sun will be shaded from the boxed bedroom window and the canopied windows on the entry deck. The lower winter rays, however, will be welcomed, to help with the heating.

Equal attention has been paid to the interior detailing of this house, beginning at the entry that keys traffic to all the first-

Solar schematic lets you adapt system to other leisure homes in this book

On four big (18″ x 30″) plans sheets, solar basics are summarized, as are instructions for calculating the size system you'd need for your home (new or existing). There's also illustrated data on collectors, storage tanks (water's the transfer medium), heat exchangers, siting for best solar exposure—and tips for working with local heating engineers (the schematic was prepared by a certified pro). The Sun-Seeker is used as an example (on sheet 4) to show how solar capabilities can be computed for a specific house in your area. The solar system detailed on these sheets is based on the one built and tested at Langley Research Center. It's intended to supplement any forced hot-air system, and should provide about 40 percent of the heat required for any home. It applies equally well to the Solar Gambrel in this chapter, as well as to other house designs. To order the Solar Schematic see page 190.

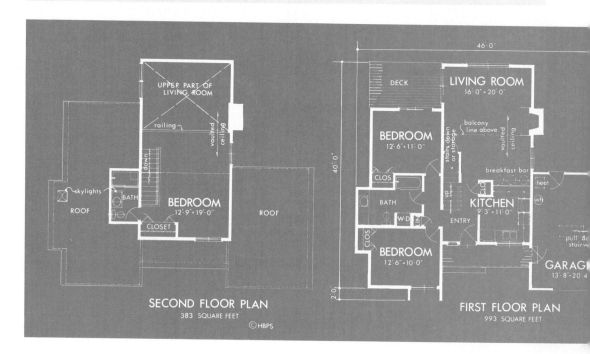

floor rooms. It's just a few steps to the U-shaped kitchen and to the bath shared by the downstairs bedrooms.

A spacious deck—built of 2x4 western lumber on edge—is shared by one of the bedrooms and the living room. The exterior of the house as shown is finished with western-wood board paneling.

The master bedroom, up an open staircase, has its own skylighted bathroom and walk-in closet. A cathedral ceiling covers both the bedroom and the living room.

5. FAR-OUT SHAPES

V-PAC was the first design source for the *Popular Science* leisure home series, and remains the most prolific: It has the largest representation in this book—you'll find nineteen houses in the grouping that follows. V-PAC's an abbreviated acronym for Vacation Plans, Products and Properties Advisory Council—an informal group (mostly manufacturers of building materials) that was formed to promote quality leisure home plans for build-it-yourself projects. The Council is under the leadership of the architectural firm of Robert Martin Engelbrecht and Associates. Mr. Engelbrecht, who administers its programs (including construction of selected designs for promotional purposes), maintains an architectural office near Princeton, N.J. where all V-PAC plans are designed. *Popular Science* has been the publishing arm of V-PAC since 1973. Sponsoring members (and their specialties) include:

American General (prefab stairs); Andersen (windows, gliding doors); Darworth Inc. (stains, preservatives); Du Pont (interior finishes); Frigidaire (kitchen appliances); GAF (roofing); Georgia-Pacific (paneling, doors); Heatilator (fireplaces); Johns-Manville (insulation); F. E. Myers & Bro. (water-pump systems); Pass & Seymour (wiring devices); Simpson Timber (decking, siding); Singer (heating); United Farm Agency (land resources); Universal-Rundle (bathroom fixtures).

The architectural renderer for all V-PAC designs is Don Scherer, whose highly-charged ink lines crackle and snap across the following pages, and whose original approach to perspective is often essential to capture the complexities of V-PAC's multi-faceted roof designs.

For ordering information on this group of plans, see page 191.

Holiday Hill for Entertaining

Ideal for holiday entertaining, this house is also designed for gracious year-round living. Though the house boasts all the amenities for family weekends and vacations at *all* seasons, its special inspiration was the occasional circumstance that puts such a strain on conventional homes: holiday entertaining.

Count those bedrooms and see how well provided each is with access to a bathroom, and with provision for privacy (count those doors, while you're at it). This

house is "upside down"—stacking major activity areas (kitchen, dining, living room) atop the ground-level "sleep cells." These flank a big family room with direct access to the outside via sliding patio doors that have a storage area between them for bulky outdoor furniture and sports equipment. This family room is an ideal "depressurizing chamber" for exuberant skiers (or hikers or swimmers or hang-glider fliers)—a place they can shuck off gear and debris before passing into dressier quarters.

A matched pair of sliding glass doors

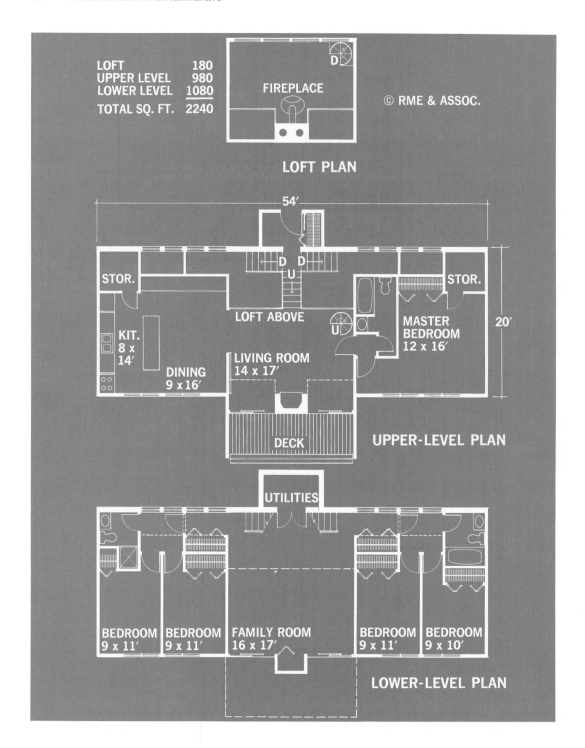

LOFT   180
UPPER LEVEL   980
LOWER LEVEL   1080
TOTAL SQ. FT. 2240

© RME & ASSOC.

FIREPLACE

LOFT PLAN

54'

STOR.

LOFT ABOVE

U

STOR.

MASTER
BEDROOM
12 x 16'

20'

KIT.
8 x
14'

DINING
9 x 16'

LIVING ROOM
14 x 17'

U

DECK

UPPER-LEVEL PLAN

UTILITIES

BEDROOM
9 x 11'

BEDROOM
9 x 11'

FAMILY ROOM
16 x 17'

BEDROOM
9 x 11'

BEDROOM
9 x 10'

LOWER-LEVEL PLAN

on the floor above is stepped forward, and gives onto a cantilevered deck that's shielded at each side from crosswinds. Behind is the "floating" living room—the heart of the house, since everything circulates from it or through it. At the front it's open to a hideaway loft, above; at the back it looks down to the lower level past a T-shaped stair. There's a mid-floor rear entry at the stair landing.

The loft (snugged into the higher peak of the house's center section and reached by a spiral stair) boasts its own fireplace— and the best views: through the rear glass wall and through novel portholes built into the chimney cricket. Note that flues are encased in an insulated full-height chase that's sheathed to match the house siding.

Holiday Hill might be termed the ultimate split-level. It adapts to sloping sites of any grade. On the fairly steep lot we've sketched, the ground floor is dug into the hillside, with the tapered concrete foundation doubling as a retaining wall. In such a case, the rear windows that light the bedroom halls would be strips tucked near the ceiling, or they could be omitted, since daylight will bounce down through the open level above. The canted sill line roughly parallels the slope to add to the geometric appeal.

Engelframe Towable

This towable two-phase is the ideal do-it-yourself house for distant sites where weekend building just isn't practical because of time and energy expended on travel.

The "starter wing" can be easily and quickly constructed in your backyard, handy to your shop—the way you'd build a boat or camping trailer. Then, rent a set of wheels and tow the assembly to your site—which you've prepared with a post-and-beam foundation.

Borrowing an idea from the Lockbox House, the decks are hinged to the floor of the unit, to double as window shutters—especially valuable, here, since they offer protection on the road. (Since the unit is only eight feet in width, no transport permit is required.)

If yours is not a large family, you may

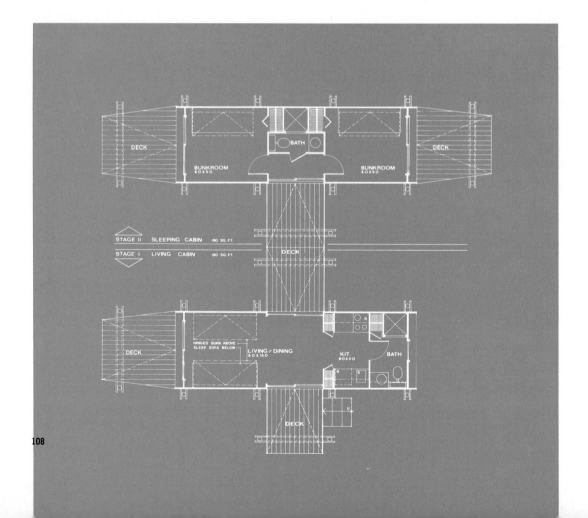

find this first wing ample for your weekend needs. It makes an ideal hunting cabin or ski retreat, with its hinged bunk beds, kitchenette and shower. But if you wish to expand, later, you just build a sleeping wing and tow it alongside.

Note that the floorplan and Phase II sketch offer a choice of arrangements:

The plan retains the hinged-deck feature of both wings, for secure closure when the house is vacant; the two side decks drop down to form a bridge. In the sketch, though, these shutters have been absorbed into a larger deck with a connecting breezeway.

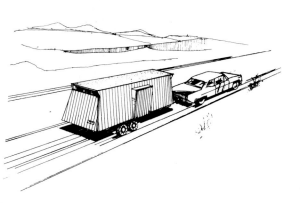

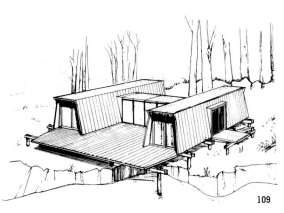

Cruciform House

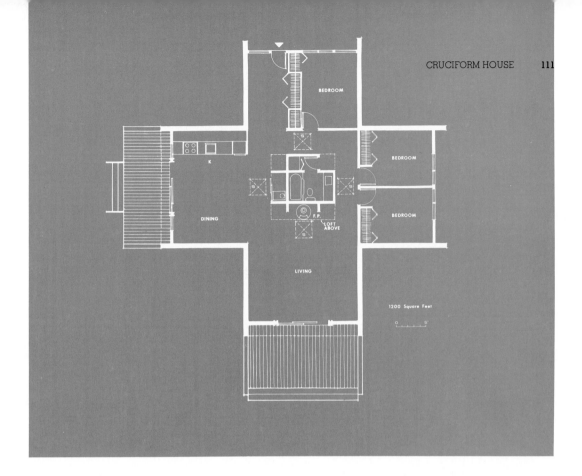

BEDROOM

BEDROOM

K

BEDROOM

DINING

F.P.
LOFT
ABOVE

LIVING

1200 Square Feet

Windows in each end wall frame a different view in this bisecting Engelframe design. Robert Martin Engelbrecht is famous as the inventor of the truncated A-frame for vacation homes. By trimming off that useless peak (wasteful of both construction materials and heat), he's able to move the sidewalls out to a steeper pitch for better utilization of floor space.

These canted walls are actually massive box beams, unweakened by window openings. Since they're strong enough to cantilever at least a third of their length—and could span up to 80 feet—they adapt to difficult sites where minimal foundation support is possible.

The Cherokee Indians, after whom this house was named by its architect, were formidable warriors against adversity—so the Engelframe Cherokee is a formidable fortress against the elements. Designed in the shape of a symmetrical cross, this steeply framed single-floor house creates a compact plan with maximum space. The open ends of the design capture the view in all directions.

Sliding glass doors lead from the living room to a deck and from the dining room to a relaxing area which can be either a patio or the raised deck shown.

A center bath and utility core screens three bedrooms from other living areas. A loft above this core can provide the second-home owner with additional storage facilities or an emergency sleeping loft for overflow guests.

Stilt House (Apache)

Architect Robert Martin Engelbrecht, famed for vacation-home designs, has chosen American Indian names for many of his houses. "Apache" is appropriate to this setting, since it means "living high on the mesa." But this floating platform house adapts to a variety of sites; it needs no level or smooth terrain and calls for only eight or ten piers, rather than a foundation. On a flat beach, it would have a short entry stairway. It could even perch on a mountain crag or bridge a brook. Window walls take full advantage of any setting.

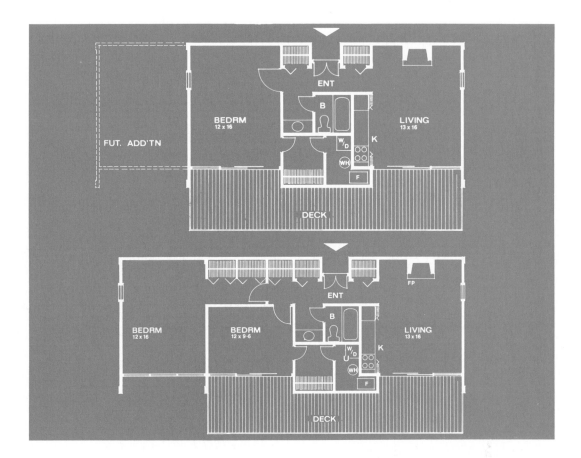

The house can be built with only one bedroom with the opportunity of future expansion. Note that the floor plans give a choice of one or two bedrooms. In the one bedroom plan its size is 12 by 16 feet, which becomes the size of the second bedroom when a hall and closets shrink the first.

The open area under the house provides storage for boats, snowmobiles, and other recreational gear; it's also a cozy play area for rainy days. The roof creates interiors of lofty distinction. The compartmented bathroom permits dual use when the second bedroom is added. Fold-ing doors hide a tuck-away kitchen in the living area.

First-stage construction suggests that the bedroom be equipped with two pair of bunk beds, and a convertible sleeping unit for the living room sleeping six altogether.

Compact inside, the house features a large redwood deck and is ideal for casual, indoor-outdoor living.

On any site the house has a lofty, airy feeling with the decks and window walls projecting into the view. The supporting structure remains exposed, as a dominant part of the rugged design.

Twin-Prow Split Level

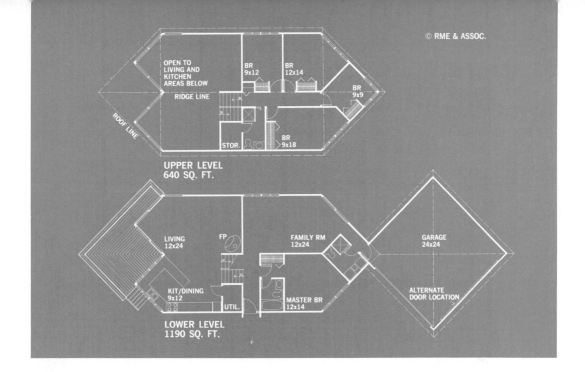

OPEN TO
LIVING AND
KITCHEN
AREAS BELOW

BR
9x12

BR
12x14

BR
9x9

RIDGE LINE

ROOF LINE

BR
9x18

STOR.

**UPPER LEVEL
640 SQ. FT.**

LIVING
12x24

FP

FAMILY RM
12x24

GARAGE
24x24

KIT/DINING
9x12

UTIL.

MASTER BR
12x14

ALTERNATE
DOOR LOCATION

**LOWER LEVEL
1190 SQ. FT.**

The story-and-a-half at the front of this house is as practical as it is dramatic. That unexpected reverse corner at the center creates *two* window bays, and splits interior space into a living room and a kitchen, both sporting two-direction views and cathedral ceilings. That deep roof overhang shields the glass from excess solar heat.

The home's stretched-hex shape boasts a unique treatment at the opposite end, as well. Here, it shares a corner with a pyramidal garage, providing an interior entry through the bath/laundry hallway. This back bathroom contains a shower and space for a washer-dryer.

It's basically a split level, with the twin-prow front rooms a half-level above the entryway. The back half of the house is a full two stories, to stack a variety of upstairs bedrooms and a third bath above the master bedroom/bath and big family room. The latter, with access to that back bathroom, can double as a guest suite; it has sliding glass doors onto a private terrace screened by the garage wall.

The big double garage can serve as a boat house, to avoid back-and-forth trailering. It's also designed for overhead storage of all the bulky items a vacation house collects. You can tuck more storage under the house ridge, above the hall ceiling.

This plan adapts to a narrow lot, and since the garage is square, you can locate the driveway approach and garage door on any of its four sides. Depending on the terrain, you can have a crawl space or full basement (with exterior access) under the living/kitchen area. The rear half of the house would most likely be erected on a concrete slab.

A short flight of stairs ascends from the entry hall to the living level; another continues upstairs. Tucked into the stairway corner is the essential fireplace.

Two-Phase Twin Ridge

We've named this house Twin Ridge because of its two wings, set at right angles. Gross floor area of Phase I is 505 square feet; the T wing adds 570 square feet, including entry connection. Wood framing is sheathed and sided in one operation with redwood plywood; you needn't even insulate or panel the inside the first year. The architect, Robert Martin Engelbrecht, suggests that you can fabricate panelized components in your backyard, cart them to your site on a rented trailer; his two-phase concept frees you from an every-weekend bondage that

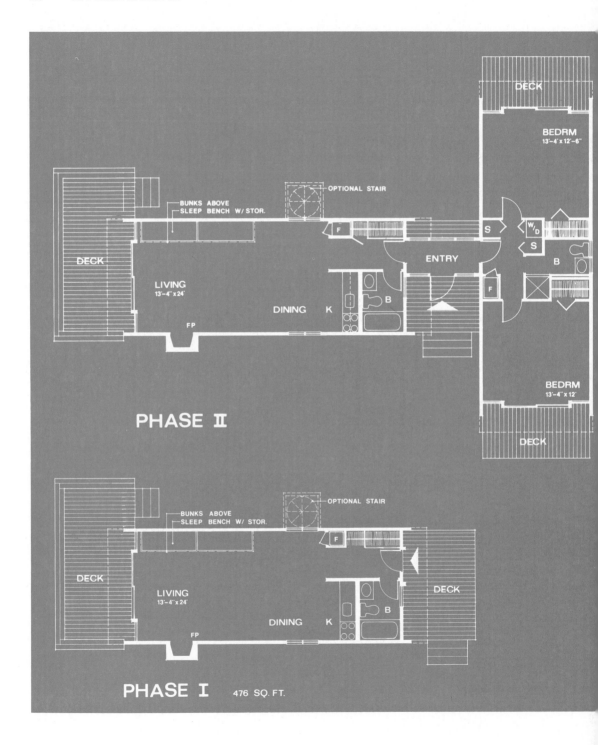

DECK

BEDRM
13'-4" x 12'-6"

OPTIONAL STAIR

BUNKS ABOVE
SLEEP BENCH W/ STOR.

F

S

W/D

S

ENTRY

B

DECK

LIVING
13'-4" x 24'

DINING   K   B   F

BEDRM
13'-4" x 12'

FP

DECK

PHASE II

DECK

BUNKS ABOVE
SLEEP BENCH W/ STOR.

OPTIONAL STAIR

F

DECK

DECK

LIVING
13'-4" x 24'

DINING   K   B

FP

PHASE I   476 SQ. FT.

can go on forever when you're building from a conventional leisure-home plan. He points out that this T-shaped house can be built in two stages, with the first stage serving to accommodate up to four people, particularly if wall-hung bunk beds are used.

Either of the two wings require a minimum of tree cutting or site disruption. They can be erected on piers, or on crawl-space, or on full basement foundations—or even, where the site permits, on a concrete slab.

The glass end walls, glass sliding doors, and decks expand the livability of

the house further. The second-stage wing is joined with a glass-walled entry corridor, and is composed of two bedrooms, an additional bath, and space for laundry equipment.

The two decks, one open and one railed with a bench, offer family and guests a choice for outdoor relaxation.

Another original touch is the optional spiral stair for basement access.

Incidentally, this was the first design published in the *Popular Science* leisure home series that followed the initial Lockbox articles reprinted in Part Two of this book.

Arrowhead Retreat

Those two striking houses perched at opposite sides of a river valley in the rendering are the same house from different angles. The novel shape suggests a blunt arrowhead, and it gives a special excitement to the interior space. Three ridges soar to a central peak, adding the interest of sloped ceilings. Roof projections at all window clusters screen the glass from high, hot summer sun.

You enter the house below floor level and either step up into the central traffic core (four bedrooms, two baths, and the living-dining area all open off it) or you descend to the game room/utility level that's tucked within the foundation pedestal. (For a flat site, of course, this lower floor could be replaced with a simple slab on grade.)

Architect Robert Engelbrecht calls his house the Tomahawk and "signs" the design with his famous cantilevered deck framed by the typical bench rail. Living and dining areas open onto it.

The master bedroom is 13 by 16 feet and has its own private bath. The three other bedrooms are served by the combination bath and laundry room. The centrally located fireplace serves both the large living and adjacent dining spaces.

This house accommodates the leisure needs of a family in a very thoughtful way, by carefully zoning various types of room use so that there's a reasonable degree of separation for various age-oriented activities. Sleeping areas are spaced from the daytime living areas, while the lower level offers an isolated location for noisy activities.

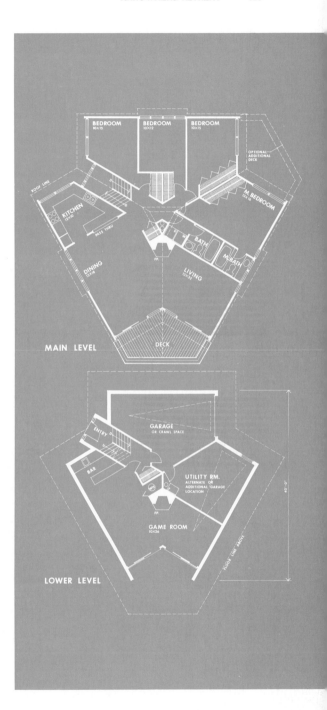

Octagon House for Tight Perch

Like a trimly cut gem, this multifaceted house makes the most of its setting—and its light. The interiors are as dramatic as the octagonal exterior. A central staircase (with skylight above) spirals down to the lower level. All ceilings—wood decking over exposed beams—taper up to the skylight. The open-plan living/dining space is further enhanced by sliding glass doors onto an elevated, cantilevered deck. The center zone also contains an efficient kitchen, defined with a pass-through eating bar. Back-to-back bath areas serve three bedrooms.

Architect Engelbrecht calls this house The Sekani—an Indian name meaning "those who live among the rocks." But it can be built on a flat site, too—with the lower level (and stairway) optional.

The down slope lower level can be built with a partial basement opening onto grade or a full basement, depending on the site. The projecting chase accommodates both upper and lower level fireplaces.

While the octagonal conformation presents some problems in furnishing the odd-shaped rooms, the compensation is that 360-degree outlook that gives every room its own view. A partially railed deck wraps nearly half the house to add space for comfortable outdoor activities.

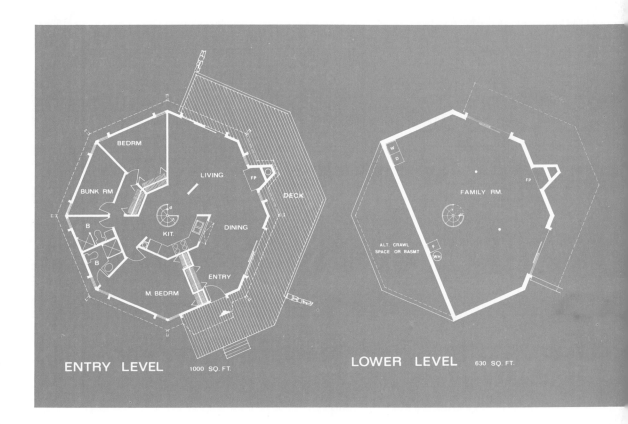

ENTRY LEVEL   1000 SQ. FT.

LOWER LEVEL   630 SQ. FT.

Bridge House for Small Stream

This leisure home capitalizes on a unique site: It's designed to span a small stream. Its architect, Robert Martin Engelbrecht, has built such a home for himself; his house handsomely bridges the neck of a pond. Says he: "Though the foundation for my house was built from scratch, my inspiration for the Bridge House was those abandoned foundations I spot along stream banks all over the country-side. In many cases where rerouting a road left a bridge unused, the bridge has deteriorated but its well-engineered foundations remain in good shape. If you can buy such a site, you've got the tough part of this job already done for you."

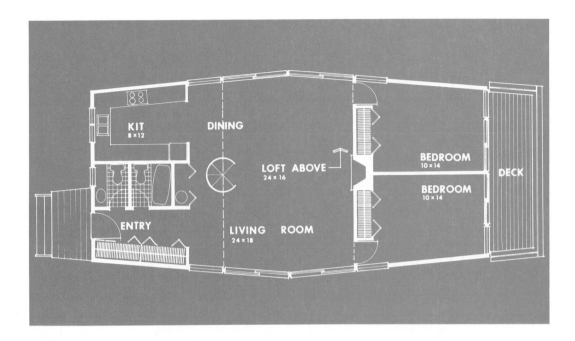

If you're not so lucky, but still have a tranquil stream or pond you'd like to span, the plans you can send for give details for embankment foundations. Be sure that wing walls of masonry or railroad ties will channel any highwater flow. It's best to check out the function of these bridge piers through a highwater season.

You'll want to be certain that the highest water level remains well below the floor span.

The house itself, though compact, is designed for expansive living. A stairway spirals to a central loft that can accommodate a large number of overnight guests, inclement weather-type leisure pursuits, or spread-out craftwork.

The staircase helps zone the open living area from the open dining area. The U-shaped kitchen is spacious.

Headroom for the loft is created by a four-way roof that sweeps up from low corners to a high center ridge. Behind the fireplace are bedrooms, which can also serve as bunkrooms, doubling the number that can occupy the house. Each bedroom (10 by 14 feet) opens out onto a large railed deck. The entrance has adequate storage for all weather gear and both a full and half bath.

Sliding glass doors are used along the peaked side walls to provide both view and ventilation. When the glass is rolled back, latched screens allow strong cross breezes without the nuisance of insects, thus turning the living space into an airy outdoor pavilion. Double glazing plus tight construction make the house a snug year-round retreat.

Stretched Hex (Omaha)

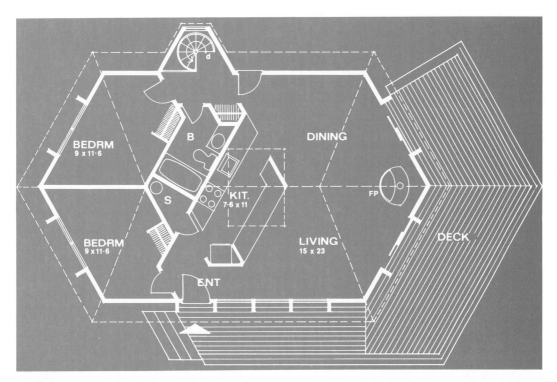

Novel in exterior shape and floor plan, this vacation house is another in the series the architect gave Indian names. This one is dubbed The Omaha. Tribal translation: "Those going against the current"—an apt description of adventurous builders who don't want a conventional house.

Two-thirds of the home's 800 square feet is one large living-cooking-dining area, with insulating-glass sliding doors opening onto a spacious deck. The ceiling slopes upward to a central skylight. The kitchen is semi-concealed by wall fins that bracket the cabinetry. Of possible locations for the prefab fireplace, most dramatic is (as shown on plan) centered between the canted glass doors.

Though polygonal, each bedroom will accommodate a double bed—or bunks if preferred. A spiral staircase beside the back exit descends to the partial basement (full basement is one of many possible options).

The prows at each end of the open-plan Omaha angle the window walls in such a way that all views are expanded.

Two distinct architectural features visually expand the house beyond its actual size: The overhang and strong eaves trim lengthen and dramatize the asphalt shingle roof. And the height of the house appears to be increased by the strong, heavy vertical jamb projection that frames each window and door opening.

The rendering shows rough-sawn redwood plywood siding with vertical battens. The large three-sided deck contains a handsome bench rail—a typical feature of houses by architect Engelbrecht.

Lean-to House

This is a steeply-roofed cabin that's reminiscent of the shelters trappers once built to protect themselves against the elements. Just as the woodsman aimed his lean-to toward the sun, we angle ours toward a dramatic wall of glass that frames the view. Built with its low back wall set into the hillside, the one-room, two-story house is entered through a raised dormer that provides headroom at the doorway.

The interior space soars dramatically upward toward strip windows that run along a full-length sleep loft. Rustic crossbeams support this loft by spanning the room from the jambs of the sliding glass doors to the back wall (dotted lines on lower level plan). For additional sleeping, built-in couches have hinged panels above that raise to form double bunks. With these, the house can sleep seven. Bathroom tucks beside a strip kitchen to put all plumbing in one wall. The spacious deck is railed for safety. The bench rail for comfortable outdoor seating is a typical feature of Engelbrecht's houses.

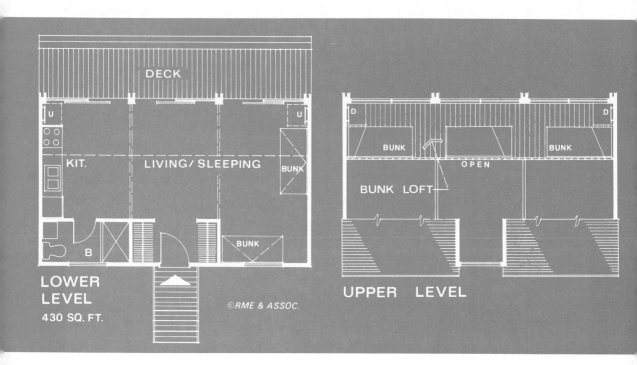

DECK

KIT. LIVING/SLEEPING BUNK

B BUNK

LOWER LEVEL
430 SQ. FT.

©RME & ASSOC.

BUNK OPEN BUNK

BUNK LOFT

UPPER LEVEL

Round House on a Pedestal

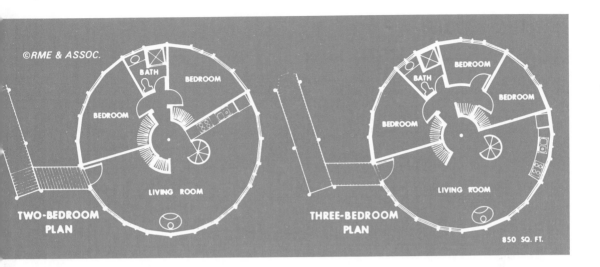

©RME & ASSOC.

TWO-BEDROOM PLAN

THREE-BEDROOM PLAN

850 SQ. FT.

Can't decide which way a house should face on your site? A round house looks in all directions. Ideal for a beach house, this "mushroom," designed for V-PAC by architect Robert Martin Engelbrecht, would also fit a rugged site with cramped level ground. Since the entire living area projects from the support core, you need no outdoor balconies. Full-height fixed-glass and screened-casement windows turn all rooms into enclosed decks. In fact, this allows the entire living area to perform as a screened outdoor room, projecting into the view.

The structural design allows interior partitions to run beneath any of the twenty-four radiating roof beams, offering great flexibility in floorplan. In the three-bedroom version, the two smaller rooms work best with bunks. A third version (not shown) is an open plan, with a single spacious bedroom between the walls of bath and kitchen.

The pedestal base consists of eight poles (or reinforced masonry piers) enclosed with wall panels to create ground-level storage accessible from above by a spiral stair. You could eliminate the catwalk and use this base as your entry, if you chose.

Of course, just like square houses, round houses come in many sizes and floorplans. We have shown only two of the plan variations possible. As always with such an unusual shape, you have to balance the difficulties of furniture arrangement (particularly in the three-bedroom floor plan) against the magnificence of that 360-degree view.

Split Gable
with Privacy Offset

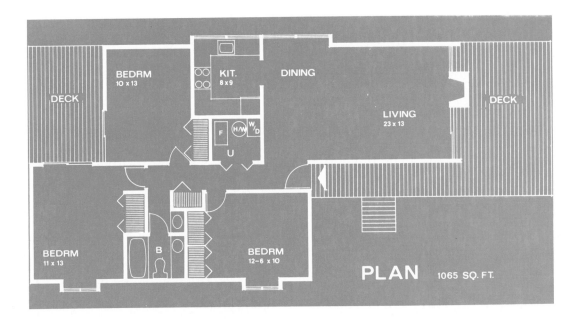

The split gable elevation is created by an offset plan which locates a protected entrance near the center of this low, long, compact vacation house. Shrewdly zoned for vacation guests, it is sliced down its ridgeboard and the halves offset to create a protected deck at front and rear. That third bedroom (at back) could be omitted if you'd prefer a larger deck area adjacent to the kitchen, with a rear entry tucked behind the utility room.

Although only a thousand-plus square feet in size, this house has a zoned plan that allows it to perform as a much bigger house. Additionally, the sloping ceilings follow the roof line to higher interior walls, giving an airy, open feeling. The front hall gives quick access to all active areas with no traffic bottlenecks.

Snow, wet leaves, sand and mud are frequent enemies of neatness and cleanliness in a vacation home; all this is min-imized here because of the protected entry which gives quick access to the utility room and to the bathroom. The efficient single bath is zoned to include an extra lavatory.

The back bedrooms, removed from the bustle, share a deck through patio doors. Similar doors, up front, expand the living room right past the fireplace chase to encompass the larger deck.

Windows are placed to offer views in all directions, yet maintain privacy and adequate wall space for furniture.

Architect Robert Martin Engelbrecht has again given a colorful name to his creation. It is called the Lenape, which you pronounce "len-a-pay."

Stacked Shack

Chop a corner off a cube, shift the ridge across the remaining pair of corners, stack an L-shaped loft at mid-height, and you've transformed a conventional box into a delightful small house. I particularly admire the cantilevered triangular deck prowing out into space, and the sliding barn-door partitions that close off the sleep zones from the circular-stair hall. At the ridge, these zones are a loft-y 10 feet high.

The lower entry level has a window-wall to frame an expansive view with a free-standing fireplace at the center. This entire level is basically one space: the spiral staircase and partial partitions zone off the entry corner with its coat closet, bath and utility rooms. The sleeping lofts are open to the two-story fireplace triangle and share the window-wall's vista. They're provided with accordion doors or drapes that can be drawn to give privacy from the living room below and from each other. If provided with two to six double bunks, these lofts could sleep four to twelve people.

In addition to the two glass sliding doors opening onto the deck, there are casement windows located to provide cross ventilation.

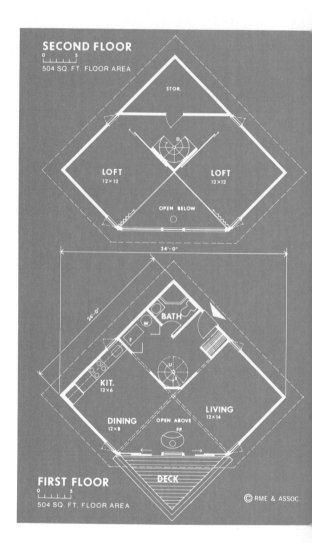

Double-Decker Salt Marsh

Architect Robert Martin Engelbrecht christened this home "The Salt Marsh," so our color rendering depicts a bayside setting with the front deck serving as a boat dock. Yet, since this three-bedroom house adapts to a variety of settings, we prefer our broader title. It has a double meaning: There are, indeed, two deck levels; and the sleeping areas are also stacked.

That front deck, flanked with sliding patio doors from master bedroom and dining areas, needn't be a dock—it might overhang a ski slope, or be laid on flat ground as a terrace. The canopy deck,

above it, provides privacy—ideal, the architect points out, for *au naturel* sunbaths.

The plan of the main level is a big H, with plumbing and traffic cores forming the crosspiece. This entry/kitchen/bath unit separates daytime-activity areas from the sleep wing. A stairway spirals up from this entry to a bunk loft (ideal for children or unexpected guests that overflow the downstairs bedrooms). The low entryway contrasts with the high, slope-ceiling areas at both sides. Though the house is small (and economical to build), space is

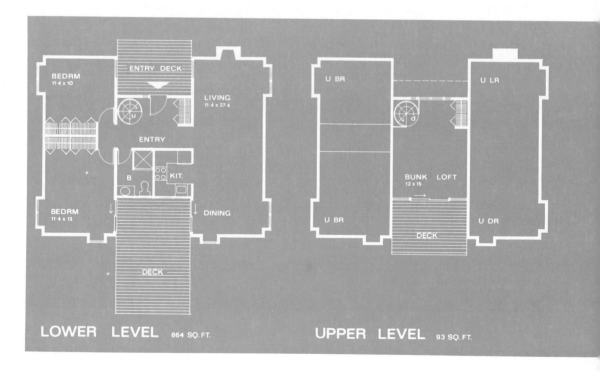

LOWER LEVEL 864 SQ. FT.

UPPER LEVEL 93 SQ. FT.

expanded by thrusting windows and fire-place beyond the wall line, creating exterior interest as a bonus.

The house sketched here is over a crawl space. That front foundation wall doubles as a retainer for land fill, letting you perch the house at water's edge or even projecting beyond. The working drawings offer several alternate foundations, including slab-on-grade or full basement.

The sleeping wing can be built with high sloping ceilings following the rafters, or with flat ceilings to create storage attics accessible from the bunk loft.

Note especially the generous size of the living/dining area: 11 feet 4 inches by 27 feet 4 inches, with a fireplace centered on the shorter side wall of the living room.

Bunk Tower: Rooms with a View

For a ski chalet—or summer guests—you can stack up as many sleep lofts as needed. A continuous stairway spirals up this tower from the entry vestibule. Identical bunk lofts are stacked beside it—one, two, three (or more) tall. Stacked sleep space makes special sense for vacation homes: The higher you go, the better the views you provide your guests. And the less site disruption for your foundation.

Since most leisure homes are built on a slope, you can tuck a partial basement under that glass-ended living room to expand the house function; use it as a game room, sauna, laundry, or storage area. Though the rest of this house has an insulated floor over crawl space, a flat site gives you the option of a full basement.

The architect calls this house the Quinipissa—an Indian name for "those who look out." The top level of the tower is provided with additional window area to create an observation lounge. Imagine yourself greeting friends on the ski slopes with: "Meet us in the tower for drinks at four."

The architectural contrast between the vertical sleep tower and the horizontal living space makes this an exciting house in any setting.

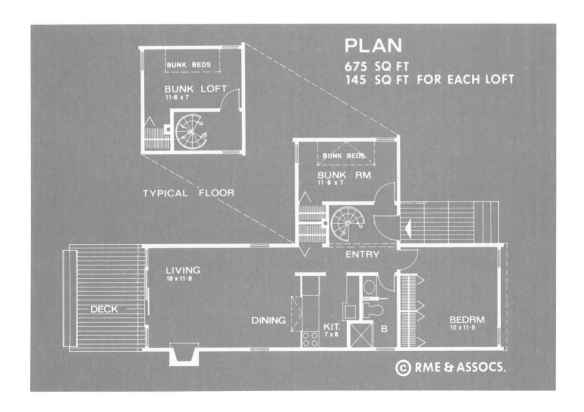

PLAN
675 SQ FT
145 SQ FT FOR EACH LOFT

BUNK BEDS

BUNK LOFT
11·8 x 7

TYPICAL FLOOR

BUNK BEDS

BUNK RM.
11·8 x 7

ENTRY

LIVING
18 x 11·8

DECK

DINING

KIT.
7 x 8

B

BEDRM
10 x 11·8

© RME & ASSOCS.

Arrowhead Lodge (Akanu)

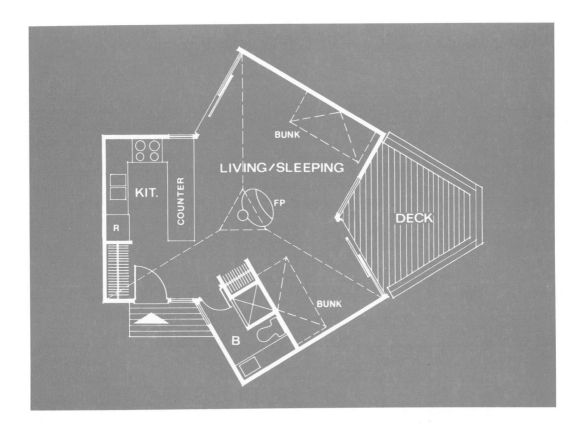

The unique floorplan, plus a pyramid roof with a chimney skylight, creates the distinctive shape of this house. The steep-pitch roof is a three-faced pyramid (dotted lines on the plan indicate ridge boards) imposed on a floorplan shaped like a blunt arrowhead. The result: an eaves line of multiple angles that looks at home in any natural setting. Inside, exposed-beam ceilings and the flue of a prefab fireplace soar toward a central skylight that's a pyramid all its own.

The only partition wall encloses the bathroom—and supports double-deck hinged bunks that fold up during the day. Across the room, two more bunks can be wall-hung to sleep a second couple. A sliding glass door gives onto the dramatically cantilevered deck—which, on a waterside site, could jut past the bank. The kitchen is more than adequate with a counter doubling as an eating-serving bar.

Architect Engelbrecht calls this house Akanu—Indian for "small lodge."

Stilt House Stacks Two Ways

This two-story, two-bedroom house is a cozy size, despite its imposing appearance. It's a veritable eagle's nest, perched on eight sturdy columns in close-set pairs, and tied to its hillside site with a dramatic catwalk. As illustrated here, the house has the living room on its upper (entry) level, connected to the lower bedrooms with a spiral staircase. But the plan is easily reversed for a more conventional stacking. You can tuck the entry floor under the bedrooms if your site is less steep.

Either way, each bedroom retains its private balcony and easy access to the bath and utility rooms. A compact kitchen is handy to the open-plan living-dining room on the other floor, flooded with light from the sliding patio doors on three sides that open the entire space to a cantilevered deck. The decks projecting from each of the bedrooms create an observation lookout for all room areas. The roof has a wide overhang to shelter outdoor activities; it pagoda-peaks to a central skylight.

Any way you stack it, this is one of architect Robert Martin Engelbrecht's most versatile homes, adaptable to many sites with minimal excavation. It's ideal for a couple with one or two small children . . . as a "shared" investment for two childless couples . . . or—eventually—as a retirement retreat with guest room.

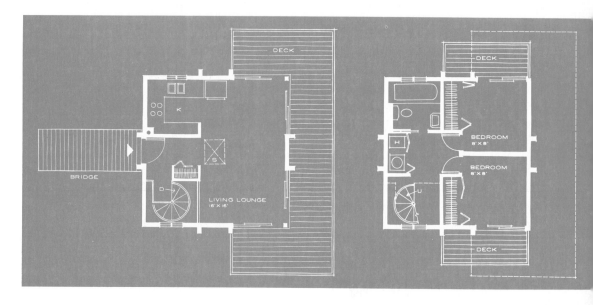

Two-Story Sleep Wing

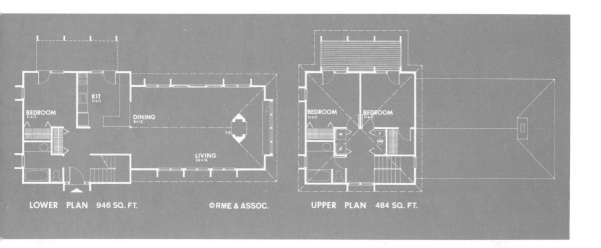

LOWER PLAN 946 SQ. FT.   ©RME & ASSOC.   **UPPER PLAN   484 SQ. FT.**

Half of this dramatic, large-scaled house consists of stacked bedrooms; the other half, a single-story wing, is a spacious living/dining area focused on an island fireplace at the far end. The square footage totals over 1500.

Both floors of the sleep wing have a similar plan: All three bedrooms are 11 feet square (served by two identical bathrooms stacked for simplified plumbing runs), and each opens directly onto a patio or deck. The upper rooms share a roofed porch that should be oriented to the best vista. The rafters of the four-way roof are left exposed as a ceiling design. The upstairs foyer tucks utilities (washer, dryer, water heater, furnace) behind folding doors.

Downstairs, the kitchen occupies one corner of this tall wing, separated from the dining area by a serving counter. The 24-foot-long living wing is bordered with glass, opening it up to light and views on three sides. Along the back, a window-wall provides a fourth entry, giving the plan an unusually flexible traffic flow. Tucked behind that two-faced fireplace and under the hip roof is a cozy window-seat alcove, sure to be a favored retreat for lovers and philosophers.

The clapboard exterior is accented with vertical trim fins flanking all window groupings. They provide draft protection and, when stained to contrast with the siding color (along with the under-window panels), dramatize the vertical thrust of the sleep wing.

6. POTPOURRI OF SPECIAL SHELTERS

Not all of the plans in the *Popular Science* collection come in clumps from predictable sources. We've had a number of special working relationships with architects and designers on individual projects.

● We met Marc Harrison of the Rhode Island School of Design through an all-metal house he and his students designed and built for International Lead Zinc Research Organization Inc. (ILZRO). A visit to this Providence project prompted us to ask Harrison to develop a solar leisure home for us, using similar industrial components.

● Jeff Milstein and Les Walker are young architects headquartered in Woodstock, N.Y. who've collaborated on books and buildings but usually work independently, on projects for a broad range of sponsors including *Popular Science* and *Family Circle*. Jeff designed our Tent Cabin; Les's major commissions from us were the Frame-Hung Dome on the following pages, and the Lockbox, detailed in Part Two of this book.

● George J. Bunzer is a building contractor specializing in vacation housing in North Carolina. Robert Gannon is a Contributing Editor of *Popular Science* who also teaches at Penn State. Bunzer designed and built his RV Chalet; Gannon involved Penn State's Architectural Engineering Department in the design of his as-yet-unbuilt house for a tropical island (as he explains on the following pages). And multi-talented Ray Pioch rendered both houses for us.

● Jersey Devil is a far-out architectural commune that moves onto the construction sites of the buildings it designs. These are the only homes in this book for which plans aren't available, since they're structured on the spot.

For ordering information on all other plans in this group, see page 192.

All-Metal Solar Wedge

Designed by Marc Harrison

Two wedges—one facing north (right), the other south (below)—differ greatly. Except for a pair of skylights, north wedge is opaque, while much of south face is glazed for passive solar gain. Strip above chimney is a bank of solar collectors.

Here's a unique house assembled from prefab metal components. There's no lumber for structural framing, no plywood for sheathing. Exterior walls are factory-finished panels with insulating foam sandwiched between metal faces.

We commissioned the design after our visit several years ago to an experimental all-metal house built by Marc Harrison and his students at Rhode Island School of Design, under the sponsorship of the International Lead Zinc Research Organization (ILZRO).

"Give us a high-tech, high-style, compact leisure home using assembly techniques similar to your Rhode Island project," we told Professor Harrison; "and let's work in both active and passive solar applications." When Harrison delivered the striking design you see here, we got back to ILZRO, challenging them to find us an industrial source for the components and a distributor who'd ship assembly kits at affordable prices. The task we set ILZRO was complicated by the fact that U.S. manufacturers of metal construction systems—the type used for quick erection of warehouses and commercial buildings as well as in the Rhode Island project—aren't ready to venture into the housing market.

ILZRO's quest for a factory to fabricate components for Harrison's design took them to Mexico's prestigious IMSA (Industrias Monterrey, S.A.). This manufacturer has vast experience in panelized structures, and sells two different kits of house parts through the Oklahoma supplier listed in our box of sources.

You'll get a house—quickly and easily—with many features that adapt it to year-round use as a leisure home. It benefits from both passive and active solar collections, and its design is compatible with either liquid or air systems—or a hybrid (see box). The south-facing greenhouse section can be sealed off from the rest of the house to confine unwanted heat and humidity, but the barrier is removed at night to take advantage of the passively stored heat. Clearstory windows siphon off the summer heat that rises to the peak.

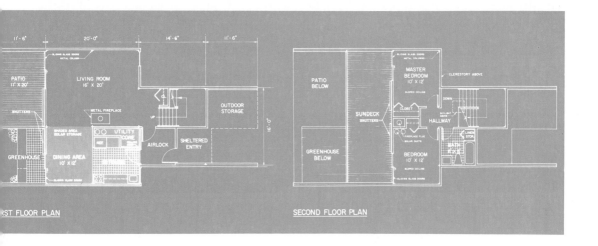

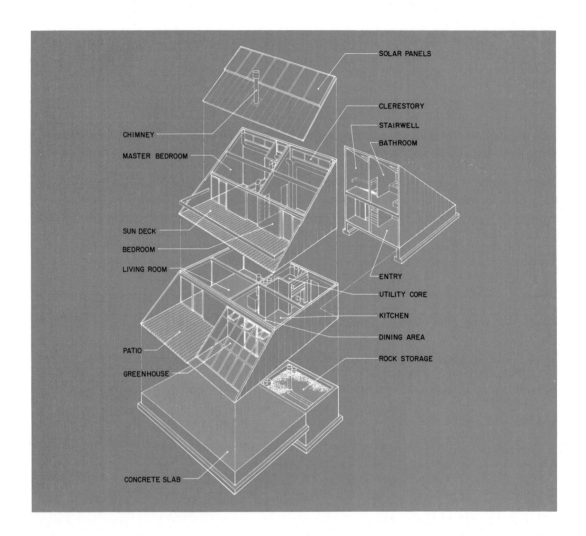

SOLAR PANELS

CLERESTORY

STAIRWELL

BATHROOM

CHIMNEY

MASTER BEDROOM

SUN DECK

BEDROOM

LIVING ROOM

ENTRY

UTILITY CORE

KITCHEN

DINING AREA

ROCK STORAGE

PATIO

GREENHOUSE

CONCRETE SLAB

You can buy kits for this house

Kit 1 includes all metal-sandwich panels (based on metric dimensions): 34.13 in. wide for walls, 31.52 in. wide for roof: $16,454 (all prices as of early 1980).

Kit 2 includes all panels plus framing to support floors on both stories: includes window frames (glass must be purchased locally): $22,720.

Total cost of erected house (including foundation, wiring, plumbing, bathroom, kitchen cabinets): $38,000 (approx., depending on location). Order construction kits from Carl Baldwin Enterprises, Box 302, Carter, Okla. 73627.

Solar gear is separate purchase

House is designed to take either air or liquid system (concrete well under floor can store heat in either rocks or—with a steel tank—liquid). Revere Copper's system collects heat in liquid, converts to hot air through heat-exchange coil; costs $8,000 to $9,000, depending on local climate (which determines collector area needed). System has "energy manager" LED readouts of temperatures in various zones so gear can be fine-tuned; runs on standard thermostat; includes domestic hot-water tank, humidity control, collectors and storage tank. Can be installed by homeowner, following manufacturer's manual. Supplier: Sun Solar Heating, Inc., North Kingston, RI 02852.

Alternate system is all air, from Solaron Corp., 720 S. Colorado Blvd., Denver, Colo. 80222. Installed cost: $6,300 for the ILZRO Wedge, including air handlers, ducts, automatic samplers, rock storage, foundation, wiring—based on 168.5 sq. ft. of collectors. Franchised installation only ("too tricky for DIY"). Optional domestic hot-water kit, $1,295 from Sunworks, Somerville, N.J. 08876, includes two collectors, 80-gal. tank, and controls.

The large south windows have enough awning-type overhang to shade them from the worst midday summer sun, as well as screens that block hot, low sunlight from east or west. The bedrooms share a shielded sundeck and their sliding glass doors can be left open to cool night breezes.

All four glass doors on this "sun face" have an exterior insulated shutter, hung from a barn-door track so it can be rolled across to shield the glass from unwanted solar radiation on summer days or heat-robbing winds on winter nights. Borrowing an idea from the Lockbox (see Part Two), these shutters also offer security, leaving no vulnerable glass exposed while the house is vacant between visits. The shutter within the greenhouse seals its only access door.

Though this is only a two-bedroom house, it can take additional overnighters on convertible couches in the living room. And the kids will likely opt for sleeping alfresco in that teepee-like, sheltered projection at the rear. It's also ideal for storing winter firewood, which is likely to be the only wood in the house.

Two people can erect the house using only a rivet gun, power drill and saw, plus miscellaneous hand tools. Two kits are offered because some builders may want to arrange for their own framing; Kit No. 1 omits framing. The framing in Kit No. 2 consists of light, square tubing of high-tensile steel. Like the panels in the kits, it's precut and numbered for erector-set assembly at your site.

Tent Cabin

by Jeff Milstein

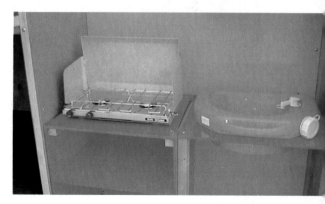

Prefabbed parts plus accessories can be brought to the site in a standard pickup (complete stack, after unloading, is shown above). Since structure—including galley cart—is designed as knock-down, it's easy to disassemble at end of season and truck away for storage. Or just close it up for winter (above right); here, deck is held up by winch ratchet alone, but for unattended closure you'll want to add three padlock hasps—one near pulley at each edge of deck, plus one on rear door. Flanged half-spheres of Plexiglas are elegant side-window option. Propane stove and Porta-Sink (right) were bought at Sears.

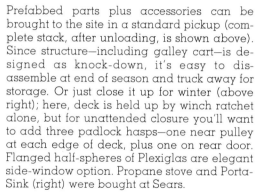

Here's a route to your first second home that's so quick, easy, and inexpensive you can move in the same month you start construction. Though this shelter offers most of the comforts of a conventional cabin or a big RV, you can build it—complete with bed, kitchen, and private potty—for around $750. And that's only the start of your savings: Instead of driving a gas-gulping motor home (or camper, or trailer) to your country site every weekend, you deliver this unit once (all parts stack in a mini pickup or rented utility trailer).

You prefab at home, truck it to a summer site, erect it in a day. Then you leave it there all year—it locks as tight as a house.

It assembles on pads or footings, then folds into a weatherproof shed when you depart. On subsequent visits (via your fuel-saving compact or motorbike) you just lower the deck and the tent erects itself with all facilities in place, ready for use. At the end of the season, you can disassemble it and truck it back home for storage—or lock it up and leave it in place

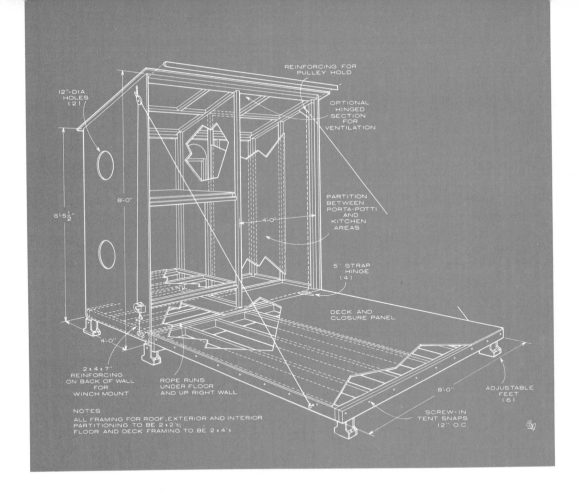

REINFORCING FOR
PULLEY HOLD

12"-DIA.
HOLES
(2)

OPTIONAL
HINGED
SECTION
FOR
VENTILATION

8'-0"

6'-5½"

PARTITION
BETWEEN
PORTA-POTTI
AND
KITCHEN
AREAS

4'-0"

5" STRAP
HINGE
(4)

DECK AND
CLOSURE PANEL

4'-0"

2 x 4 x 7"
REINFORCING
ON BACK OF WALL
FOR
WINCH MOUNT

ROPE RUNS
UNDER FLOOR
AND UP RIGHT WALL

8'-0"

ADJUSTABLE
FEET
(6)

SCREW-IN
TENT SNAPS
12" O.C.

NOTES
ALL FRAMING FOR ROOF, EXTERIOR AND INTERIOR
PARTITIONING TO BE 2 x 2's;
FLOOR AND DECK FRAMING TO BE 2 x 4's

With tent off to show interior, architect Milstein demonstrates folding bed. Platforms for bed-rolls are hinged at midpoint; front sections drop flush with stationary rear, bringing ladder along.

Here flap is being unzipped to convert to awning supported by take-apart aluminum pole seen in large color photo. Tent section folds inside shed.

1) Prefabbing side panels is simple matter of attaching 2-by-2's with construction adhesive and galvanized nails. 2) Attach wall panels to edge of deck; note framed rear door—it's shown open, from back, at 3) along with framing for Plexiglas roof. 4) Add bed parts, then kitchen built-ins. 5) Galley rolls out on casters, end leaves rise and lock.

for next summer. (Though our plans call for simple wooden feet, you could anchor the shed to concrete piers.)

The unit serves various needs:

● As a temporary residence on property to which you have access for only one season.

● As a movable structure for trying different house sites on newly purchased land, so you can choose at leisure the best place to build.

● As a construction hut you can live in comfortably while building your permanent leisure home.

● As a guest cottage for an existing—but overcrowded—cabin.

It's shrewdly designed for easy building. Wall panels and partitions are ⅜ inch plywood, the deck is ½ inch. For the "weather" walls, we chose rough-sawn cedar siding but any APA-grademark EXT will do. The roof is ¼ inch clear Plexiglas. As shown, there's a center vent attached with a poly-hinge, but you could apply the roof in a single sheet. The skylight effect keeps the snug interior from seeming cramped.

Frame-Hung Dome

Designed by Les Walker

Shop-made panels and conduit frame pieces stand ready for dome assembly. Electrical conduit frame (above right) is plumbed automatically by the radially framed flooring system. Note threaded rods at all frame joints; they bolt frame and support dome panels. Five working louvers at top of completed dome (below) give efficient ventilation during warm summer months. Exterior frame doubles as scaffolding.

You can prefab it—its exoskeleton supports stressed-skin panels—insulated for year-round living. Its design high points are:

- Simple prefabrication. You can prepare all parts in your spare time over the winter.
- Simple erection.
- Interchangeable panels. You design your own window layouts.
- Operable louver system.
- 100-percent-seamless exterior panels, fully insulated.
- Adjustable hubs that tighten panels together to prevent leaks.
- Permanent exterior scaffolding.

We commissioned this dome from Lester Walker, architect of our Lockbox House, who tells the step-by-step construction story:

"Once we had our basic design on paper, we turned to testing. A 3-foot model gave us an overview of the project and a small-scale check of dimensions. We made full-scale mockups of the important parts and tested them for strength.

"Confident in our research and testing,

Working in winter workshop (above), Walker pre-insulated stressed-skin panels by sandwiching glass wool between the skins. Small boat winch and a system of nylon cords (top) operate the watertight louvers, which are mounted with plastic hinges. Above left, architect Walker takes a rest in his just-completed dome.

we started the actual construction. About 300 hours' fabrication time later the frame and panels were ready to erect, and 250 man-hours after that the dome was finished. Just in time for ten days of rain and heavy winds. The dome didn't leak a drop.

1. Three-foot model was the first check on my calculations and design. Next I made full-scale mockups of all important parts and tested them for strength. The stressed-skin panel supported 100 pounds per square foot without breaking. Other tests led me to choose marine paint, silicone caulk, foam tape, and aluminum tape for the four-way sealing system.

2. Panel struts were no trouble. I ripped them to right size and angle on a 10″ table saw, then moved to a radial arm to cut them to length. Note use of a stop-block system to assure strut uniformity. I cut the ¼″ plywood skins (four at a time) using a portable circular saw, guided by a special jig described in the plans for this dome.

3. Panels went together like this: Julian Olivas, here, helped fasten skins to struts with 3M panel adhesive and 1½″ galvanized nails, 6″ o.c. We sandwiched foil-backed fiberglass insulation between skins, then finished each panel with polyurethane marine enamel. All panels are designed so their outer skins are 100-percent seamless.

4. Next—the conduit frame. I cut the ¾″ EMT conduit to length with a hacksaw. I crimped the ends halfway in a heavy vise, flattened them all the way with a hammer. After drilling the hole in each end of each strut, I cleaned the metal with an acid wash, primed, and painted with enamel. All conduit struts were labeled to avoid erection mixups.

5. The fun begins with the assembly of the exoskeleton. With help of Ed Fuller, a Woodstock friend, I completed the tube frame in about an hour and a half. Next we dug 15 holes for the foundation posts. We made these holes a foot and a half across and deep enough to pass the frost line. Then we attached the posts to the tube frame and suspended them in their holes. Next came the floor joists. We set all 15 of the 2-by-10 joists on a center post, then fastened them to their respective foundation posts via joist hangers. We leveled the floor by raising or lowering the foundation posts in the holes, blocking them in position when the joists were level. Once the joists were level, the exoskeleton was level, too. Its base was not perfectly circular—our next step would take care of that.

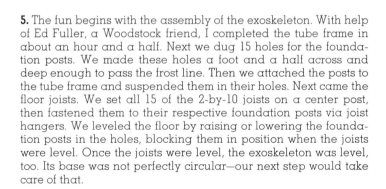

6. A plywood circle, wedged between the tips of the joists resting on the center post, forced the dome into a perfect circle. Then we spiked another larger plywood circle over the hub we'd just formed, a nail into each joist. This made sure that nothing would shift when we moved on to the next operation.

7. Concrete footings for the foundation posts came next. I used about 1¼ yards of concrete for the job. Ready mix is easiest way to get the job done, but if you build on a remote site you may have to mix your own. To make 1¼ yards you'll need eight bags of cement, about 1800 pounds of sand, and 2500 pounds of gravel. Here's a rough guide to mixing a batch for one footing: Use a half bag of cement, 100 pounds of sand, and 140 pounds of gravel. Three gallons of water complete the mix—never use more or strength of the concrete will suffer. We mixed our concrete so stiff we had to help it out of the mixing trough and into the holes, as we're doing here.

"Building a dome is simple—too simple in some ways. Hour after hour of repetitious operations can get to your head after a while. That's why we designed this dome as a workshop prefab. You can spread the work out over an entire winter, working in your shop whenever you get the chance. Come spring, all that's left is a simple job of assembling the parts you've been making. In a few days the dome is ready to live in. That's the way we built this prototype."

Hubs provide the link between exoskeleton and the dome panels, and let you "squeeze" the dome together for a tight fit by tightening the nut on the outside. Rubber washers, aluminum flashing, plus caulk and sealant, all serve to keep the hubs watertight.

Foundation posts are the key to the self-leveling dome. Each post supports not only the conduit outer frame, but a floor joist and part of three panels as well. Note the use of joist hangers—they're easier than toenailing, and stronger, too.

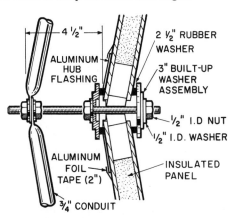

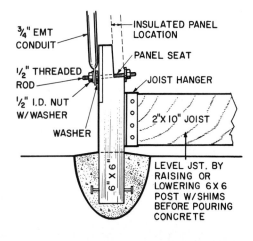

8. Panel placement can begin as soon as footings have set. We started by placing the base row of 15 panels—those with vertex pointing up—then added second row of 14 with vertex pointing down, plus the door panel. Temporary hubs of plumber's strap held things as we worked.

9. Foam tape goes on edges of all panels as part of sealing system. When all panels were in place we tightened the hub assemblies from outside the dome, forcing all panels tightly together. Then we went back to each hub to install aluminum flashing as detailed in the plans.

10. Our floor was 2-by-6 tongue-and-groove spruce, spanning from joist to joist over 6″ of insulation. We supported the insulation on ½″ plywood nailed to the bottom of the joists. A rented floor sander smoothed the flooring and brought it all to a uniform color. Two coats of urethane varnish was the finish.

Roof plan of the Frame-Hung Dome shows the window and louver layout used to erect the prototype. Glazing used is Eastman Chemical's Uvex, a low-cost alternative to acrylic or polycarbonate.

11. Aluminum tape goes over all seams and over the edges of all the flashing. But before we put on the tape we applied silicone caulk to seams and flashing, being careful not to smear the caulk (tape doesn't stick to it very well). Our dome was up and gleaming! We set to for one final step: Burnishing the tape with a blunt wood instrument to ensure a good seal against weather.

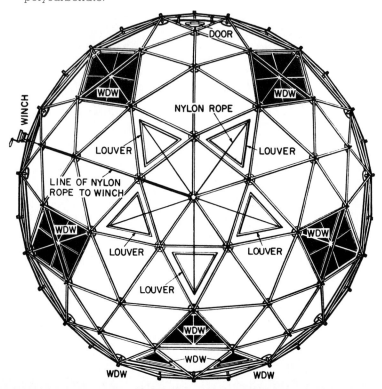

Planning a practical interior for a 24-foot-diameter dome—laying out living areas that convert it into a home—isn't as simple as it might seem. There's little previous data to research—beyond some very personal schemes shown in *Domebook II*—and one of our requirements was that any partitioning must preserve that unique sense of free overhead space that led you to choose a dome in the first place.

Who better to solve these problems than the architect we had commissioned to design our frame-hung dome, especially since he built it himself and lived in it for several years? Les Walker comments: "The two schemes I evolved are meant to be frameworks for the dome-builder to use in constructing the kind of environment he wants in a leisure home. For a more open floorspace in the Family Plan, he might want to eliminate the solid walls around the bedrooms (and use the lofts for sleeping), in which case he'd simply provide post-and-beam support for the inner edges of the loft flooring. Or he may wish to add up to four privacy partitions, radiating out like spokes from the Couple Core pentagon.

"My idea was to stimulate the builder's ingenuity with two widely different schemes. I can attest that my dome kept very warm all winter with only an Ashley wood-burner. My dome's insulated wall panels really pay off. One tip: To adjust to any partitioning, builders may want to change window panels from the positions shown on my original plans. No sweat, since they're interchangable with wall panels."

Standard 2x4-stud wall construction is used for all partitions. Note that 2x8s are fastened to the upper 2x4 of the top plate

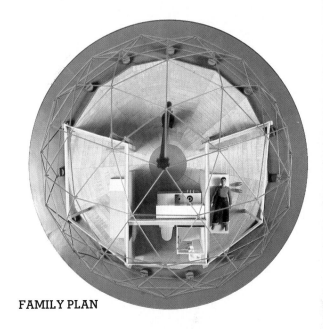

FAMILY PLAN

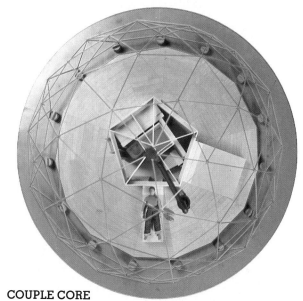

COUPLE CORE

to serve as floor beams. For best appearance and strength, make this assembly *before* installing the upper 2x4 (taking care to drive fasteners flush with its bottom face), then nail this 2x4 securely atop its mate.

161

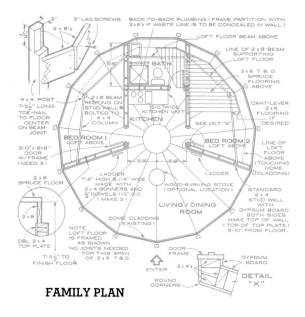

FAMILY PLAN

COUPLE CORE

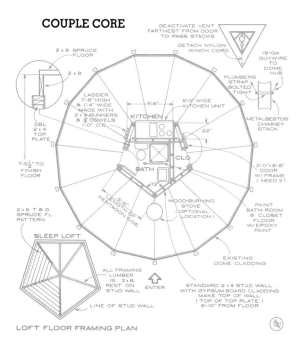

LOFT FLOOR FRAMING PLAN

The 2x6 tongue-and-groove flooring is capable of spanning up to 6½ feet—but be sure it's thoroughly seasoned before installation. If not, shrinkage could pull tongues from grooves, reducing structural effectiveness. With care, you can angle all your nails through the tongues and into the 2x8 beams (prior to placing the grooved adjacent plank). This keeps the face free of nailheads. You can get by with 3 inch (10d) common nails for tongue-nailing, but 16d hot-dipped galvanized are better—especially if any face-nailing is required.

Sand the flooring after installation, and apply three coats of polyurethane varnish. If loft railings are desired, install after floor is finished. They could be panels of ½ inch A-C plywood, bolted to beam faces so as to extend 2 feet above floor level—or 1 inch galvanized pipe with fittings.

Walker has called for standard 6'8" doors, 2 feet wide, on both plans. Buy the prehung type and install in your rough framing before you apply wall cladding. This could be drywall, Homosote, prefinished hardboard, plywood or rough-sawn lumber. All fixtures are standard, with the exception of the kitchen unit. Several manufacturers make these compact combos, which include range, refrigerator, and sink. Walker worked with one from Dwyer Kitchen Products; it's available with or without the attached upper cabinets.

Stove pipe—Metalbestos or equivalent—and a vent stack from the bathroom both exit at the dome's top, through a deactivated vent.

Partitioning into privacy zones without destroying the "spatial domeness" was a problem in two-bedroom plan. Rooms are "roofed," creating U-shaped loft that can sleep up to three more people. If extra sleep space isn't needed (right photo), loft becomes platform for spread-out activities, bulky storage, or playroom (add solid-panel railing). Though

not shown in model, flooring can project beyond perimeter beams to touch dome wall. No joists are needed between these beams and inner support walls if t&g flooring is properly installed. Cladding is left off inside walls, here, to show framing. Where privacy isn't a factor, partitions can be omitted for more open plan, replaced with post-and-beam supports.

Simpler plan for young couple with small child tucks all utilities into pentagon core, with open kitchen at rear and doors to closet (left) and bathroom (top right). As with Family Plan, loft offers option of additional sleeping or play space (note mitered butt of t&g flooring). To split floorspace into living areas, beams could project from pentagon points to dome hubs to take tracks for hanging accordion doors—where figure is standing between the beds, for instance.

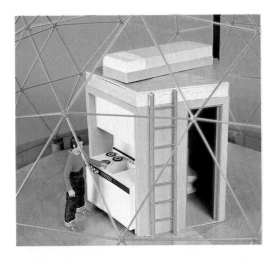

RV Chalet

Designed by George J. Bunzer

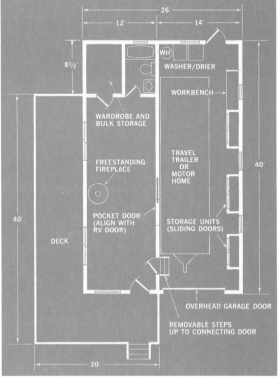

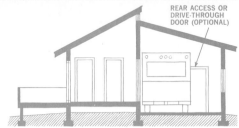

Stepped ridge provides clerestory window above partition, as shown in section through connecting door.

We all know vacationers who can't make up their minds. They like the mobility—the leave-on-impulse freedom—of a rec vehicle; but they also yearn for their own place in the country, where they can settle in on those holiday weekends without having to fight for campground space.

This clever structure offers the best of both leisure worlds. Your motor home or trailer doubles as a functional part of a vacation cottage. Your RV carries you to the site, then hooks up to become a working part of the house. This avoids costly duplication of facilities. Since most of today's travel trailers and motor homes sport full cooking gear, you can save the staggering cost of installing a kitchen in the cottage. Furnish the cottage with a convertible couch (as shown at right) or bunk beds, and you can sleep all the guests you want. The small bathroom in your RV then becomes a private bath for that "master bedroom," while the new bath is for daytime use.

Where the site permits, a drive-through arrangement is ideal; it spares you the backing maneuver to snug the RV against the partition wall. You just put pivoting panels or an overhead garage door at *both* ends of the RV space, moving the water heater and laundry units to the side wall.

The partition wall can be conventionally framed and—for winter use—insulated. In our artist's rendering, we've pierced the partition with only two doors: a hinged one for direct access between the two spaces, and a pocket sliding door

Hidden doors blend into house wall (above) but swing smoothly open (below) for RV exit. Specially designed hinges support the heavy doors. To preserve the illusion of an unbroken exterior, the knobless door opens only from the inside.

aligned with the RV's entry. (Check local codes to see if they require a fire wall separating what they'd classify as a garage from the rest of the house. If so, you can face the RV side of the partition with noncombustible panels; if not, you could even omit the wall, substituting a railing along the edge of the stepped-down floor.)

The RV section is equipped with all the hookups you'd have in a commercial campground—water, electricity, drain (the latter can be tied into the permanent waste system or run to its own dry well). Gas kitchen appliances can be hooked into a propane tank outside the structure. You can leave the RV hooked into the house and travel back and forth in a gas-stretching compact. Yet the RV is ready to roll on longer trips.

The RV Chalet was conceived by George J. Bunzer who has since built a number of them in the Southeast.

Trying to conceal the two large doors on these structures led Bunzer to search for the perfect pivot. His original plans called for an RV-sized overhead garage door, but he later thought doors that matched the reverse board-and-batten siding would be more handsome. He also wanted the doors to match the paneled interior of the house.

But when he looked for hinges that would be both invisible and able to support the weight of these massive doors, he found none available. The solution—galvanized pipe fittings. From ¾-inch pipe flanges and matching nipples he constructed heavy-duty pivot hinges that allow the doors to open exactly 90 degrees. Since there is absolutely no play in the doors, the threaded nipples should outlast the occupants!

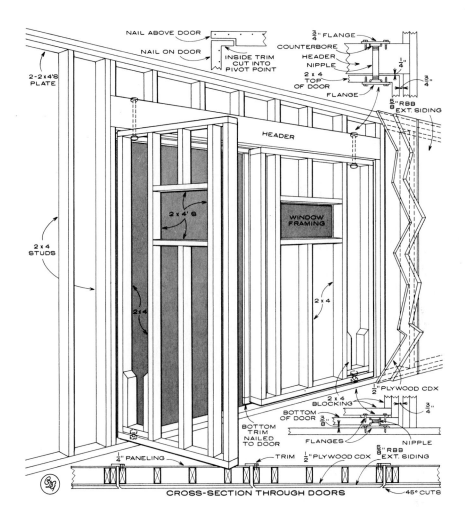

CROSS-SECTION THROUGH DOORS

The length of the nipples is important to ensure proper spacing after they are hand-tightened to the flanges. The ¾-inch flanges make a good fit to both the underside of the header and the top of the 2x4 sill plate. This sill presents no obstacle to our RV's wheels, but the plate can be eliminated, and the flanges fastened directly to a concrete floor if desired.

To make the doors "invisible" on the inside of the house, Bunzer nailed paneling and trim to their inner faces. For the doors to pivot properly, this trim must be cut precisely to fit the pivot point; then part of the trim must be nailed to the wall (see diagram). To assure proper fit, this tricky cutting job is best tried out first on scrap pieces.

The ¾-inch gap on either side of the doors is essential—it allows the doors to pivot. But gusts of cold air can't get through. Mitered siding joints as well as weatherstripping around the doors make the opening snug.

The miter joint between the doors also helps keep them tightly shut, as do the foot bolts on the top and bottom of the inside left-hand door.

Cool House for a Hot Climate

Text by Robert Gannon

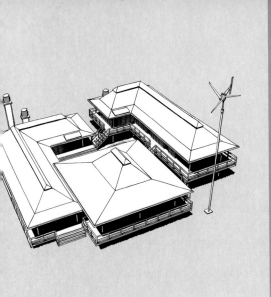

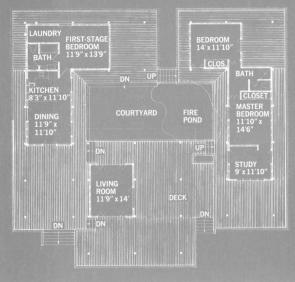

All roof areas are "phantomed" in color rendering, facing page, to reveal three separate elements of house. Sketch above shows how roof extensions shelter entire deck area. L-shaped section at left will be built first. When right-hand bedroom section is built, first bedroom will convert to storage/utility.

My site is spectacular—a sun-drenched bluff overlooking the azure Caribbean, with coconut palms framing waves breaking on a distant coral reef. But the climate is that of a greenhouse—hot and wet. Temperatures average 81°F, humidity usually hovers in the 90's.

The site is at Port Royal on Roatan, an island off Honduras, and it is here that an environmentally oriented house was planned as a future test site for such alternate-energy gear as wind generators (the trades average about 20 mph) and solar equipment (the sun beats down with near-equatorial intensity).

Most of the vacation homes in the *Popular Science* collection have been designed for cold-weather climates: The emphasis is on keeping heat *in*. But many southern readers have the opposite heat problem. This house is planned to let the heat *out*, by coaxing a flow of cool breezes.

When we looked for basic house plans for a really hot climate, we found few, and none of them included the ideas we wanted to incorporate. So we asked the architectural engineering department of Pennsylvania State University to help us develop our own. For nearly a year, three teams of students worked on the project, using a systems approach. What resulted is the Penn State/*Popular Science* tropical house.

First requirement: a house as self-sufficient as possible, one to work with and take advantage of the environment. It *has* to be independent. The island has no power lines, no water lines, no sewers. In fact, because the site is atop a bluff, even digging a well is impractical; a cistern is the only answer.

The original idea called for a plan that could also be adapted to climates that at times are relatively cool. But as the design developed, we found that to do that we'd

169

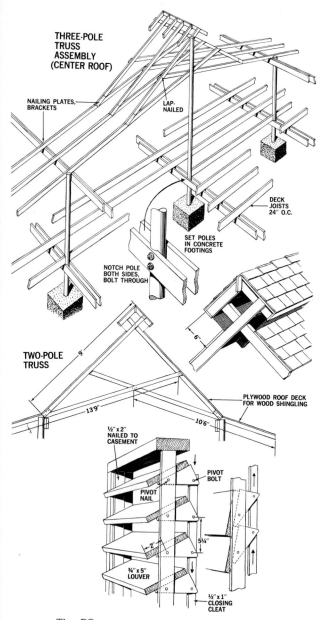

THREE-POLE
TRUSS
ASSEMBLY
(CENTER ROOF)

NAILING PLATES,
BRACKETS

LAP-
NAILED

DECK
JOISTS
24" O.C.

SET POLES
IN CONCRETE
FOOTINGS

NOTCH POLE
BOTH SIDES,
BOLT THROUGH

TWO-POLE
TRUSS

PLYWOOD ROOF DECK
FOR WOOD SHINGLING

6"

13'9"

10'6"

½" x 2"
NAILED TO
CASEMENT

PIVOT
BOLT

PIVOT
NAIL

2"

5¼"

¾" x 5"
LOUVER

½" x 1"
CLOSING
CLEAT

The PS commitment to post-and-beam for leisure-home construction dates back to the
Lockbox house, which uses the technique to
float a structure above a steep "unbuildable"
site (see Part Two of this book). The reasons
for going post-and-beam for our tropical
house are equally persuasive: By lifting the
mass above ground winds, we make fullest
use of natural air circulation. By the same token, post-and-beam offers best anchorage in
storm winds; it won't present a solid barrier,
but lets winds pass under and around. Most
walls consist of adjustable louvers shown at
right; air currents flow through and out
screened ridge vent.

have to compromise major innovations.
The final decision: This house would focus
on hot-weather living. The design can be
adapted to the Gulf Coast and Southwest
desert states, of course—you don't have to
own a tropical island.

The prime consideration was air-flow.
Unless heavily insulated, most U.S. homes
act as summer ovens. We wanted the
breeze to flow right through this house.

So we opened nearly all walls, using
screened, floor-to-ceiling wood louvers, a
conventional 19th-century Caribbean
design feature. Only two glass windows
will be installed: in the kitchen, so the
stove won't blow out during wind storms
and the chef can look outside; and in the
study, so papers won't blow.

To open the house even more—and to
produce a feeling of living out-of-doors—
we separated the structure and exploded
it into three distinct living sections that
are linked only by deck space and roof
projections. In the center we placed a 16-
by-36-foot garden that nearly every room
looks onto. The result will be like a small
village of clustered huts.

The design has the added advantage
of being adaptable to three-stage construction. The first stage is the kitchen-
storage-bathroom section; the second, the
living room; and the third, the sleeping
wing. While the second and third stages
are going up, the occupants will sleep in
the storage room.

To further capture the wind, the sections are on three levels, allowing
prevailing currents to breeze through
two-foot open steps. An added benefit is
that one of the breaks isolates the "private wing"—bedrooms and one bath—
from wandering visitors.

Finally, the whole structure will sit atop a huge deck supported by poles to let wind sweep underneath and be forced upward with air scoops into the rooms, up into peaked ceilings, and out ridge vents. On breezeless days, ceiling fans will stir the air.

For cool sleeping, air will flow through the beds. The springs will be padded, slatted wood (we plan to use bases from Lattoflex models), and each unit, boxed in, will spread over a large trap door lowered to capture the breeze under the house. On extremely hot nights the sleeper can rest directly on the foam-covered springs, with cool air continually wafting up.

Circulation isn't the only reason the design uses pole-house construction. It's also less expensive, easy to erect, and one of the best structural modes for hurricane protection—something to think about in the Caribbean. (Fasteners and pole-base footings will be extra heavy for the same reason.)

The main lumber for the structure will be Honduran pine. It's somewhat stronger than the standard American variety, but the engineering specs are based on conventional U.S. stock. We ordered it through a Honduran subsidiary of the Atlanta-based Caribbean Lumber Co.

All wood will be pressure-treated with Kopper's Wolman CCA (chromated copper arsenate) at the rate of 0.25 to 0.6 pound per cubic foot (depending on whether it's general lumber or ground-contact poles) to guard against wood rot and termites—important anywhere south of, say, Atlanta, but essential in the high-humidity tropics. Here, the homeowner fights not only wood-burrowing insects but fungus and bacteria as well.

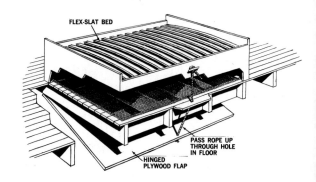

Air scoop beneath built-in bed captures night breezes passing under house, directs them upward through screened opening and between slats of bed.

How the Cool House Grew

Author Gannon proposed this project to the teaching staff of the Penn State architectural engineering department. They assigned 60 advanced students, in groups of three, to draw up plans. Three months later, the PS editorial staff picked the best of the 20 concepts. Winner was a preliminary design by John Walker, Steve Kalista, and Carol Axenfeld.

Back at Penn State, Walker continued as head designer, while Kalista concentrated on working out ecological systems and building the model. Joe Gottardy was recruited to study wind and solar power. The graphics from which artist Ray Pioch worked were supplied by Jim Vogel and Darrell Kratzer.

Finally, through a series of two dozen weekly meetings of students, professors, and editors, the energy and ecological systems were integrated with the basic floorplan presented here.

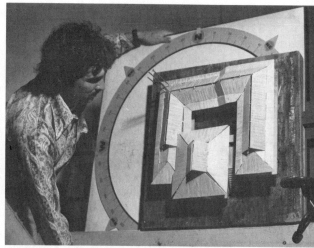

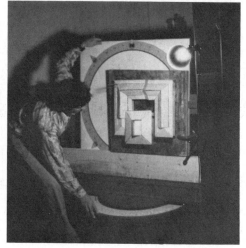

To test airflow, model of house is placed in Penn State's low-speed wind tunnel by students Steve Kalista and John Walker. They tracked flow through transparent roof by attaching lengths of yarn to all major points, outside and in.

To check siting and roof projection, model with opaque roof was mounted on school's heliodon—a compass-like tilting table adjustable to various latitudes and seasons, against which an artificial sun is directed, as Walker demonstrates in these two photos.

And for the Roatan location, treated poles and crawl-space joists aren't enough. *Everything*, right up to the ridge vents, is potential termite food. Those Honduran beasts will build their wood-and-saliva tunnels up slivery corner cracks to the roof, and we've heard tales of them even hollowing out dining-room tables.

We checked around for finishes, but following Kopper's suggestion, decided to do nothing. We'll let sea breezes weather the light-green Wolmanized lumber to a silvery gray.

We'll be using Canadian white cedar shakes, a material that's recently been catching on in the Bahamas. They're about one-third cheaper than red cedar, and should weather well in humid, sun-bleaching climates, we're told. The shakes, too, will be Wolmanized.

To test for airflow, Penn State engineers built a model and bolted it to the floor of the aeronautical engineering department's low-speed wind tunnel. With

pieces of yarn (see photo) and, later, ⅛-inch soap bubbles of helium, we checked air-current paths through the house and made sure the roof wouldn't intensify the wind so much that sitting in the garden would be uncomfortable.

Putting the Wind to Work

Is it possible to get along comfortably on a 600-watt, 12-volt electric system without such energy-hungry appliances as electric ranges, dryers, and irons? We think so—at least in a leisure home. So we selected the C-9 Wind Wizard, manufactured by Aero-Lectric (see address list at end of text), even though larger, more powerful units are available. The basic price (around $1000) is in a range where many readers can afford to experiment, and the simple design seems to be rugged, well-thought-out, and easy to maintain.

The whole unit weighs only about 50 pounds, so no elaborate tower will be required. Assembly of the basic unit is easy: Kevin Moran, Wind Wizard's designer, put our model together for a Penn State demonstration in only 15 minutes.

Recreational vehicles have made 12-volt appliances plentiful. For refrigeration, we'd be using a combination 12-volt DC/120-volt AC/propane unit made by Dometic Sales Corp. For some equipment—a saber saw, for instance—standard 115-volt AC current may be necessary. A $20 RCV inverter should do the job.

We also plan to place a watt-hour meter in the circuit to check on power use, and a Heathkit strip chart recorder (IR-18M) hooked to Heath's Five Function Weather Station to see what actually happens in what winds. In addition to monitoring wind speed and direction, the Heath unit checks indoor/outdoor temperature and barometric pressure. On an isolated Caribbean island, weather suddenly becomes very important.

The generator should start producing when winds hit 12 mph, providing nearly 400 watts at 17 mph, and more than 500 at 25 mph. Energy can be stored in standard auto batteries, but the constant charge/discharge cycle will kill them fast. Deep-cycle batteries, for golf carts and fork lifts, are made for such punishment. So we'd use Gould's heavy-duty PB-220's. They'll give 220 amp-hours or more than 2400 watt-hours of energy storage, enough to keep a 50-watt refrigerator going for two days in a dead calm.

Golf-cart batteries are expensive, but under charge/discharge conditions they should have four times the life of automobile batteries. We plan to use two sets connected in parallel by a double-pole switch; while one set of batteries is being used, the other set is charging.

The generator is a standard General Motors Delco alternator. The windmill's nine-foot, hand-carved birch blades (each costs $100) drive the alternator at a 9.2-to-1 ratio. When windspeed tops 26 mph, the spring-loaded blade assembly begins to fold out of the wind, effectively slowing itself. Otherwise it could pull down the mast or tear itself apart; in a 26-mph wind those blade tips, at 408 rpm, are traveling at 130 mph. The tail is also spring-loaded; a sudden side gust simply swivels it away for a moment.

For maintenance, we will provide a tilting-top mast. Main items of service are the belt and the blades. Belts need periodic adjustment; if blowing sand begins wearing the blades, their leading edges may have to be covered with urethane tape.

The tests led to interesting design changes. We found that despite ridge vents, wind grabbers, and level changes, airflow through the kitchen-bath-storage unit was sluggish, even though the wind whistled outside at scale 50 mph.

But when a skirt of cardboard was held against the northern pole bases, the interior yarn bits suddenly came alive; air was flowing at just the right speed. So the working design includes a canvas windskirt along the north side. If it is as necessary in real life as it seemed in the tunnel, we'll probably make a permanent skirt of ¼-inch marine plywood.

Tests also showed that our original placement of the windmill—on a tripod of poles at the northwest corner—was the worst choice we could have made: The upwind roof generated a variety of unpredictable eddies and vortices. So we moved it to the opposite, prevailing-upwind corner where currents were smooth. We also detached it from the house structure to avoid sympathetic vibrations.

For protection against the broiling sun, the roofs are huge, shading the decks and also shielding them from the frequent tropical downpours. We made sure that the roof overhang was correct by putting a model of the house on Penn State's heliodon (see photos, page 172).

In the central garden will be planted broadleaf trees that eventually will spread their shade over a good section of roof.

Such a stretched-out house—actually separate buildings huddled together—would ordinarily be expensive; the costs of decking, roof materials, and the labor for making louvers add up. (Costs could be shaved by shrinking the deck space,

or by adding decking only as funds become available.) Walls are only one board thick, however—no outer covering or standard sheathing to pay for, no sub-sheathing, no insulation, no interior plasterboard, no storm windows. No fear of water pipes freezing, either, and no worries about snow load—so roof rafters can be 2x4s.

At first, the water-supply situation looked as if it might give problems. Roatan has a 67-inch average annual rainfall, however, and that 4000-square-foot roof could collect some 22,300 cubic feet of water a year. We figure that an 8-by-10-by-14 foot cistern, holding 8100 gallons, will carry a three-member family through a 90-day dry spell.

It wouldn't sustain an average American household, however, which uses some 90 gallons of water a day per person. But about 40 percent of that simply flushes down the toilet. (According to one estimate, the typical flush toilet uses 13,000 gallons of water a year to carry away 165 gallons of body waste.) By eliminating water-operated toilets and substituting the Mullbank composting privy—formerly called the Ecolet—we reduced the need for water to a maximum average of only 36 gallons a day, well within the limit. In theory, we'll have something like five times the water we'll need.

The Mullbank toilet ordinarily speeds the decomposition process by the use of resistance-wire heat. But because the location of this house produces virtually free hot water, we'll have the only solar-powered john we've heard of, with hot water running through the plastic-coated copper pipes that were designed to carry heating coils. (Though it isn't shown in the diagram, we'll probably add a small heat

Solar-Powered Toilet

That shiny porcelain symbol of civilization, the flush toilet, uses five gallons of pure water to flood away a half-pint of urine. It has instituted an enormous waste of water, staggering sewer systems, and costly waste-treatment plants.

One alternative: the composting toilet. We're installing the Swedish-built polystyrene Mullbank. Some of its advantages:

● A standard toilet uses some 750 gallons of water a month per user; a composting toilet, none.

● A composting john needs no septic tank, no drain field.

● It presents no chemical or incineration worries.

● It provides the homeowner with one of the finest garden fertilizers available.

● Including the holding tank, it's not much bigger than a tall flush toilet.

The Mullbank principle is simple. The waste decomposes, while odors are wafted up a ventilating pipe by a small, internal fan. To quicken decomposition, heating coils snake across the inner floor, and a fan sucks air through the waste, providing oxygen for aerobic bacteria.

The normal ratio of people's solid to liquid waste is ideal for decomposition. Amazingly, at the end of a year, claims Recreation Ecol-

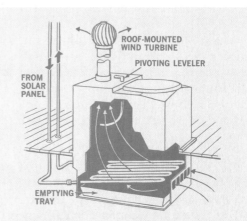

ROOF-MOUNTED WIND TURBINE

PIVOTING LEVELER

FROM SOLAR PANEL

EMPTYING TRAY

ogy Conservation of U.S., the waste of a family of three has broken down to a soil-like residue that will fit into a coffee can.

For our tropical house, we'd modify the unit a bit. We'd pull the electric wires from the PVC-coated copper tubes and attach our solar hot-water generating system. We'd keep warm water circulating through the toilet pipes with the aid of a tiny, 12-volt pump.

To the exhaust tube we'd add a $30 Triangle Engineering Company wind-driven turbine ventilator, and a spring-loaded switch. When breezes blow across the roof, the ventilator will spin, drawing air up through the waste; when the turbine stops, the switch will automatically turn on the fan.

exchanger to guard against contamination should a leak develop within the toilet.)

So-called gray water, from showers, sinks, and washing machine, will flow out across the ground through a pebble field. The sun should dispose of it nicely, and any phosphates deposited will sink into the soil, where they belong. At least, that's the theory. We may find that a residue will build up, so we included a ten-cubic-foot settling tank in the plan, just in case.

Water is collected by roof gutters. (In a less rainy climate, a tile drain field could be laid out on the uphill side.) Water will be stored both in the cement-block cistern and in insulated hot-and-cold-water holding tanks atop the house.

For cold water, we originally thought of a pressure tank buried in the ground. Then we realized that ground-water temperature equals the mean annual above-ground range in any climate. So on Roatan, no matter how deeply we buried a tank, the water would still be 81°F—not refreshingly cool.

Water pressure will be sustained by gravity. Any extra rainwater will overflow into a deep pond that's built at one end of the central garden both for esthetics and—a consideration in all remote locations—fire protection. The idea isn't new; Frank Lloyd Wright placed a fire pond in the lobby of Tokyo's Imperial Hotel. We'll have a self-priming Homelite (Model XLS 1½) gasoline-powered pump standing by. It's capable of throwing more than a gallon a second and weighs only 25 pounds.

Hot water will be stoked by the sun. For a home farther north, we'd recommend a small, auxiliary, propane hot-water heater, but for this island location we'll probably have all the hot water we'll need from a couple of homemade collector panels. As in most Caribbean areas, the sun broils down a good part of almost every day.

The hot-water gear starts with the two flat-plate collectors—one for the east bath, another for the west kitchen and bath. By the thermosiphon principle, the hot water will gravity-flow to an insulated drum higher on the roof, and somewhat cooler replacement water will be tapped from the drum's bottom. As hot water is drawn off, it will be replaced by cool water from another tank that's tucked between the tower legs. One nice thing about using collectors in the tropics: No antifreeze is needed, so a heat exchanger is unnecessary; you can use hot water directly from the collectors.

Except for the copper collectors, we'll be using the Connex-All polybutylene system for all our supply plumbing plus the Fit-All plastic tubular drain system—mainly because of ease of installation and resistance to oxidation and corrosion.

For a main power supply we selected the 500-watt, 12-volt-DC Wind Wizard (see box). With the nearly constant trade winds, we hope to run a number of 12-volt, van-type appliances—lamps, radio, fans, water pumps, and a Dometic refrigerator.

As a backup, we'll have one of Homelite's 170A15 generators. It's designed for 120-volt-AC use (and will be handy to power construction tools) but also comes equipped with a 12-volt-DC charger—fine for charging windmill batteries when doldrums settle in.

I'd planned to build the Cool House with neither professional help nor elaborate tools, to prove that a well-designed, hot-weather leisure home can be constructed by a weekend carpenter. My thought was that if I could do it on a site as remote as Roatan Island, any reader of this book can tackle a U.S. adaptation confidently.

The two years that have now passed since the working drawings were completed have confirmed this view. My Roatan project remains grounded, while I receive frequent (and frustrating) reports from purchasers of the plans on how "their" Cool House projects are progressing.

Residents of Honduras and neighboring countries have an expression applied to those frustrating events commonplace in the tropics, but difficult for time-sensitive North Americans to accept. The expression is "Well, cawa," said with a shrug of the shoulders. It's an acronym for "Central America wins again." We've had many opportunities to use the term in our attempt to build Cool House. For example:

The first load of poles, shipped from the Honduras mainland to Roatan, disappeared. We were told that they were "lost at sea," whatever that meant.

Finally, after a year and a quarter, the poles arrived, along with most of the rest of the stage-one lumber. Our island representative (have you ever tried to work with an island representative two thousand miles away?) stacked the materials nicely on the shore. But then Hurricane Greta came along and washed most of it to sea. Much of the rest was—er—borrowed by locals to repair their storm-damaged houses. But at least the poles were safe.

Knowing how quickly things work, we reordered the lumber two months in advance of our next visit. We figured on a trade-off: While the material sat on shore, some of it would walk off, but enough would remain to do the framing and flooring of stage one. But when we arrived, the lumber still hadn't been delivered. We sent a message to the supplier on the coast, and waited, and waited, and finally discovered that the captain of the ship had sold the wood in the town down the coast. He had received a higher price. He paid us back, but no lumber. So again, we reordered.

In the meantime, we planned to emplace the poles, so we made arrangements for the only bulldozer within 30 miles to pull them up the mountainside to the building site. The dozer broke down, of course, and another three months sped by before it was again mobile. And then, two days before the big event, the operator (the only bulldozer operator on that end of the island) was involved in a machete fight, effectively putting him out of commission. He went off to a mainland hospital and hasn't been seen since. And the poles still rest on the shore. Cawa.

But, as I said, I've received progress reports from Tonga, Wake Island, Belize, Costa Rica, British Virgin Islands—and from a retired couple in Florida who are installing double-glazed window-walls inside the louvers, using the louvers in place of drapes. So the plans are practical—anywhere but Roatan.

PRODUCT SOURCES, CREDITS:
AeroLectric, 13517 Winters Ave., Cumberland MD 21502 (Wind Wizard windmill); **Caribbean Lumber Co., Inc.,** Box 8367, Savannah GA 31402 (poles and other lumber); **Chicago Specialty Mfg. Co.,** 7500 Linder Ave., Skokie IL 60076 (Connex-All polybutylene water system and Fit-All drain system); **Dometic Sales Corp.,** 2320 Industrial Pkwy., Elkhart IN 46514 (combination electric/propane refrigerator); **Gould Inc.,** Box 3140, St. Paul MN 55165 (deep-cycle batteries for windmill); **Heath Co.,** Benton Harbor MI 49022 (five-function weather station and strip chart recorder); **Homelite Division of Textron, Inc.,** Box 7047, Charlotte NC 28217 (120-VAC/12-VDC generator; fire-protection pump; Super E-Z chainsaw); **Honduras Information Service,** 501 Fifth Ave., New York NY 10017 (travel arrangements); **Koppers Co., Inc.,** Forest Products Div., Koppers Bldg., Pittsburgh PA 15219 (Wolmanized pressure-treatment for lumber); **Lattoflex, Inc.,** 285 Palisade Ave., Cliffside Park NJ 07010 (flexible slat beds); **Recreation Ecology Conservation of United States, Inc.,** 9800 West Bluemound Rd., Milwaukee WI 53226 (Mullbank composting toilets); **Triangle Engineering Co.,** 11600 Big John Blvd., Houston TX 77038 (turbine roof ventilator and generator).

Leisure Homes from Catalog Components—designed by Jersey Devil

Construction camp for most recent house project is on ridge above California's Skyline Drive. Jersey Devil's Badanes (top) leans against collector for solar shower; windmill pumps water into 8000-gallon redwood tank behind him. At right is self-contained towable he lives in. Campsite can be seen again in distance of photo below, where work crew moves dirt onto roof deck.

If you don't choose to build your own leisure home—using one of the professional plans listed in this book—there's another route to a distinctive house (a house that won't look like every other one the local contractor has erected): Import a designer-builder.

While the team described in the report that follows can't be said to be typical—and would doubtless be difficult to approximate in your locale—you may find it instructive to learn how their unique custom homes are built. Their designs are so unconventional, the team moves to their client's site for as long as it takes them to build each project.

There are five of them now, scattered down both U.S. coasts. I've romped through three—after watching the latest sprout, like a sod-capped fungus, from the crest of a windy ridge between San Francisco Bay and the Pacific.

The wild custom homes shown on these pages have nothing in common except that they've all sprung from a collective creative force that dubs itself Jersey Devil. It's an informal association of architectural designers, spark-plugged by youthful, rangy Steve Badanes. Originally headquartered in New Jersey, the partnership took as its professional trademark the name and image of an imp that dates back, in local folklore, to the early 1800's. Differing accounts of the Jersey Devil have the creature (reddish fur, bat wings, cloven hoofs, horns, forked tail)

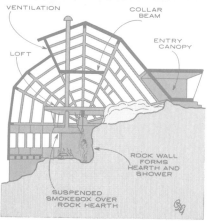

VENTILATION

COLLAR BEAM

LOFT

ENTRY CANOPY

ROCK WALL FORMS HEARTH AND SHOWER

SUSPENDED SMOKEBOX OVER ROCK HEARTH

HELMET HOUSE

Jersey Devil didn't set out to anchor a giant knight's helmet to a rock outcrop in a New Hampshire forest overlooking a lake; that's just how the design concepts added up. Framed in laminated "Gothic" rafters and 2x4's in a spiderweb pattern (lower left), the house literally grows from the granite ledge, which remains the rustic floor of much of the interior. As the sketch shows, there's a floating loft but no interior walls: The toilet is tucked behind a boulder; shower is a rock niche off living area; kitchen, built against the ledge, has rock storage nooks. To this site, Jersey Devil took a trailer for the crew office, and portable kitchen hut; pitched tents in the woods.

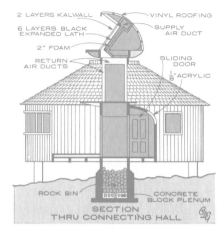

SILO HOUSE

Though in the midst of woods (near Lambertville, N.J.), this is only active solar house Jersey Devil has built. Huge air collector across top grabs enough sun in winter, when trees are bare, to take chill off house. Each of three separate living zones has wood-stove backup. They're modified prefabs from Unadilla Silo Co., joined by skylighted airlock entries (seen from rear, left).

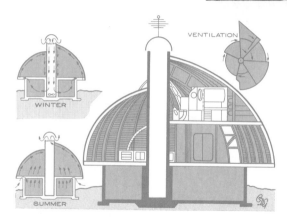

SNAIL HOUSE

Audaciously ambitious for a first house-building project, this shell-like home was erected in '73 in the Jersey Pine Barrens, with ascending series of barn rafters fanning around a con-crete core. Note vertical and horizontal air-flow schemes above, left. (Other photos page 185.)

hopping about the state from mischief to mischief. "That seemed appropriate to our *modus operandi,*" says Badanes.

The group has ranged wide, going wherever its commissions take it. "That's what makes us unique," Steve tells you. "We're not office architects. We first work up a structural image—which is always geared to the site and the client, so is never duplicated. Since our concepts are usually unlike anything that's been done before, we must first do our basic engineering to see if they'll work. Then we take the design directly to the site to work out details."

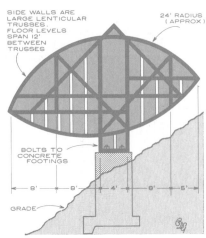

SIDE WALLS ARE
LARGE LENTICULAR
TRUSSES.
FLOOR LEVELS
SPAN 12'
BETWEEN
TRUSSES

24' RADIUS
(APPROX)

BOLTS TO
CONCRETE
FOOTINGS

8'   8'   4'   8'   5'

GRADE

FOOTBALL HOUSE

Actually a guest cottage connected to an existing house (off right, above) by a flying covered catwalk, this structure cantilevers forward and back from tiny (but deeply rooted)
pedestal. Author found interior a cozy delight;
it's stepped, and flows out onto an open deck
that floats in space. The house is a bold solution to an "unbuildable" slope and it tucks in
among California redwoods without site disruption or root damage. Framing is like that of
pier-support bridge: All weight hangs from
central uprights.

Surprisingly, Jersey Devil—unlike your
average architect or builder—isn't content
with a part-time commitment to its current
project. The designer and his associates
literally set up a construction camp and
live with the house from site preparation
right through to whatever level of completion the client wants (some prefer to do
all interior finishing themselves). The
client—who pays for this "live-in" setup, of
course—may be invited to double as contractor, or to pitch an adjacent tent and
pitch in with carpentry help. "We're filling
a gap," says Steve, "by offering quality
custom housing without an architect."
(Although the partners—and some of their
pick-up crew members—have architectural degrees, none of them cares to be
licensed.)

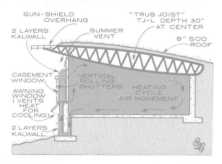

SKYLINE HOUSE

Most recent project is flat, bowed home dug into top of ridge that's backbone of peninsula south of San Francisco. Since Skyline Drive authorities won't issue permit for structures that spoil visual sweep of ridge, owner of this lofty site appealed to Jersey Devil for a self-effacing home that would sacrifice none of the ocean view. Catalog trusses fan across between entry patio at rear and window wall, leaving interior open and creating vast roof deck for sodding. Trombe wall below expanse of windows supplies heat. Wood stove and few electric baseboards are backup.

Helmet House gets protective ferro-cement skin—¼" layer—over sheathing of Homasote and Styrofoam.

Football House has preformed one-piece sky-light across ridge—made possible by special pier-support framing. Badanes stands in front of cedar-sided house (bottom photo), set in coastal redwoods.

"I think we started well, back in '72," says Badanes, "by establishing our on-site development technique with our first major project—the Snail House. We built it for a New Jersey steam fitter who'd do the plumbing, heating, and electrical himself, after we'd finished the shell. He had a small lot in light woods, and it was obvious he'd soon have close neighbors, so privacy was a big factor."

The snail-shell structure spirals up from east to west, letting sunlight enter continuously as the sun arcs around it. There's operable Plexiglas glazing at each interface of adjacent shell segments. These resulting steps in the structure also create a natural ventilator effect, with fresh air scooped in low and exhausted high, at the column's top. In winter, air is recirculated down the column by a fan at its base.

"We sheathed this first house in t&g red cedar, which serves as the interior finished surface, with all those laminated curved rafters exposed, as shown in one

of the photos. Insulation was applied to the *outside*, where it's most efficient: Three inches of urethane foam was sprayed over the entire exterior. Then a cement stucco was troweled on as a weathercoat. The thermal efficiency of all this means the house can be heated by a central wood stove on winter weekends."

This first house established the policy of using humble, off-the-shelf materials in unusual ways, as photos at right and the list on page 187 attest.

"We like to use materials that are made for some other purpose," says Steve. "They often turn out to be the cheapest solution. One of our best working relationships with a materials source has been with Unadilla Silo Co. in a New York village of that name. They make not only wood-stave farm silos but laminated barn rafters. We've adapted their catalog modules to several of our projects. When my focus shifted to the West Coast, I began searching out similarly unexpected sources."

(While working in California, Badanes terms his enterprise "Jersey Devil/West." His partner, John Ringel, keeps home fires burning back east. The two of them collaborated on the eastern houses shown here. For the two California homes, Badanes' design associate was Jim Adamson.)

Snail House erection began with structural/ mechanical core-column, 32' high, made by stacking standard 4'x4' manhole sections, using rented crane (top). This was ringed with circular concrete foundation, and joists were fanned across basement level, with bridging as shown at center. Varying lengths of laminated rafters were erected from edge.

And the pattern of client participation also persisted into subsequent projects. Helmet House client Nash Glynn was an active partner in the whole process, in New Hampshire in '74. And the couple for whom the Silo House was created, the following year, were just back from a sojourn in Tanzania and eager to help with the work. They were homesick for round African huts, and wanted to retain the simpler lifestyle they'd adopted abroad. They opted for solar heat, backed up with wood stoves.

This is actually primary housing. (Jersey Devil doesn't specialize in leisure homes; they'll tackle anything on a challenging site.) The three-silo plan gave the couple zoned activity areas (sleep/living/office) that are thermally and acoustically isolated. The timber truss that rides across the center of the peaked roofs not only carries the clamshell collector and air ducts; it provides operable clerestory windows for air.

This house is Jersey Devil's only effort at active solar, and the distribution system is impractically attenuated. I accompanied John Ringel on one of his "call-backs" to tune up the fans. Though the long-trough rock storage is ingenious and the fans have now been enlarged to make the system practical, this was higher technology than Jersey Devil likes to deal in. Their other houses stuck to passive systems, with thermal efficiency designed in, not mechanically imposed.

Their best passive example to date was only recently completed. I've visited this Skyline project three times. First, before the spectacular site had been touched (to the west, a broad sweep of the Pacific; to the east, the whole of the Bay; north,

along the peninsula's spine, San Francisco bristling from its tumble of hills). Then again after the site had been leveled for the slab pour. And, finally, back to see the ridge restored—with a Trombe-wall house tucked beneath it! I can't imagine better evidence of what "live-in architects" can pull off.

They've been able to "tune up" the passive-solar concepts as they built (see the color photograph of the double foundation). On the blustery March day of my most recent visit, the system's performance was impressive. The sharp ocean sun sliced through the Kalwall glazing below that long strip of windows, heating up the black-painted, 14-inch-thick concrete wall behind. Inside the house, cool floor air enters the system through perimeter vents along the base of the window seat. Dipping down the foundation trench and through vents along the footings, it rises through the heated chamber between Kalwall and concrete, then reenters the house through window-seat vents.

In addition, heat from the low winter sun slants through the south and west windows and is stored in the quarry-tile-on-slab floor, to be radiated into the living space at night.

For summer sun control, there's a shading overhang plus shutters. The bermed wall helps cool the home by natural air convection.

Jersey Devil worked this site for over two years; what they accomplished couldn't have been done any other way. If you want a distinctive leisure home but lack the skills to build it yourself—and can finance such costly customizing—you'd do well to search out a group of creative itinerants like this one.

OFF-THE-SHELF OR CATALOG COMPONENTS FOR FIVE HOUSES

HELMET HOUSE
"Gothic" barn rafters
Pre-painted Homasote sheathing
Styrofoam (with ferro-cement skin)

SILO HOUSE
Prefab wood silos (for three cylinders)
Kalwall glazing
Vinyl car roofing (for collector)
Mason's mahogany floats (sliding door handles)

SNAIL HOUSE
Stacking manhole sections
Laminated barn-rafter arcs
Sprayed urethane insulation

FOOTBALL HOUSE
Ridge skylight
Aluminum sliding glass doors
Corrugated FRP (catwalk roof)

SKYLINE HOUSE
Trus-Joist (roof supports)
Precast catch basins (1' dia., for porthole windows,
    light recesses)
Terracotta flue tile (mortared for built-in wine rack)
Kalwall glazing (Trombe wall, skylight)
Stock windows (Andersen awning and casement,
    AWS circular)
Bottle bottoms (laid in mortar or cast in panels for
    clerestory windows, dividers)
Manhole riser (2' high x 6' dia., patio planter)
Vertical rolling exterior shutters (Sunegar)
Dryer duct, PVC pipe (exposed utility chases)

7. ORDERING INFORMATION FOR ALL HOUSE PLANS

This chapter contains all prices and addresses you need to follow up on your selection of a leisure home from the preceding pages of this book. Prices for plans are all correct as we go to press and our sources will hold them at this level as long as possible. However, because of increases in printing costs and postage, prices are subject to change, particularly beyond a year after the book's copyright date. In such cases, the source to which you mail your check will notify you of any additional amount due, but you will have the option to cancel the order if you do not wish to pay the requested sum.

ORDERING INFORMATION FOR ALFREDO DE VIDO HOUSES

Address: Alfredo De Vido, 699 Madison Avenue, New York, N.Y. 10021. Check or money order is to be payable to Alfredo De Vido.

Page No.	Name of house	Price 1 Set	Price 4 Sets
4	Biosphere	$60	$75
8	Underground Solar House	$60	$75
12	Sun Trap	$60	$75

ORDERING INFORMATION FOR WILLIAM J. WARD, JR., HOUSES

Make check or money order payable to Idea Enterprises, Box 1720, Grand Central Sta., New York, N.Y. 10017. (See exception below.) Plans sent postpaid by first-class mail.

Page No.	Name of house	Price 1 set	Price each add'l set	Comment
18	Atrium House	$40	$10	Plans include elevations of exterior and atrium walls, full foundation plan and a progressive materials list that lets you estimate what each stage will cost
22	Four-Module Pin-Wheel	$40	$10	Complete working drawings and materials list
26	High-Security Weekend Retreat	$40	$10	Complete working drawings and materials list
30	Two-Phase Contemporary	$40	$10	Plans include typical outside wall sections, full foundation plan, and a dual materials list that lets you estimate what each phase will cost
34	One-Room Leisure Home Sleeps Ten	$50	$65 for 3 sets $75 for 5 sets	For this Ward house send check or money order to Vacation Plans Service, Box 426, Kingston, N.J. 08528. Specify The Sleeps-Ten-House VPS 29

A materials list is $10 with a plans order.
Sources for Skylids, Beadwall and other special materials are included in the materials lists.

ORDERING INFORMATION FOR SAMUEL PAUL HOUSES

Address: Homes for Living, Inc., 107–40 Queens Blvd., Forest Hills, N.Y. 11375. Check or money order payable to Homes for Living, Inc. Materials list and specifications are included at no extra cost. A mirror reverse print can be ordered for $10. Add $3 for postage and handling.

Page No.	Name of house	Architect's name for house	Price 1 set	Price 5 sets
40	Suncrest: Passive Solar-Plus	same	$65	$95
44	Skewed-Prow	Candlewood	$65	$95
48	Multi-Level Lodge	Hampton	$65	$95
52	Sky Vista	same	$65	$95
56	Modified Saltbox	Nantucket	$65	$95
60	Expandable Retreat	Greenwood	$65	$95
64	Split Pavilions	Twins	$65	$95
68	Fireproof Retreat	Hummingbird Plan No. 9214	$65	$95

ORDERING INFORMATION FOR HOME BUILDING PLAN SERVICE (HBPS) HOUSES

Address: Home Building Plan Service, 2235 N.E. Sandy Blvd., Portland, Or. 97232. Check or money order to be payable to Home Building Plan Service. A building materials list for any house is $15. Plans will be reversed, side-for-side for $20. Plumbing and wiring diagrams are $6 each. Give both name of house and HBPS number. (The Solar Schematic shown in a box with the Sun Seeker (page 102) is free with an order for 4 sets of plans, otherwise $10.)

Page no.	Name of house	HBPS number	Price 1 set	Price 4 sets
72	Six-Way House	894–1A without basement; bedroom/bath on second floor	$80	$100
		894–2A without basement; dormitory on second floor	$80	$100
		894–1B with standard basement, bedroom/bath on second floor	$95	$120
		894–2B with standard basement; dormitory on second floor	$95	$120
		894–1C with daylight basement; bedroom/bath on second floor	$95	$120
		894–2C with daylight basement; dormitory on second floor	$95	$120

Page no.	Name of house	HBPS number	Price 1 set	Price 4 sets
74	Energy-Saver	1392–2A specify wood or concrete foundation	$80	$100
78	Gambrel Frame	892–1A without basement	$105	$130
		892–1 with standard basement	$120	$150
		892–1B with daylight basement	$120	$150
82	Sun Cottage	916–1A without basement	$80	$100
		916–1 with excavated basement	$95	$120
84	Gambrel with a Solar Wall	909–1A without basement	$90	$110
		909–1 with basement	$105	$130
88	Vertical House	935–1A without basement	$105	$135
		935–1 with basement	$125	$150
90	Hexagon House	899–1A	$125	$140
94	Peak House on Stilts	111–1	$95	$120
96	King Post Pagoda	913–1A	$80	$100
98	Upside-Down Retreat	896–1 for a sloping site	$80	$100
		896–2 for a level site	$80	$100
100	Sun Seeker	920–1A without basement	$80	$100
		920–1 with basement	$95	$120

ORDERING INFORMATION FOR V-PAC HOUSES

Address: Vacation Plans Service, Box 426, Kingston, N.J. 08540. Check or money order to be payable to Vacation Plans Service. Prices for all V-PAC Houses: $50 for 1 set, $65 for 3, $75 for 5. Exception: Engelframe Towable (VPS 22) which is $35 for 1 set, $50 for 3 sets, $60 for 5. Include $2.00 postage and handling for plans to the continental U.S.A.; $3.00 for same outside the continental U.S.A. (U.S. funds only.)

Page No.	Name of house	V-PAC name	V-PAC number
104	Holiday Hill	same	VPS 31
108	Engelframe Towable	same	VPS 22
110	Cruciform House	Engelframe Cherokee	VPS 26
112	Stilt House	The Apache	VPS 15
114	Twin-Prow Split Level	same	VPS 33
116	Two-Phase Twin Ridge	same	VPS 5
120	Arrowhead Retreat	The Tomahawk	VPS 45
122	Octagon House	The Sekani	VPS 16
124	Bridge House	same	VPS 28
126	Stretched Hex	The Omaha	VPS 12
128	Lean-to House	same	VPS 25
130	Round House	same	VPS 27
132	Split Gable	The Lenape	VPS 1
134	Stacked Shack	same	VPS 43
136	Double-Decker	The Salt Marsh	VPS 4
138	Bunk Tower	The Quinipissa	VPS 6
140	Arrowhead Lodge	Akanu	VPS 24
142	Stilt House	The Olympic	VPS 21
144	Two-Story Sleep Wing	The Pawnee	VPS 36

ORDERING INFORMATION FOR INDEPENDENT PROJECTS

Page No.	Name of house	Name of Architect or Designer	Prices for Plans	Addresses or Information
148	All-Metal Solar Wedge	Marc Harrison (built for ILZRO-International Lead Zinc Research Organization, Inc.)	$40 per set $60 for 3 sets	Send check to ILZRO, 292 Madison Ave., New York, N.Y. 10017. For sources of kits and solar gear, see boxes with text
152	Tent Cabin	Jeff Milstein	$25 per set $40 for 2 sets	Send check or money order to Jeff Milstein, 429 Zena Rd., Woodstock, N.Y. 12498

Page No.	Name of house	Name of Architect or Designer	Prices for Plans	Addresses or Information
156	Frame-Hung Dome	Les Walker	$40 per set $70 for 3 sets	Send check or money order to Les Walker, Box 678, Woodstock, N.Y. 12498
164	RV Chalet	George J. Bunzer	$35 per set $50 for 4 sets; $10 for materials list	Send check or money order to George Bunzer, Rte 6, Box 384, Murphy, No. Carolina, 28906
168	Cool House for a Hot Climate	Robert Gannon	$50 per set $10 for ea. add'l set with original order	Send check or money order to Tropical House Plans, 114 Buffalo Run, Port Matilda, Pa. 16870
178	Far-Out Leisure Homes from Catalog Components	Jersey Devil	No plans available. See text	

PART TWO

THE POPULAR SCIENCE LOCKBOX HOUSE

1. Erecting the Pole-and-Beam Skeleton (with complete plans)

Modesty be damned: We rate our Lock-box as the wildest do-it-yourself leisure home ever built for publication. We'd carefully considered such a project for several years, in response to repeated requests for house plans. But we saw no need to rush into a field already served by government agencies and plans ser-

vices, until we had a unique and exciting concept—a truly innovative design you could find only in *Popular Science*. Such houses, we told ourselves, don't grow on trees. (As it turned out, ours *did!*) We decided the only way we'd get the house we wanted to publish was to build it ourselves.

Total-security concept of our Lockbox House includes designed-in shuttering system. Front corner—an open, two-floor well—is glazed with four wood sliding patio door units, to "prow into" the canyon view. One panel of each unit slides to provide fully adjustable ventilation. But so much exposed glass leaves the house vulnerable, while vacant, to storm, accident, casual vandalism, forced entry. So each window sports its own shutter: The three 8-footers have a plywood panel hung alongside, from a barn-door track. Rollers catch the bottom edge. The shutter for the 12' door is a pair of crossbuck-braced sections of the deck. With these rections raised, the naked deck joists discourage passage and prevent banking of snow against this entry. Whether closing for a weekend or a winter, you have no heavy panels to wrestle out of storage. Just slide or hoist, and latch from inside.

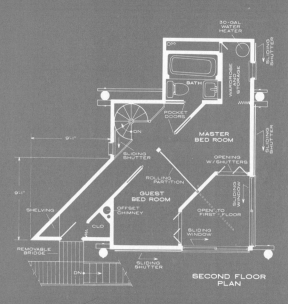

SECOND FLOOR PLAN

Labels on second floor plan: 30-GAL. WATER HEATER; SLIDING SHUTTER; BATH; WARDROBE AND STORAGE; POCKET DOORS; MASTER BED ROOM; DN; SLIDING SHUTTER; OPENING W/SHUTTERS; SLIDING SHUTTER; ROLLING PARTITION; GUEST BED ROOM; SLIDING WINDOW; OFFSET CHIMNEY; OPEN TO FIRST FLOOR; CLO; SHELVING; SLIDING WINDOW; REMOVABLE BRIDGE; DN; SLIDING SHUTTER; 9'-1"; 9'-1"

Choose your entry level: Catwalk from hill path brings you to solid fiberglass door—only entry when house is shuttered. If hinged deck is down, you can descend to sliding-glass entry. All exterior construction is Garden Grade redwood. Partition between bedrooms floats forward in well when not needed.

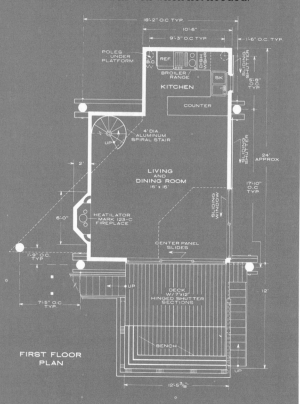

FIRST FLOOR PLAN

Labels on first floor plan: 18'-2" O.C. TYP.; 10'-6"; 9'-3" O.C. TYP.; 1'-6" O.C. TYP.; POLES UNDER PLATFORM; REF.; DISH WSHR; SLIDING SHUTTER; BROILER/RANGE; SK; 5'-8" TYP.; KITCHEN; COUNTER; 4' DIA. ALUMINUM SPIRAL STAIR; UP; LIVING AND DINING ROOM 16' x 16'; 24' APPROX; SLIDING SHUTTER; 2'; 17'-10" O.C. TYP.; HEATILATOR MARK 123-C FIREPLACE; SLIDING WINDOW; 6'-0"; CENTER PANEL SLIDES; 1'-9" O.C. TYP.; UP; DECK W/7'x12' HINGED SHUTTER SECTIONS; 12'; 7'-5" O.C. TYP.; BENCH; UP; 12'-5 5/8"

The magazine's Centennial provided the occasion (see Introduction). And our previous small-project work with prize-winning architect Lester Walker indicated he was just the man to put our house ideas into a workable package. But first those ideas needed firming up.

We decided we could make the most significant contribution to house design in the area of the "second" home—the weekend cottage, fully winterized for year-round recreation and retirement option. Our research revealed that half of all second homes are now built at least 100 miles from the primary residence. The frontiers are fast retreating from all population centers. As choice recreation land is gobbled up by large summer-home developers, what's left for the private builder? Ever more remote and unbuildable parcels. Designing a house for such plots isn't easy.

There are built-in paradoxes to vacation-home design and construction: You're building on your site, in the first place, because you love it just as it is, and long to live in harmony with it. Yet most homes require elaborate grading and foundation work that does violence to the naturalness you'd hoped to enjoy. Also, you choose a site that offers maximum privacy so you can open the house up to the view. Yet in doing so, you make the house vulnerable to pilferers, vandals, and irresponsible hunters while you're away.

One more thing: You quickly become an ecology nut when it's your *own* nest you'd be fouling. A nonpolluting waste-disposal system gets high priority—at further potential hazard to the site (drain-field installations for conventional septic systems can wreak havoc with a rustic plot).

The sum of all our solutions to such problems is what makes the Lockbox unique. It grows naturally from the site— it's not imposed upon it by force. The shuttering system explained in an earlier caption lets you close the house with confidence. And the aerobic tank, tucked in a shed under the front corner, will harmlessly dispose of sewage in a rocky clay soil that would make a septic system doubly impractical—from the standpoint of both excavation and percolation.

POLE-AND-BEAM SYSTEM

After trying several scale models, architect Walker and I chose pole-and-beam construction. It offers unique advantages for vacation homes:

● Minimal site preparation. To erect our prototype in deep woods, we felled only one tree, dug only seven holes.

● Ideal for steep sites, unstable soils. Since the house perches on "stilts," framing is self-leveling. You're spared the expensive and time-consuming buildup of a foundation.

● Fine for wooded slopes. Since it's something of a "tree house," it looks at home. And you'll need nearby trees to rig your block-and-tackle. Point each pole downhill toward its hole and it's already part way erect. (To erect the poles on a flat plot, you'd have to rent a small crane for a weekend.)

● No heavy equipment needed. No bulldozers for grading, no concrete trucks, if you're willing to mix your own batches for setting the poles. As a challenge, we chose a site nearly 150' down a mountain from our access road.

● Faster cover. Conventional framing builds toward the roof; this delays shelter till the bitter end, exposing construction to the vagaries of weather (particularly risky for mountain or lakeshore sites). With poles, you can erect rafters before framing any walls, then work under a giant treetop umbrella.

● No fret about header spans above windows. With conventional framing, this would be critical in a glass-walled house. Here, structural load is borne by the poles: You're dealing with a "curtain-wall" construction not unlike that employed in modern skyscrapers. This fact also lets you start erecting your "closing" walls anywhere you wish. We began at the top and worked down!

Since pole-and-beam construction offers many advantages, it's surprising the technique isn't better known. Until recently, of course, poles set in the earth were thought to be temporary—they'd have to be replaced eventually, like telephone poles. So pole construction used to be confined to inexpensive outbuildings.

Modern advances in wood-preservative pressure treatments have changed all that. We shipped in Koppers construction poles of southern yellow pine, treated (in Alabama) with pentachlorophenol, by means of the Cellon process. This is a dry method that gives the deepest penetration yet achieved. The solvent carrier for the penta is LPG—injected into poles under pressure in a cylinder, then evaporated to lock in the penta as a solid crystalline preservative that can't bleed from the wood.

Cellon-treated poles average from $4 to $4.50 per foot, depending on the length. (A 60' pole runs more per foot than a 30-footer because it's harder to handle and treat. As our pole-and-beam-skeleton sketch indicates, the longest pole re-

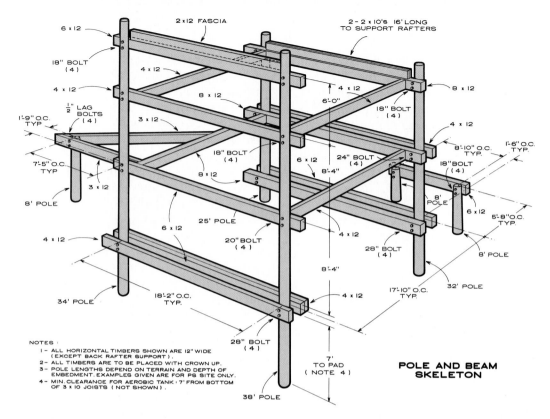

POLE AND BEAM SKELETON

quired for our site was 38'. Today, it would run you about $150.)

There are other preservative treatments that leave poles clean and odorless—but creosoting isn't one of them. *Don't* try to buy poles from local utilities; they're likely to be rejects, or used poles that were replaced because they're near the end of their design life. If they can't be trusted to carry a telephone cable, you certainly don't want to hang a house on them!

Until now, little has been published on pole-and-beam techniques. There's an FHA reprint you can get for 50 cents from American Wood Preservers Institute, 1651 Old Meadow Rd., McLean, Va. 22101. It's skimpy on specific how-to, but it has some good embedment tables and back-filling tips. A more sophisticated manual, with good illustrations (including photos) is

Low-Cost Pole Building Construction by Doug Merrilees and Evelyn Loveday ($5.95 from Garden Way Publishing, Charlotte, Vt. 05445).

Setting the poles. The spacing shown on our diagrams is approximate. These poles taper from 7″ tips to as much as 12″ at their bases, so diameters at various connection points differ. The site may also require adjustment of hole location. Placement of the four major poles is flexible—within limits: They must stand outside the basic 16′ cube. You'll note we set the front-right pole further out to accommodate a platform for the lower stairway.

The recommended method for connecting beams to poles is by means of a special "spike grid" system from Teco (address in co-sponsors list). It involves the elements shown in one of the photos:

● ¾″ threaded rod; you'll need sixteen 2′ lengths (to be trimmed to various lengths after assembly) plus eight 3-footers hacksawed in half to create sixteen 18″ bolts.

● ¾″ nuts and 2″ washers for each end of each rod length.

● Single-curve spike grids, to insert between pole and beam (curved face toward pole, flat toward beam). Using a pair at each connection, you'll need 44.

● Special applicator (which you can rent from Teco outlets).

● Two wrenches, one to fit bolt nuts, one to fit applicator's draw nut.

● Our personal addition to the system: Teco's Ten-Con angles—a pair per beam. These are for convenience in positioning the heavy beams. You apply the angles first, after carefully marking the poles you're spanning, to determine the exact height you want the *bottom* of the beam. Check the two pole markings to make certain they're level; we filled a 30′ clear plastic tube with water to serve as a level. Now, spike the pair of support angles to the posts using the special cut nails provided (no need to fill all the holes in the angle—seven to ten nails should be plenty).

With a tape, measure center-to-center distance between poles the beam is to span. Center this spacing on the beam length and square your drilling lines across the face of the beam that will go toward the poles. Drill two holes through the beam on each line, about 3″ from each edge.

Hoist the beam (with a block-and-tackle rig from each pole) until it rests on the angles. Drill for and drive bolts through (page 201), inserting spike grids between beam and pole so that bolt passes through their center hole. Apply a washer and snug up a nut on the emerging end.

Excavating is limited to pole holes. Our rocky site called for blasting. Jackhammer was fed by 150′ hose from compressor.

Husky rigging—like that on a ship's mast—is secret of pole raising. Two block-and-tackle rigs to nearby trees do best job.

Two up, two to go: Position poles uphill of their holes; raise and guy downhill poles first. Note two hoist ropes on pole at right.

Fast action with concrete assures firm embedment. This hole, blasted into boulder, couldn't go 6' depth so was filled flush.

Alternate connection system involves notching pole. Terrain forced us to set this rear pole out of line, so we notched beam, too.

Needed for connections (l-r): Teco Ten-Con angles with nails, 2' and 3' lengths ¾" bolt rod, spike grids, two wrenches, applicator.

Drill beams before hoisting. Though too short to pass through, ¾″ machine-spur bit in ½″ drill starts holes square to face.

Using drilled beam as template, bore on through pole with ¾″ spade bit in extension shank. Back out often to clear chips.

Sledge bolts through holes predrilled in beam(s) and pole, while beams are lashed in position. Double nuts protect threads.

Compacting is done by threading applicator socket onto projecting end of bolt and wrenching draw nut, as author does here.

Hoist roof beams with double block-and-tackle rig; this 8x12 is first raised to second floor. Polyethylene pad helps it slide.

Topping out skeleton, front 6x12 is raised from attic floor. Temporary platform projects at corner for pole drilling, bolting.

As first winter fell, skeleton was complete up to rafters. Cube at front of first floor is fiberglass tub/shower to be raised to second floor through corner-well opening above it.

Attach the applicator to the rod bolt (whichever end is most convenient) and draw joint tight as you can by turning the applicator nut with a wrench. (Stop pressure when washer on opposite side embeds itself in the beam.) This squeezes members together, forcing the spikes on the grid's curved face into the pole, and those on the flat face into the beam.

Insert a second wrench through the open side of the applicator (page 201, bottom right) and re-snug the nut against the washer. Back off the applicator nut and detach the unit. Repeat for each bolt—that's two compactions per joint. The carrying capacity of a double-grid connection is over 7,500 pounds.

You'll note in one photo that we notched a misaligned rear pole to bring that beam parallel to the front beam. You can, however, use notching as a substitute connection method, if you don't want to buy spike grids.

In this case, you simply set the beams into snug notches and secure with bolts. Notching does weaken a pole somewhat—especially if you must notch both sides—but this isn't critical if the notch isn't over 2″ deep. Notching the beam, as well, is recommended only where required for alignment. (In that same photo, a water-repellant wood preservative is being brushed onto all notched areas—always a good practice.)

A thinking man's project. Lockbox construction must proceed in logical sequence, since you're raising heavy (and therefore potentially dangerous) timbers to considerable heights. Let's go back to the start and establish the order for the first 15 steps:

1. Stake positions for the four major poles that support the basic 16′ cube. Dig (or blast) holes 4′–6′ deep with a minimum diameter of 2′ at the bottom. Pour an 8″-thick bearing pad; when concrete has set, drop in pole and guy erect with at least three ropes to surrounding trees or well-anchored stakes.

We'd recommend ½″ hemp, both for the block-and-tackle rigs and the guys. The first pole we erected—our 38-footer—was guyed with ¼″ rope. A worker brushed one of the guys before we embedded the base, jarring the pole enough to break it loose from the other two. It crashed back to earth, grazing our associate architect; a few inches difference would have flattened him. We took no further chances

dictated by economy—and, incidentally, never saw the associate again.

2. Bolt on the first-floor beams and install joists and plywood floor to create a working platform.

3. Project perimeter lines from this platform (using twine run out to stakes, batter boards or trees, and equipped with a line level) for the two wings (kitchen/bath and entry) to determine locations for the three final poles. Set poles on below-frost footings.

4. Frame the second floor. This is the tricky one, with doubled and tripled joists, 45-degree angles, open corners. To avoid the complexity of intersecting ledgers (and for a less-cluttered visual effect, since all these joists remain exposed), we suspended this entire floor from Simpson joist and purlin hangers. Simpson won't supply individual builders direct. And some of the hangers we call for (skewed 45 degrees) are special-order.

Your best bet is to contact Seidel Co., 4110 Dumbarton Rd., Houston, Tex. 77025. This shipper handles Teco building hardware, as well, if you prefer the convenience of a single source. Write them for a quantity takeoff on the hardware required for this house. (You can, of course, install all your joists with Simpson or Teco hangers if you wish to avoid notching for ledgers.)

5. Frame kitchen wing, complete with joists for bathroom floor. (More about the two wings in the next chapter.)

6. Pass the plywood panels for the attic floor up onto the second-floor joists, tacking them temporarily to create a second-level work platform. (Those open corners require temporary supports for the plywood.) Permanently apply flooring to wing joists only—and to the entry triangle, if you decide to frame it at this time for later access to the attic level.

JOIST AND RAFTER FRAMING

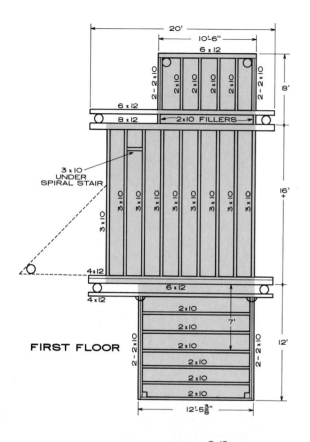

FIRST FLOOR

- 20'
- 10'-6"
- 6 x 12
- 2 - 2 x 10
- 2 x 10
- 8'
- 6 x 12
- 8 x 12
- 2 x 10 FILLERS
- 3 x 10 UNDER SPIRAL STAIR
- 3 x 10
- 16' +
- 4 x 12
- 6 x 12
- 4 x 12
- 2 - 2 x 10
- 2 x 10
- 7'
- 12'
- 12'-5 3/8"

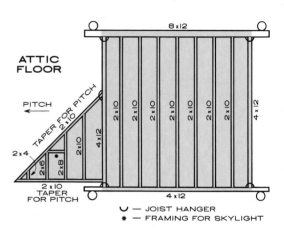

ATTIC FLOOR

- 8 x 12
- PITCH
- TAPER FOR PITCH
- 2 x 10
- 4 x 12
- 2 x 4
- 2 x 6
- 2 x 8
- 2 x 10
- *
- 2 x 10 TAPER FOR PITCH
- 4 x 12

∪ — JOIST HANGER
* — FRAMING FOR SKYLIGHT

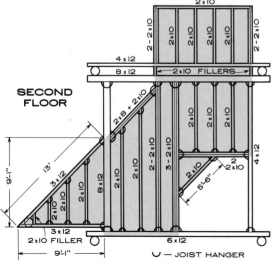

SECOND FLOOR

- 2 x 10
- 2 - 2 x 10
- 2 x 10
- 4 x 12
- 8 x 12
- 2 x 10 FILLERS
- 2 x 8 + 2 x 10
- 2 x 10
- 2 - 2 x 10
- 3 - 2 x 10
- 13'
- 9'-1"
- 3 x 12
- 8 x 12
- 2 x 10
- 2 x 10
- 5'-6"
- 2 - 2 x 10
- 4 x 12
- 3 x 12
- 2 x 10 FILLER
- 9'-1"
- 6 x 12

∪ — JOIST HANGER

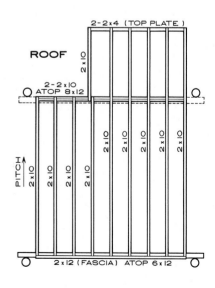

ROOF

- 2 - 2 x 4 (TOP PLATE)
- 2 x 10
- 2 - 2 x 10 ATOP 8 x 12
- PITCH
- 2 x 10
- 2 x 12 (FASCIA) ATOP 6 x 12

Glued plywood floor speeds assembly of sturdy cage

The ideal complement for pole-and-beam construction is the diaphragm floor system developed by American Plywood Assn., detailed in our sketch and photos, right. It's the fastest floor you ever laid—and a rugged, immediately usable working platform for framing the next-higher floor. We used this plywood system on first and attic floors only. The unique second floor—a "bridge" across the cube, open at two corners—is 2x6 t&g western softwood, preferably white or Douglas fir. The exposed underside serves as a beamed ceiling for the first floor. To avoid warping from weather exposure, this flooring should be applied (and coated with urethane finish) after roofing is on.

No such precautions need be taken with the plywood floors, however. Ours weathered a winter during which they were alternately sheathed with ice or under several feet of snow. Once we completed our siding job the following summer, we just went over them with a belt sander to prepare them for the Armstrong cushioned-vinyl sheet and tile flooring.

The secret of APA's Glued Floor System lies in the new elastomeric adhesives. APA issues a list of some 20 approved types. (Our choice: Franklin Construction Adhesive; it comes in 11-oz. cartridges for standard caulking guns.) A strong glue-bond joins floor and joists into an integral T beam that increases stiffness up to 70 percent over conventional floor construction—without bridging (that one crosspiece in our lower photo is at the spiral stair location). There's less vibration and bounce, too—and no nail popping or squeak (you use 80 percent fewer nails than in a two-layer floor).

Procedure is simple: Snap chalk line 4' from front edge of beam, apply glue to lay one panel; second panel completes front course. Nail each as it's laid. Cut third panel in half to stagger end joints. For second course, run bead of glue in groove of front course's rear edge, in addition to joist-top beads. Lay panel in place and sledge its tongue into this groove, using a 2x4 along the driven edge.

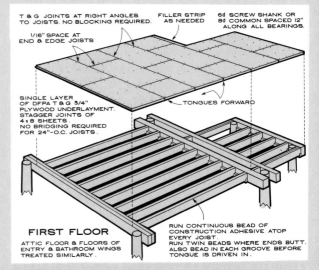

Frame first floor by notching 3x10s over 2x4 ledgers bolted to beams (top photo). Then apply t&g underlayment in three steps shown simultaneously, right: Run glue along joists, in groove; nail.

7. Hoist the attic floor beams onto second-level platform, then raise and bolt them across front and rear pairs of poles.

8. Hoist top purlin (6x12) to this second-floor level.

9. Apply Simpson hangers for two 4-x-12 crossbeams; hoist these in place.

10. Hoist (by tipping one end higher) the top purlin through these crossbeams, to rest across them. (Set ends on blocks to create work clearance underneath purlin.)

11. Install half of attic floor joists. Detach and pass up plywood beneath them. Complete joist installation, pass up balance of panels; lay upper plywood floor.

12. Hoist and bolt top purlin to poles.

13. Frame second floor of kitchen/bath wing to establish rear support for full-length rafters.

14. Install double 2x10s atop upper 8x12 to support rafters, using two to four Ten-Con flat connectors.

15. Hoist rafters to attic floor. Set one 26-footer in place across three support points, mark for birds-mouths. Cut, trial-fit, use as template for other rafters; install.

From this point, plan your "closing" to avoid any need for scaffolding—in other words, so that you can assemble your walls *inside* and tip them in place. Installed scaffolding for our steep site would have run nearly half the total materials cost of the house itself!

Yes, the Lockbox is a thinking man's house—right from the initial planning stages. We'd recommend that you think of it as a two-summer project. You could—with dedicated use of your weekends and vacation—get the structure roofed during the first summer, then close it with a reinforced-plastic film (such as Griffolyn) and

continue work through the winter when the temperature permitted.

DO-IT-YOURSELF?

A recent survey shows that *over half* of today's vacation homes are entirely or substantially owner-built. The Lockbox—because of its unique design and heavy timbers—is something of a special case. But if you can count on the help of husky teenaged sons (or boyfriends of daughters), you'll be able to swing it. A minimum crew of four (preferably five) is essential for wrestling up the pole-and-beam skeleton.

Don't make the mistake of assuming friends will offer help. I'm sure you've often read—as I have—of do-it-yourself house projects that were crawling with willing volunteers, eager to get involved. Unless I have unusually inept or self-protective friends, such accounts must be set down as myth. My experience has been that friends make themselves scarce while a muscle project of this magnitude is in the works. My own father—a professional carpenter—canceled a visit when he learned what I was up to.

My building partner, Ron Nelson, and I were able to manage with periodic student help from the architectural school where Les Walker was teaching at the time. The heroes of this crew were Bill Bobenhausen, Larry Cohan, and Nick Todaro whose sustained interest in the project through drizzle, downpour, and blizzard helped us meet our prove-out construction deadline.

There is, of course, the very real possibility that you may *have* to do the work yourself. In remote vacation areas, what little professional help you may find is likely to run scared if presented with an unusual site or structure. Their confidence is in the humdrum routine. To check this point, we invited one of the best builders in our mountain area to visit the site and have a look at our plans. We explained that the worst construction weather on record (ten consecutive weekend work sessions rained out) had put us behind schedule, and we sought a professional crew to help us meet our editorial deadline. He gulped at our mountainside, bugged his eyes at our poles, and beat a hasty retreat. Thereafter, he wouldn't even answer our letters.

So: to demonstrate that you *can* go it alone, we erected our entire pole-and-beam skeleton—and roofed it—without letting a professional touch the project. The only exceptions:

● A licensed dynamiter to blast the holes for our four major poles. (Getting a jackhammer to the site for setting the charge was no problem: Country pros are used to working at great distances from their compressors; our man thought nothing of unreeling 150′ of air hose.)

● The manufacturer of the aerobic system enclosed the tank in an insulated plywood shed.

● A crew of electricians ran our 220 power line down the mountain. (Another important advantage of pole-and-beam construction is that you "top out" the structure when you raise your first pole; as soon as you've locked any pole into the grid, you've provided a sturdy attachment for your entry cable. Without a dependable power source, early on, you'd be lost. This is a portable-power-tool project; whether you buy or rent, you'll need at least a 7″ circular saw, a saber saw, a ½″ drill, a belt sander.)

Be assured of one thing: For challenge and reward, raising the Lockbox is an adventure to match Everest. In our next chapter, we'll take you further into the construction by detailing the triangular-entry and kitchen/bath wings. And then we'll demonstrate the new roofing systems we applied to the house. The Lockbox is a showcase of innovations in building techniques and products. We'll be sharing them all with you until, by the end of this book, the house is completed.

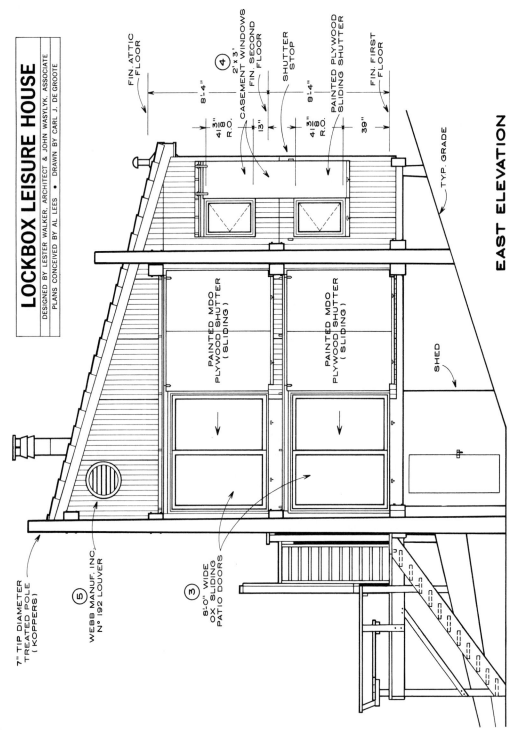

LOCKBOX LEISURE HOUSE

DESIGNED BY LESTER WALKER, ARCHITECT & JOHN WASYLYK, ASSOCIATE
PLANS CONCEIVED BY AL LEES • DRAWN BY CARL J. DE GROOTE

FIN. ATTIC
FLOOR

8'-4"

2' x 3'
CASEMENT WINDOWS
FIN. SECOND
FLOOR

4⅛"
R.O.

13"

SHUTTER
STOP

⓸

8'-4"

4⅛"
R.O.

PAINTED PLYWOOD
SLIDING SHUTTER

FIN. FIRST
FLOOR

39"

T.Y.P. GRADE

PAINTED MDO
PLYWOOD SHUTTER
(SLIDING)

PAINTED MDO
PLYWOOD SHUTTER
(SLIDING)

SHED

7" TIP DIAMETER
TREATED POLE
(KOPPERS)

WEBB MANUF. INC.
N° 192 LOUVER

⓹

8'-0" WIDE
OX SLIDING
PATIO DOORS

⓷

EAST ELEVATION

208

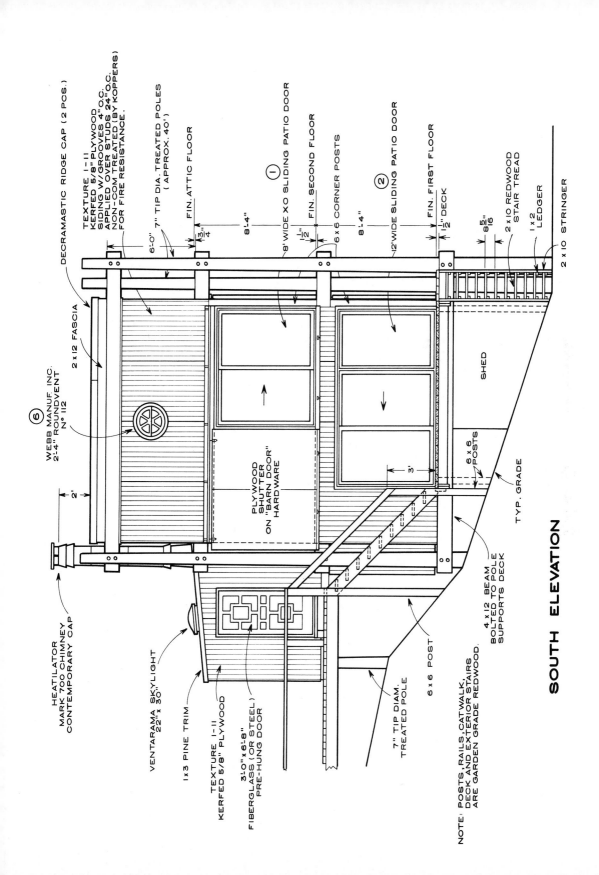

DECRAMASTIC RIDGE CAP (2 PCS.)

TEXTURE 1-11 KERFED 5/8" PLYWOOD SIDING W/GROOVES 4" O.C. APPLIED OVER STUDS 24" O.C. NON-COM TREATED (BY KOPPERS) FOR FIRE RESISTANCE.

7" TIP DIA. TREATED POLES (APPROX. 40')

FIN. ATTIC FLOOR

6'-0"

3" / 4

8'-4"

8' WIDE XO SLIDING PATIO DOOR

1" / 2

FIN. SECOND FLOOR

①

6 x 6 CORNER POSTS

8'-4"

12' WIDE SLIDING PATIO DOOR

②

FIN. FIRST FLOOR

1" / 2

1" DECK

8 5" / 16

2 x 10 REDWOOD STAIR TREAD

1 x 2 LEDGER

2 x 10 STRINGER

2 x 12 FASCIA

⑥

WEBB MANUF. INC. 2'-4" ROUNDVENT N° 112

2'

SHED

6 x 6 POSTS

3'

TYP. GRADE

PLYWOOD SHUTTER ON "BARN DOOR" HARDWARE

HEATILATOR MARK 700 CHIMNEY CONTEMPORARY CAP

VENTARAMA SKYLIGHT 22" x 30"

1 x 3 PINE TRIM

TEXTURE 1-11 KERFED 5/8" PLYWOOD

3'-0" x 6'-8" FIBERGLASS (OR STEEL) PRE-HUNG DOOR

4 x 12 BEAM BOLTED TO POLE SUPPORTS DECK

6 x 6 POST

7" TIP DIAM. TREATED POLE

NOTE: POSTS, RAILS, CATWALK, DECK AND EXTERIOR STAIRS ARE GARDEN GRADE REDWOOD

SOUTH ELEVATION

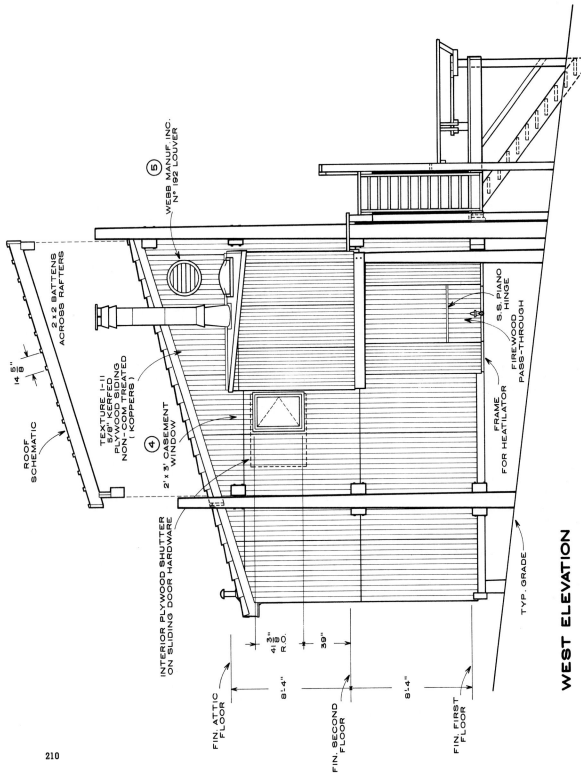

WEBB MANUF. INC.
Nº 192 LOUVER
⑤

2 x 2 BATTENS
ACROSS RAFTERS

14 5/8"

TEXTURE I-II
5/8" KERFED
PLYWOOD SIDING
NON-COM TREATED
(KOPPERS)
④

2' x 3' CASEMENT
WINDOW

ROOF
SCHEMATIC

INTERIOR PLYWOOD SHUTTER
ON SLIDING DOOR HARDWARE

S.S. PIANO
HINGE

FIREWOOD
PASS-THROUGH

FRAME
FOR HEATILATOR

TYP. GRADE

4' 3 1/8"
R.O.

39"

8'-4"

8'-4"

FIN. ATTIC
FLOOR

FIN. SECOND
FLOOR

FIN. FIRST
FLOOR

WEST ELEVATION

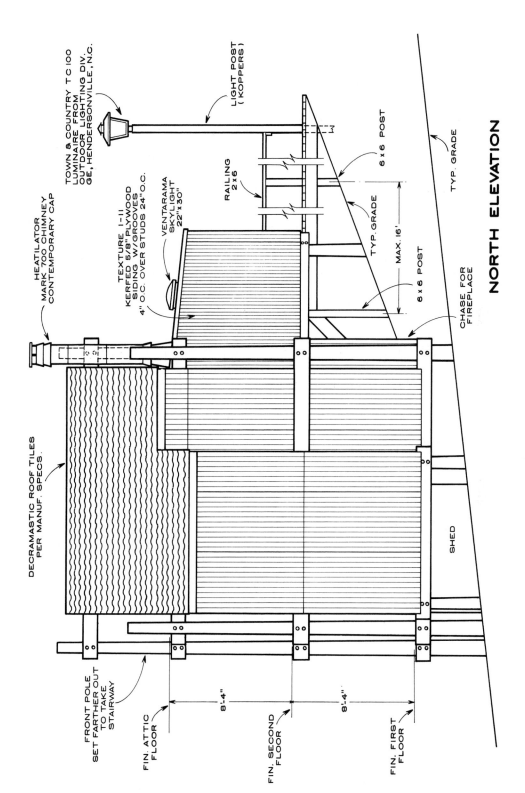

TOWN & COUNTRY T C 100
LUMINAIRE FROM
OUTDOOR LIGHTING DIV.,
GE, HENDERSONVILLE, N.C.

LIGHT POST
(KOPPERS)

HEATILATOR
MARK 700 CHIMNEY
CONTEMPORARY CAP

RAILING
2 x 6

TEXTURE 1-11
KERFED 5/8" PLYWOOD
SIDING W/GROOVES
4" O.C. OVER STUDS 24" O.C.

VENTARAMA
SKYLIGHT
22"x30"

6 x 6 POST

TYP. GRADE

TYP. GRADE

MAX. 16'

6 x 6 POST

CHASE FOR
FIREPLACE

DECRAMASTIC ROOF TILES
PER MANUF. SPECS.

NORTH ELEVATION

SHED

FRONT POLE
SET FARTHER OUT
TO TAKE
STAIRWAY

FIN. ATTIC
FLOOR

8'-4"

FIN. SECOND
FLOOR

8'-4"

FIN. FIRST
FLOOR

211

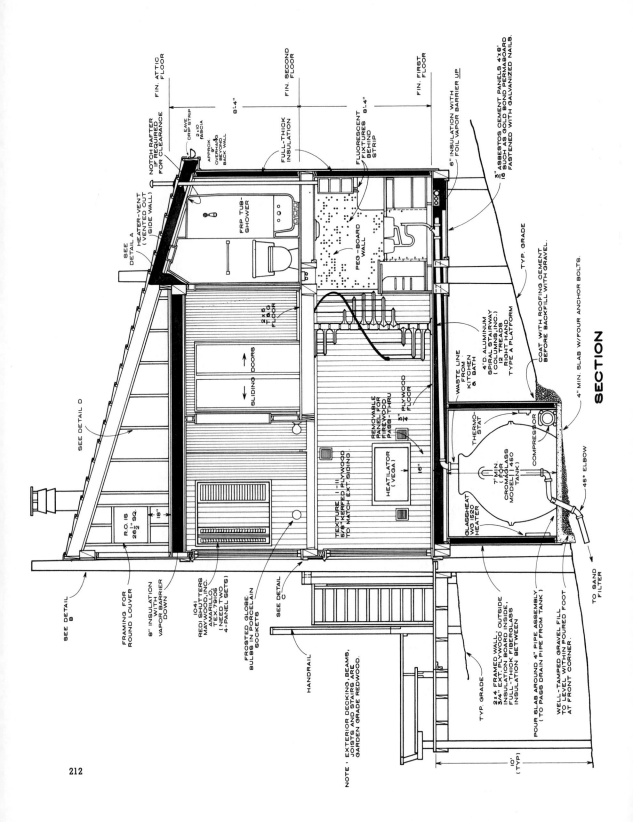

SECTION

FIN. ATTIC FLOOR

FIN. SECOND FLOOR

FIN. FIRST FLOOR

8'-4"

8'-4"

NOTCH RAFTER (IF REQUIRED FOR CLEARANCE)

EAVE DRIP STRIP

2 x 10 FASCIA

APPROX 9" OVERHANG BEYOND BACK WALL

FULL-THICK INSULATION

FLUORESCENT FIXTURES BEHIND STRIP

6" INSULATION WITH FOIL VAPOR BARRIER UP

3" ASBESTOS CEMENT PANELS 4'x8' SUCH AS GOLD BOND PERMAGARD FASTENED WITH GALVANIZED NAILS.

HEATER-VENT (VENTED OUT SIDE WALL)

SEE DETAIL A

FRP TUB-SHOWER

PEG-BOARD WALL

TYP. GRADE

2 x 6 T&G FLOOR

SLIDING DOORS

SEE DETAIL D

WASTE LINE FROM KITCHEN & BATH

4" D. ALUMINUM SPIRAL STAIRWAY (COLUMNS, INC.) 12 TREADS RIGHT HAND TYPE A PLATFORM

REMOVABLE PANEL FOR FIREWOOD PASS-THRU

¾" PLYWOOD FLOOR

COAT WITH ROOFING CEMENT BEFORE BACKFILL WITH GRAVEL.

4" MIN. SLAB W/FOUR ANCHOR BOLTS

TEXTURE 1-11 ⅝" KERFED PLYWOOD TO MATCH EXT SIDING.

THERMO-STAT

COMPRESSOR

R.O. IS 26½" SQ.

18"

HEATILATOR (VEGA)

16"

GLASSHEAT WG 1520 HEATER

7" MIN. FOR CROMAGLASS MODEL 1 450 TANK)

45° ELBOW

FRAMING FOR ROUND LOUVER

8" INSULATION WITH VAPOR BARRIER DOWN

(104) REDI SHUTTERS MAYWOOD, INC. AMARILLO, TEX 79105 (NEED TWO 4-PANEL SETS)

FROSTED GLOBE BULB IN PORCELAIN SOCKETS

SEE DETAIL C

TO SAND FILTER

SEE DETAIL B

HANDRAIL

TYP. GRADE

NOTE: EXTERIOR DECKING, BEAMS, JOISTS AND STAIRS ARE GARDEN GRADE REDWOOD.

2 x 4 FRAMED WALL, OUTSIDE ¾" EXT. PLYWOOD, INSIDE INSULATION BOARD. FULL-THICK INSULATION BETWEEN.

POUR SLAB AROUND 4" PIPE ASSEMBLY (TO PASS DRAIN PIPE FROM TANK)

WELL-TAMPED GRAVEL FILL TO LEVEL WITHIN POURED FOOT AT FRONT CORNER.

10' (TYP)

212

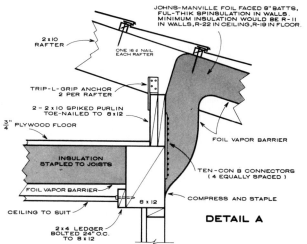

JOHNS-MANVILLE FOIL FACED 8" BATTS,
FUL-THIK SPINSULATION IN WALLS.
MINIMUM INSULATION WOULD BE R-11
IN WALLS, R-22 IN CEILING, R-19 IN FLOOR.

2 x 10 RAFTER

ONE 16 d NAIL EACH RAFTER

TRIP-L-GRIP ANCHOR 2 PER RAFTER

2 - 2 x 10 SPIKED PURLIN TOE-NAILED TO 8 x 12

¾" PLYWOOD FLOOR

INSULATION STAPLED TO JOISTS

FOIL VAPOR BARRIER

FOIL VAPOR BARRIER

TEN-CON 8 CONNECTORS (4 EQUALLY SPACED)

CEILING TO SUIT

COMPRESS AND STAPLE

8 x 12

2 x 4 LEDGER BOLTED 24" O.C. TO 8 x 12

DETAIL A

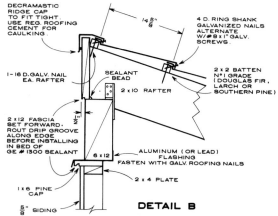

DECRAMASTIC RIDGE CAP TO FIT TIGHT. USE REG. ROOFING CEMENT FOR CAULKING.

14 ⅝"

4 D. RING SHANK GALVANIZED NAILS ALTERNATE W/#8 x 1" GALV. SCREWS.

I-16 D. GALV. NAIL EA. RAFTER

SEALANT BEAD

2 x 2 BATTEN Nº1 GRADE (DOUGLAS FIR, LARCH OR SOUTHERN PINE)

2 x 10 RAFTER

2 x 12 FASCIA SET FORWARD. ROUT DRIP GROOVE ALONG EDGE BEFORE INSTALLING IN BED OF GE #1300 SEALANT

1½"

6 x 12

ALUMINUM (OR LEAD) FLASHING FASTEN WITH GALV. ROOFING NAILS

2 x 4 PLATE

1 x 6 PINE CAP

⅝" SIDING

DETAIL B

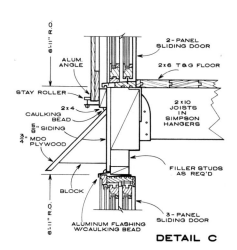

6'-11" R.O.

2-PANEL SLIDING DOOR

2 x 6 T & G FLOOR

ALUM. ANGLE

STAY ROLLER

2 x 4

CAULKING BEAD

⅝" SIDING

¾" MDO PLYWOOD

BLOCK

2 x 10 JOISTS IN SIMPSON HANGERS

FILLER STUDS AS REQ'D

3-PANEL SLIDING DOOR

6'-11" R.O.

ALUMINUM FLASHING W/CAULKING BEAD

DETAIL C

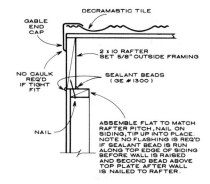

DECRAMASTIC TILE

GABLE END CAP

2 x 10 RAFTER SET ⅝" OUTSIDE FRAMING

NO CAULK REQ'D IF TIGHT FIT

SEALANT BEADS (GE #1300)

NAIL

ASSEMBLE FLAT TO MATCH RAFTER PITCH, NAIL ON SIDING, TIP UP INTO PLACE. NOTE NO FLASHING IS REQ'D IF SEALANT BEAD IS RUN ALONG TOP EDGE OF SIDING BEFORE WALL IS RAISED AND SECOND BEAD ABOVE TOP PLATE AFTER WALL IS NAILED TO RAFTER.

DETAIL D

12'-0"

3"

THIS SIDE DOWN

7'-0"

DECK SECTION
SHUTTER

2 x 6 REDWOOD DECKING GALV. NAILED TO 2 x 6 REDWOOD FRAME.

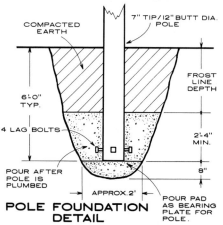

COMPACTED EARTH

7" TIP/12" BUTT DIA. POLE

6'-0" TYP.

FROST LINE DEPTH

4 LAG BOLTS

2'-4" MIN.

POUR AFTER POLE IS PLUMBED

8"

APPROX. 2'

POUR PAD AS BEARING PLATE FOR POLE.

POLE FOUNDATION
DETAIL

NOTE: THIS FOOTING DESIGN IS FOR SOIL CONDITIONS AND GEOGRAPHICAL LOCATION OF POPULAR SCIENCE SITE. AT OTHER LOCATIONS, DESIGN FOR LOCAL CONDITIONS IN ACCORDANCE WITH "FHA POLE HOUSE CONSTRUCTION." FOR SITES WHERE LARGE ENOUGH HOLES CAN NOT BE DUG OR BLASTED SEE "ALTERNATES" IN SAME BOOKLET. 50¢ FROM AMER. WOOD PRESERVERS INSTITUTE, 1651 OLD MEADOW RD., McLEAN, VA. 22101

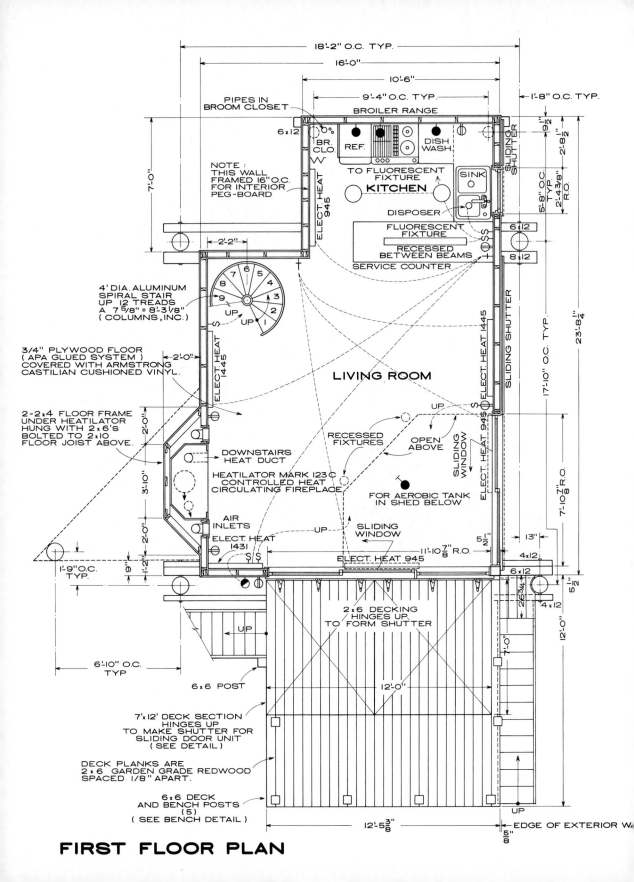

FIRST FLOOR PLAN

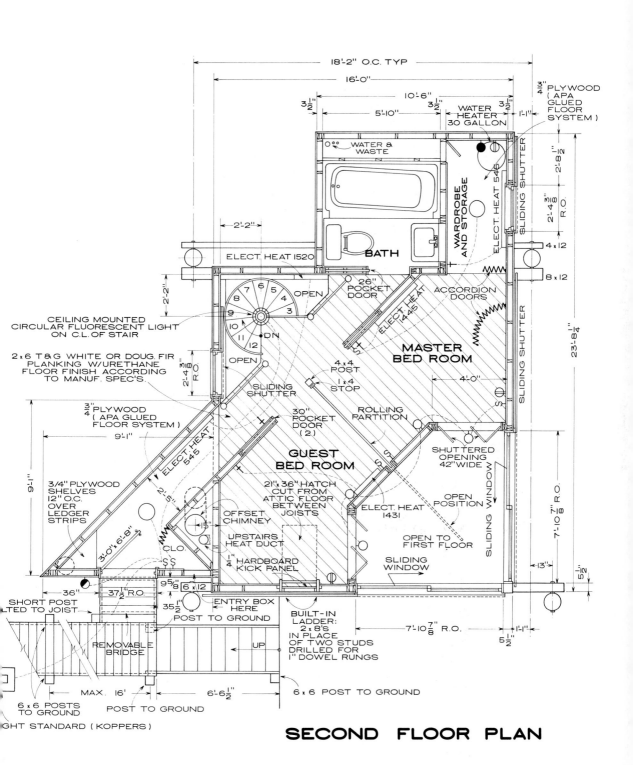

18'-2" O.C. TYP

16'-0"

10'-6"

3½

5'-10"

3½

WATER HEATER 30 GALLON

3½

1'-1"

¾" PLYWOOD (APA GLUED FLOOR SYSTEM)

WATER & WASTE

2'-8½"

2'-4¾" R.O.

SLIDING SHUTTER

4 x 12

8 x 12

WARDROBE AND STORAGE

ELECT. HEAT 545

BATH

2'-2"

ELECT. HEAT 1520

OPEN

26" POCKET DOOR

ELECT. HEAT 1445

ACCORDION DOORS

SLIDING SHUTTER

23'-8¼"

2'-2"

7 6
8 5
9 4
10 3
11
12 • DN

OPEN

CEILING MOUNTED CIRCULAR FLUORESCENT LIGHT ON C.L. OF STAIR

2'-4¾" R.O.

OPEN

SLIDING SHUTTER

4 x 4 POST

1 x 4 STOP

MASTER BED ROOM

4'-0"

2 x 6 T&G WHITE OR DOUG. FIR PLANKING W/URETHANE FLOOR FINISH ACCORDING TO MANUF. SPEC'S.

¾" PLYWOOD (APA GLUED FLOOR SYSTEM)

9'-1"

30" POCKET DOOR (2)

ROLLING PARTITION

SHUTTERED OPENING 42" WIDE

ELECT. HEAT 545

GUEST BED ROOM

OPEN POSITION

9'-1"

3/4" PLYWOOD SHELVES 12" O.C. OVER LEDGER STRIPS

2'-5"

21"x 36" HATCH CUT FROM ATTIC FLOOR BETWEEN JOISTS

ELECT. HEAT 1431

7'-10⅞" R.O.

SLIDING WINDOW

OPEN TO FIRST FLOOR

3'-0"x 6'-8"

OFFSET CHIMNEY

UPSTAIRS HEAT DUCT

CLO.

¼" HARDBOARD KICK PANEL

SLIDING WINDOW

13"

5½"

36"

37½" R.O.

9⅝"

6 x 12

35½"

ENTRY BOX HERE

POST TO GROUND

BUILT-IN LADDER: 2 x 8'S IN PLACE OF TWO STUDS DRILLED FOR 1" DOWEL RUNGS

7'-10⅞" R.O.

5½"
1'-1"
5½"

SHORT POST TED TO JOIST

REMOVABLE BRIDGE

UP

6 x 6 POST TO GROUND

MAX. 16'

POST TO GROUND

6'-6½"

6 x 6 POSTS TO GROUND

POST TO GROUND

GHT STANDARD (KOPPERS)

SECOND FLOOR PLAN

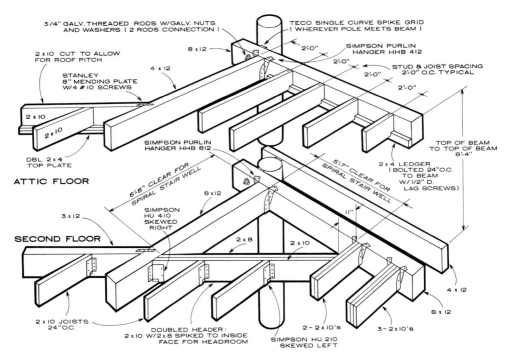

3/4" GALV. THREADED RODS W/GALV. NUTS
AND WASHERS (2 RODS CONNECTION)

TECO SINGLE CURVE SPIKE GRID
(WHEREVER POLE MEETS BEAM)

2 x 10 CUT TO ALLOW
FOR ROOF PITCH

8 x 12

2'-0"

SIMPSON PURLIN
HANGER HHB 412

STANLEY
8" MENDING PLATE
W/4 #10 SCREWS

4 x 12

2'-0"

STUD & JOIST SPACING
2'-0" O.C. TYPICAL

2'-0"

2'-0"

2 x 10

2 x 10

DBL 2 x 4
TOP PLATE

TOP OF BEAM
TO TOP OF BEAM
8'-4"

SIMPSON PURLIN
HANGER HHB 812

2 x 4 LEDGER
(BOLTED 24"O.C.
TO BEAM
W/1/2" D.
LAG SCREWS)

ATTIC FLOOR

6'-6" CLEAR FOR
SPIRAL STAIR WELL

5'-7" CLEAR FOR
SPIRAL STAIR WELL

8 x 12

SIMPSON
HU 410
SKEWED
RIGHT

11"

3 x 12

SECOND FLOOR

2 x 8

2 x 10

4 x 12

8 x 12

2 x 10 JOISTS
24"O.C.

DOUBLED HEADER :
2 x 10 W/2 x 8 SPIKED TO INSIDE
FACE FOR HEADROOM

SIMPSON HU 210
SKEWED LEFT

2 - 2 x 10's

3 - 2 x 10's

NOTE : FOR READOUT OF JOIST HANGERS AND OTHER SIMPSON AND TECO HARDWARE USED IN THE LOCKBOX ,
WRITE SEIDEL CO., 4110 DUMBARTON RD., HOUSTON, TEX. 77025 .

FRAMING AT NORTHWEST (STAIRWAY) CORNER

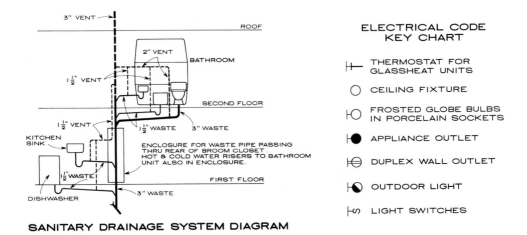

3" VENT

ROOF

2" VENT

BATHROOM

1 1/2" VENT

SECOND FLOOR

1 1/2" VENT

1 1/2" WASTE

3" WASTE

KITCHEN
SINK

ENCLOSURE FOR WASTE PIPE PASSING
THRU REAR OF BROOM CLOSET .
HOT & COLD WATER RISERS TO BATHROOM
UNIT ALSO IN ENCLOSURE.

FIRST FLOOR

1 1/2" WASTE

DISHWASHER

3" WASTE

SANITARY DRAINAGE SYSTEM DIAGRAM

ELECTRICAL CODE
KEY CHART

THERMOSTAT FOR
GLASSHEAT UNITS

CEILING FIXTURE

FROSTED GLOBE BULBS
IN PORCELAIN SOCKETS

APPLIANCE OUTLET

DUPLEX WALL OUTLET

OUTDOOR LIGHT

LIGHT SWITCHES

AN UPDATE ON SUPPLIERS

Inevitably, with any project on this scale, spanning several years from initial planning to final publication, the vicissitudes of marketing will outdate some of the materials and accessories involved. This was especially true of our Lockbox project, for two reasons: This house was to be a showcase of brand-new concepts and products (a few of which were so new and novel they never made it past test-marketing, and others of which weren't promoted properly and have since been withdrawn). And, secondly, since a major point of our project was to demonstrate that inexperienced, amateur carpenters could erect a truly original home on an unbuildable site by working weekends and holidays only, the project took longer to complete than a professionally built home; so products involved in the final installments of our long-running series had to sustain an extended market performance.

The following suppliers list, then, represents the sponsors of this project much as they were last credited in the magazine series (with addresses updated). All crucial sources have been checked as this book goes to press; all essential materials are currently available. A few of the products listed here (and shown in subsequent photographs) are no longer sold, but equivalents can be found in all but a few cases:

● On the end wall of our kitchen, we used a "wainscot"-pattern prefinished Peg-Board (the holes are attractively clustered and the lower third of the panel is unperforated)—a product that Masonite inexplicably dropped. Other prefinished "perf-boards" are still marketed, but if you have trouble locating one, substitute ordinary Peg-Board and paint it with a long-nap roller.

● From Armstrong, we chose a then-brand-new slate pattern for the vinyl floorcovering downstairs, only to have the company drop it from its line before we got into print (amusingly, the pattern has since reappeared in the Armstrong catalog in other sheet vinyl lines). We've completely revised our chapter on Armstrong's Integrid ceiling to reflect their revised installation system (though the original system is still serving us well at the Lockbox).

● Owens-Corning offered us their new molded-Fiberglas entry door to introduce nationally; I later learned (when *Popular Science* readers clamored to buy one) that only two had been manufactured: Ours, plus one for trial display at builders' shows. No wonder they could only supply us a pre-hung version hinged on the wrong side!

● Cromaglass no longer promotes our six-foot sphere for single-family sewage treatment (see Chapter 15), proposing instead a larger-model cylinder of the type we show as an alternate. But they'll still sell you our tank (they make them to ship to the Virgin Islands) and it continues to perform well at the Lockbox, six years after its hookup.

● But the worst blow of all was Crane's surprising decision to discontinue their unitized bathroom—a cleverly designed fiberglass unit with molded-in tub and vanity which we'd purchased early to design our upstairs around—precisely because we felt the Unette was ideal for a small leisure home and was the wave of the future. But Crane plumbing dealers had no idea how to merchandise the concept, so the Unette didn't catch on. When Crane's marketing executive broke the news of its discontinuance to me, he commented:

"Look at it this way, Al: You're the owner of a true American artifact." To some degree, that can be said of the Lockbox as a whole: It's a showcase that can never be duplicated—at least not in precise detail. We have sadly banished the Unette from our pages, redrawing all the floorplans to show an assembly of conventional bathroom fixtures. I'd recommend that you go the route of a molded-fiberglass tub/shower, however, since there is no equivalent of the Unette made today. Which only goes to prove that the customer is *not* always right—at least, not until he's educated as to his options.

The few other discontinued items are less critical: We originally furnished our whole kitchen (excluding range) from the Sears catalog, but in the last year or so Sears has revamped its merchandising policies, dropping many Lockbox items from its listings. Sears no longer catalogues the cabinets or the compact refrig-

erator we chose (a great little Italian import). You can secure a unit of similar size from various sources; Hotpoint offers a 10.6-cubic-foot compact that almost fits here (it's 3″ wider). If you want a larger refrigerator, you'll have to sacrifice the adjacent broom closet.

Your other option? Make the kitchen wing wider. But it's not as simple as it may sound. This is a very tightly designed house, and if you adjust one dimension, you'll find it necessary to adjust many more.

I once tried to modify the plans for a reader who wanted larger bedrooms. Fine; you just go to a basic 18′- or 20′-square floorplan instead of our 16′ cube. But, then—just how does the entry hall splice on—and how do you recalculate the roof pitch? At any rate, all our span calculations are for the 16′ plan. If you extend any of these, you'd better check with a structural engineer.

All the chapters that follow—each treating a specific aspect of the Lockbox project—have been updated where necessary.

MATERIALS SUPPLIERS

American Plywood Assn. P.O. Box 11700 Tacoma, Wash. 98441	*¾″ t&g flooring and MDO for shutters*	Columns, Inc. P.O. Box 895 Pearland, Tex. 77581	*aluminum spiral stair*
Armstrong Cork Co. Lancaster, Pa. 17604	*vinyl flooring, acoustical ceiling*	Continental Radiant Glass Heating Corp. 215-B Central Ave. E. Farmingdale, N.Y. 11735	*electric heat panels and thermostats*
Automated Building Components Inc. 7525 N.W. 37th Ave. Miami, Fla. 33159	*Decramastic roof-tile system*	Cromaglass Corp. Box 3215 Williamsport, Pa. 17701	*aerobic waste system*
California Redwood Assn. 1 Lombard St. San Francisco, Cal. 94111	*exterior stairs, fold-up deck*	Gaco Western, Inc. P.O. Box 88698 Seattle, Wash. 98188	*Gacotred roof system (entry triangle)*

Heatilator Fireplace Div. *Mark 123c heat-*
Vega Industries, Inc. *circulating fireplace*
P.O. Box 409
Mt. Pleasant, Iowa 52641

Hough Manufacturing *accordion doors*
Janesville, Wisc. 53545

Iron-A-Way Inc. *built-in ironing center*
220 W. Jackson
Morton, Ill. 61550

Jenn-Air Corp. *self-venting range*
3035 Shadeland
Indianapolis, Ind. 46226

Johns-Manville Corp. *fiberglass insulation*
Greenwood Plaza
Denver, Colo. 80217

Koppers Co. Inc. *construction poles,*
Forest Products Div. *light standard,*
Pittsburgh, Pa. 15219 *Non-Com treatment*
for siding, shutters

Masonite Corp. *paneling, Peg-Board*
29 No. Wacker Dr.
Chicago, Ill. 60606

Murphy Door Bed Co. *pull-down coil-spring*
40 E. 34th St. *bed frame*
New York, N.Y. 10017

National Woodwork *sliding glass doors,*
Mfgs. Assn. *casement windows,*
355 Lexington Ave. *attic vents, louvered*
New York, N.Y. 10017 *bedroom shutters*

Sears Roebuck & Co. *kitchen appliances*
Sears Tower *and cabinets, in-wall*
Chicago, Ill. 60684 *vacuum, water heater,*
shutter hardware, deck
winches, tools

Stanley Works *hand and power tools,*
New Britain, Conn. 06050 *interior hardware*

Ventarama Skylight Corp. *double-dome skylight*
75 Channel Dr.
Port Washington,
N.Y. 11050

Western Wood *t&g floor planks*
Products Assn.
1500 Yeon Bldg.
Portland, Ore. 97204

Additional Materials

For freeze-proof waterline: Accessible Products Co., 1350 E. 8th St., Tempe, Ariz. 85281 *(Thermazip insulation jacket);* Chromalox Div., Emerson Electric, 8100 Florissant, St. Louis, Mo. 63136 *(heat cable);* Clow Corp. Plastics, Box 626, Pell City, Ala. 35125 *(polybutylene pipe).* Also: Amos Molded Plastics, 600 So. Kyle St., Edinburg, Ind. 46124 *(readymade drawers);* Dow Chemical U.S.A., 2020 Dow Ctr., Midland, Mich. 48640 *(Styrofoam insulation);* Du Pont Co., Wilmington, Del. 19898 *(Corian);* Franklin Glue Co., 2020 Bruck St., Columbus, Ohio 43207 *(construction adhesive);* General Electric Co., Silicone Products Dept., Waterford, N.Y. 12188 *(construction sealant)* and Lighting Systems Dept., Hendersonville, N.C. 28739 *(post-lamp luminaire);* Gossen Corp., 2004 W. Bender Rd., Milwaukee, Wisc. 53209 *(pre-mitered casing);* Griffolyn Co., Box 33248, Houston, Tex. 77033 *(reinforced film for weather closure);* Kwikset Div., Emhart Corp., Anaheim, Calif. 92803 *(entry locks);* National Gypsum Co., 325 Delaware Ave., Buffalo, N.Y. 14202 *(Gold Bond asbestos-cement board);* Pyrotronics, 8 Ridgedale Ave., Cedar Knolls, N.J. 07927 *(Pyro-Guardian fire detector);* Rohm & Haas, Independence Mall W., Philadelphia, Pa. 19105 *(Plexiglas diffuser);* Sherwin-Williams Co., Cleveland, Ohio 44101 *(polyurethane varnish);* Simpson Co., 1470 Doolittle Drive, San Leandro, Calif. 94577 *(joist hangers, post bases);* 3M Co., 3M Center, St. Paul, Minn. 55101 *(mastic adhesives);* Tiger Teeth Inc., Box 8314, Charlotte, N.C. 28209 *(insulation supports);* Teco, 5530 Wisconsin Ave., Washington, D.C. 20016 *(framing anchors, spike grids)* and Eastman Kodak Co. *(security camera)*

2. The Lockbox Spreads Its Wings

Unlike basic cube, the wings projecting beyond four support poles are of more conventional platform framing. Entry triangle perches stork-like on one leg.

Two-story kitchen/bath wing stands on two short poles set into concrete footings.

The two wings jutting from the 16' cube are also pole-supported, but their construction is of more conventional platform type: The kitchen walls, for example, bear the weight of the bathroom and an extension of the main roof. The other wing—a single-story projection from second-floor level—is a triangular entry that merely supports its own roof.

Our architect, Lester Walker, included that unique entry at our insistence. It gives character to the house, and pro-vides a skylighted hall that's an ideal approach to our circular stair. And that 45-degree projection serves a practical purpose as well, knifing into and dividing downhill winds that would otherwise "flat out" against this blind wall of the house.

The 45-degree corner didn't prove difficult to frame, as Walker feared (photos right), and the lower top plate of both walls is securely spiked up into the bottom of the 4x12 attic-floor beam of the basic cage.

Entry pole is shoulder notched at 45° to take band joists (one notch complete, above). Concrete footing has embedded galvanized holddowns through which pole will be bolted. Pole location was found by projecting line from stairwell header (photo right). Skewed hanger for entry's band joist is mounted just outside line.

Author perches on completed floor, using it for stud layout. Wall units that flank entry door are framed in two sections.

Siding is fitted before erection; note angle on outer stud and ply panel.

Rear wall, assembled flat, is tipped into place, notched down to its top plate to clear beam above.

It was no great trick to lay out the three additional pole holes required. On our mountain site, both wings projected toward steep slopes, so we could run out lines at proper angles to the main-cage beams, staking the far ends to the hillside at heights dictated by line-levels, hooked on once the cords were taut.

For the wall set at 45 degrees, we simply extended the line already established by our second-floor framing of the stairwell header. Where this line intersected the line run out perpendicular to the beam, we dropped a plumb bob and dug a hole about 18″ in diameter.

Since the placement of this pole is critical (it is shoulder-notched at 45 degrees to take the 3x12 band joists), we left ourselves some flexibility by *not* embedding it in concrete. Instead, we poured a below-frost footing column and at the top embedded a pair of L-shaped steel hold-downs with holes at the top through which—after the pole was set between them and drilled to match—we ran ¾″ threaded rod (left over from pole-and-beam assembly). No wind will lift *that* pole!

Both the hold-downs and the pocket-type joist hangers shown in photos—including those skewed 45 degrees for the entry joists—are available from the Simpson Co. (See address in Chapter 1, and write them for a complete readout of Simpson and Teco hardware for the Lockbox.)

We gave the shorter poles, set at the outer corners of the kitchen/bath wing, a different treatment, as the photos show.

One of the hazards of building in a forest is root damage. One of our footings had to be sunk right beside a good-size tree. Just over a foot beneath the surface, we found a network of major roots crossing the hole we had to dig for a below-frost footing. We continued digging and poured our 8″-thick footing at the bottom. When it had set, we placed several assemblies of foot-long steel pipe nipples and floor flanges (page 225) on the footing, projecting up past the root bridge.

We wrapped the roots in damp burlap and filled the hole with a rich concrete mix, filling the pipes, too, as if they were lally columns. Before the mix stiffened, we embedded another nipple-and-flange unit with the flange up, centered under the pole base. A length of commercial concrete form (18″-dia. Sonotube) was set over the hole and the pour continued. The pole was positioned in the form by means of nailed-on cleats bridging the tube's rim. When the pour was complete, the braced pole was left in place until the concrete was fully set and the form could be stripped.

At our site, these footings anchor the rear of the house to the steep slope, letting us get by with less than the 6′ embedment recommended for the four major poles.

Simpler footings for platform poles usu-ally will suffice. (Prototype houses are always overbuilt. You could surely do with less than that 6x12 beam our plans show across the kitchen poles. But its mass weights the back of the house and ties the wing in, visually, to the basic cage.)

We recessed screw-plates (Stanley's 8″ mending plates with four #10 screws each) at each band-joist-to-basic-cage connection to humor our structural engineer, but our plywood glued-floor system (see previous chapter) ties wings to cage even better. Note that the plywood floor

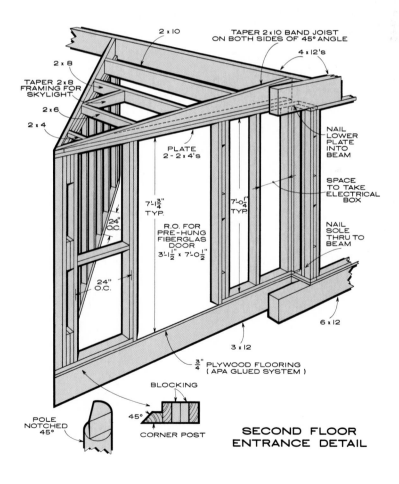

SECOND FLOOR ENTRANCE DETAIL

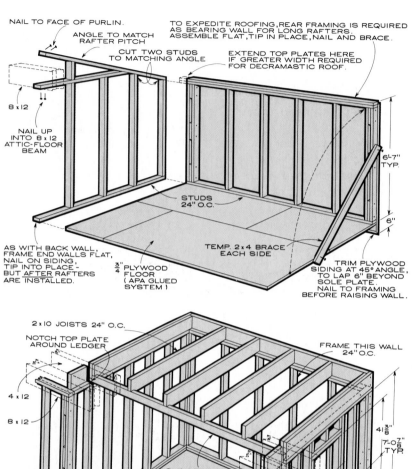

NAIL TO FACE OF PURLIN.

ANGLE TO MATCH
RAFTER PITCH

CUT TWO STUDS
TO MATCHING ANGLE

TO EXPEDITE ROOFING, REAR FRAMING IS REQUIRED
AS BEARING WALL FOR LONG RAFTERS.
ASSEMBLE FLAT, TIP IN PLACE, NAIL AND BRACE.

EXTEND TOP PLATES HERE
IF GREATER WIDTH REQUIRED
FOR DECRAMASTIC ROOF.

8 x 12

NAIL UP
INTO 8 x 12
ATTIC-FLOOR
BEAM

6'-7"
TYP.

STUDS
24" O.C.

6"

AS WITH BACK WALL,
FRAME END WALLS FLAT,
NAIL ON SIDING,
TIP INTO PLACE-
BUT AFTER RAFTERS
ARE INSTALLED.

3/4" PLYWOOD
FLOOR
(APA GLUED
SYSTEM)

TEMP. 2 x 4 BRACE
EACH SIDE

TRIM PLYWOOD
SIDING AT 45° ANGLE,
TO LAP 6" BEYOND
SOLE PLATE.
NAIL TO FRAMING
BEFORE RAISING WALL.

2 x 10 JOISTS 24" O.C.

NOTCH TOP PLATE
AROUND LEDGER

FRAME THIS WALL
24" O.C.

4 x 12

8 x 12

4'-1 3/8"

7'-0 7/8"
TYP.

2 x 4 LEDGER
FASTEN WITH
5" LAG SCREWS
INTO
4 x 12 BEAM

41"

FRAME
THIS WALL ONLY
16" O.C.
FOR PEG-BOARD
PANELS (2)

BLOCKING

CORNER POST
3 - 2 x 4's

3/4" PLYWOOD FLOOR
(APA GLUED SYSTEM)

KITCHEN AND BATH WING DETAIL

system is used *only* in the second-floor wing sections. The floor of the main cage, added later, is 2x6 t&g planks, laid diagonally (see Chapter 6).

Actually, you need only erect the *rear* wall of the kitchen/bath wing to provide support for the long (nearly 26') rafters. We enclosed the entire wing to make a two-story shed to store materials and appliances as they were delivered to the site.

We applied the second-floor Texture 1–11 siding first, letting it project 6″ below the framing sole and beveling it 45 degrees toward the rear face.

The *top* edge of the panel below, then, is beveled toward the front face and a generous bead of construction sealant (such as GE's #1300) is run along this

Experimental footing to save critical roots calls for 1½″ nipple-and-flange units set in concrete for base of pole to bear on.

Tubular cardboard form strips away, once concrete sets, to leave below-frost footing with pole partly embedded. Backfill firmly.

Outer doubled joist of kitchen/bath wing ties into rear beams of cage via recessed metal plate and 2x10 between 4x12 and 8x12.

For plywood floor, construction adhesive is run along top of each joist. Joists rest on top plate at back wall, this end unnotched.

End walls are framed flat and plywood siding nailed on. Here, hole is cut to match rough opening framed for top casement.

And up it goes. Siding extends 6″ beyond sole plate to lap joist. Bevel bottom edge 45° for no-flashing joint with lower panel.

bevel before the panel is butted up under the top panel and anchored with nails angled through both bevels. Such a joint—not difficult with a portable circular saw—lets you omit obtrusive Z flashing or battens at horizontal joints.

The front wall of the triangle gave us the ideal spot to locate our entry box when we brought electricity to the structure to operate our power tools. Enclosure, here, let us apply a roof that doubles as platform access to the attic during construction, since it's decked with ¾″ t&g plywood.

3. Two Unique Roofing Systems

NEOPRENE COATS

METAL TILE

No ordinary roof would do for the Lock-box—the design and technique had to be as innovative (and as practical for do-it-yourself application) as the pole-and-beam structure itself. And the roofing had to fit our total-security concept—which meant, for leisure homes in remote areas, nonflammable, maintenance-free materials.

Since one of the major advantages of pole-and-beam design is that it gets you under shelter fast (you can erect your roof before your walls) we needed *quick* systems that eliminated the usual fussy details.

We also decided that a do-it-yourself roof for the main house had to be applied without scaffolding, and preferably without our having to scramble up and down the pitch.

So we discarded our architect's specs and went in search. For the main roof, we chose a metal tile system—handsome as it is novel—that gives the heavy butt line of Spanish tile without the weight (only 180 lbs. per square). The units are formed from 28-gauge galvanized steel, coated with bituminous compound, covered with ceramic chips in your choice of nine colors (we chose the rich Sable Brown) and

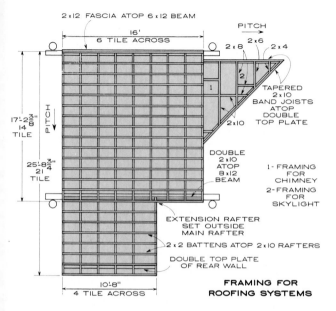

2×12 FASCIA ATOP 6×12 BEAM

PITCH →

16'
6 TILE ACROSS

2×8   2×6   2×4

2

1

TAPERED
2×10
BAND JOISTS
ATOP
DOUBLE
TOP PLATE

2×10

PITCH ↑

PITCH ↓

17'-2⅜"
14
TILE

25'-8¾"
21
TILE

DOUBLE
2×10
ATOP
8×12
BEAM

1- FRAMING
FOR
CHIMNEY

2-FRAMING
FOR
SKYLIGHT

EXTENSION RAFTER
SET OUTSIDE
MAIN RAFTER

2×2 BATTENS ATOP 2×10 RAFTERS

DOUBLE TOP PLATE
OF REAR WALL

10'-8"
4 TILE ACROSS

**FRAMING FOR
ROOFING SYSTEMS**

Entry triangle and main roof present different problems. Latter has substantial pitch but is relatively inaccessible. Entry is minimal-pitch deck, pierced by skylight and fireplace chimney.

treated with weather- and fungus-resistant sealer. The system is called Decramastic, and it's available from Automated Building Components Inc., 7525 N.W. 37th Ave., Miami, Fla. 33159. Everything you need for the Lockbox main roof should run you under $350.

Here's what you get when you order your Decramastic materials for the Lockbox: 120 tile (3.9 sqs.); 20 lin. ft. of ridge cap, specially pre-bent for this application; 20 lin. ft. of 2″x3″ eave drip and 42 gable end caps (21 each, right and left). All these units are the coated sheet metal described above. You'll also receive an installation kit containing hex-head screws and ring-shank nails, 2 qts. emulsion, 10 lbs. granules, plus a spray can of

PVA sealer. The last three items are for patching any tile damaged in transit or installation—though you'll note that more tiles are provided than the sketch at left calls for. This gives you the option of adjusting courses, as we'll discuss later.

Each tile is 2'10¼″ wide and has four valleys; with side laps, it takes six tiles to cross our 16' cube. Since four tiles make up a 10'8″ width, we adjusted the roof framing over the rear extension so as to avoid any cutting. Though the system is engineered around whole tiles, you can trim Decramastic units with tin snips. (For clarity in our sketch at left, the extension rafter at the right side of the kitchen/bath wing is shown detached from the rafter above it. For strength, it's best to cheat the latter over enough to spike these lapped ends together. You may, if you wish, equalize spacing between the balance of the rafters, instead of maintaining a rigid 2'-on-center positioning.)

Spacing of the 2x2 battens is critical, since the tile flanges are formed to bridge 14⅝″. You anchor each butt flange with a screw or nail driven just off-center of each valley. Each fastener (we used two screws and two nails per butt) pierces the butt flange *and* the top flange of the tile in the course below, securing tiles into one big leakproof metal membrane. For driving the screws, you'll need a standard screwdriver accessory for your electric drill—one capable of about 1,700 rpm—plus a hex-head socket driver. No predrilling is required for either screws or nails, though you may prefer to drill through the four layers where the flanges of two tiles and two end caps must overlap.

The ridge cap and eave drip come as a pair of 10' strips, each with provision for the lap joint that's necessary at both the

Predrill 2x2 battens for single 16d hot-dripped-galvanized common nail at each rafter crossing. Co-builder Ron Nelson has marked one batten in place on rafters, now uses it as template for drilling others.

Spacing is critical as battens must be an accurate 14⅝" o.c. for metal tile to fit. Here, author uses two 2x2 blocks (one shows at nailing position, other is off right) cut to length that provides that spacing.

Work from eaves up on lower part of roof. Student helpers, above, are starting new course: Bill is driving self-tapping screw through gable end cap (similar to unit Larry holds) that fits over end of tile.

Work from ridge down on upper part of roof. Fastest anchoring is by means of 1" hex-head self-tapping screws and driver accessory in portable drill. Alternate fastener is black galvanized ring-shank nail.

The finished roof of mineral-coated galvanized steel tiles is handsome and durable.

top and the bottom of the roof. The end of one strip in each pair is taped for easy stripping of the emulsion/granule coat to bare metal. Apply roofing cement to this lap before seating the extension strip atop it.

As with other roofing applications, don't tackle the job at high noon on a bright day; roofing's a hot job, and heat tends to soften this emulsion so the toes and heels of your shoes can gouge the granule coating. It's possible to walk on a Decramastic roof (and our slightly under 4:12 pitch is a comfortable one). You place your feet in the valleys just above the butt line; never step on the crowns or on unsupported between-batten areas.

To patch, spread emulsion on bare spots, press granules into surface, spray with sealer.

Since precisely dimensioned plans for a pole-and-beam structure just aren't practical, eave overhang treatments can vary. Assuming that poles are set at varying levels on a steep site, each pole will taper a different amount between equiva-

lent vertical points. The taper also makes it difficult to set posts exactly plumb (clapping a level against a tapered pole doesn't tell you much). It's best if the poles lean slightly inward—that is, toward the cube they're supporting. This could mean that the horizontal front-to-back dimension at the attic-floor level may be less than at the first-floor level. In our prototype, the first-floor measure is 16'10"; but the attic floor, front-to-back, is just under 16'4".

To superimpose the precise Decramastic grid on so flexible a cube, you may have to adjust your eaves projection or alter the course count (only six deep over kitchen/bath wing, instead of our seven). Photos and sketch (right) show how we utilized overhang of short rafters as an above-insulation vent. Lower eave has a longer overhang, and is boxed.

But how did we get square corners with a rear wall slanted inward? We erected our short rear wall plumb. This created a sub-eave at second-floor ceiling level with the wall extending under the purlin

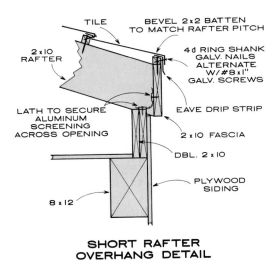

TILE

BEVEL 2×2 BATTEN
TO MATCH RAFTER PITCH

2×10
RAFTER

4 d RING SHANK
GALV. NAILS
ALTERNATE
W/#8×1"
GALV. SCREWS

LATH TO SECURE
ALUMINUM
SCREENING
ACROSS OPENING

EAVE DRIP STRIP

2×10 FASCIA

DBL. 2×10

8×12

PLYWOOD
SIDING

**SHORT RAFTER
OVERHANG DETAIL**

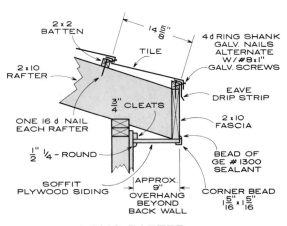

2×2
BATTEN

$14\frac{5}{8}$"

TILE

4 d RING SHANK
GALV. NAILS
ALTERNATE
W/#8×1"
GALV. SCREWS

2×10
RAFTER

$\frac{3}{4}$" CLEATS

EAVE
DRIP STRIP

ONE 16 d NAIL
EACH RAFTER

2×10
FASCIA

$\frac{1}{2}$" $\frac{1}{4}$- ROUND

BEAD OF
GE #1300
SEALANT

SOFFIT
PLYWOOD SIDING

APPROX.
9"
OVERHANG
BEYOND
BACK WALL

CORNER BEAD
$1\frac{5}{16}$" × $1\frac{5}{16}$"

**LONG RAFTER
OVERHANG DETAIL**

beam, beyond the roof's drip line. Though an application of Gacotred's Contourflash (see below) took care of weather leaks, we wished to avoid drain-splash on this ledge. So, we installed a vinyl gutter and downspout here.

The pair of elbows that form the familiar S below a collector outlet are designed to move a downspout back from an eave projection for wall mounting. In our case, we reversed the assembly to float the downspout *forward*, to drop be-

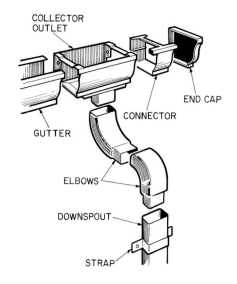

COLLECTOR OUTLET

END CAP

CONNECTOR

GUTTER

ELBOWS

DOWNSPOUT

STRAP

tween the beams that flank our rear poles. The strength and lightness of vinyl—plus sturdy assembly methods using PVC cement and Pop-rivets—make this possible. For a manual covering conventional installation of the components, write Bird & Son, East Walpole, Mass. 02032. The system shown in the final photo of the roll-roofing series—and laid out in the photo above—is from Plastmo Inc., 920 Shelley St., Springfield, Ore. 97477. It's available in dark gray.

THE ENTRY TRIANGLE

The separate roof over our triangular entry called for a different treatment. This is virtually a deck, with about a 1:12 pitch to prevent puddling. Plywood sheathing was fine, here—but what surfacing would be practical for a small, flat roof that supports both a skylight and the flashing cone for our fireplace chimney? A neoprene system—Gacotred—comes from Gaco Western Inc., P.O. Box 88698, Seattle, Wash. 98188. Enough materials to complete our triangle add up to around $70.

When you order Gacotred materials for this job, you'll get: 2 gallons each of Gacoflex N–114 brown neoprene and granules; 1 gal. N–450–1 thinner; 1 qt. each of N–7 neoprene adhesive and N–74 flashing compound, plus a roll each of Contourflash elastomeric sheet (12″ wide) and R–68 joint fabric, a polyester tape 4″ wide.

A well-supported deck is important; framing details for the joists shown in dotted lines at right were given in the previous chapter. Use only hot-dip galvanized nails (6d or 8d common) to anchor the ¾″ plywood, spacing them every 6″ at panel edges, 12″ elsewhere. For extra rigidity, we treated this deck like our APA glued floors (see first chapter), running beads of construction sealant along the beveled or tapered edges of all support members before laying the plywood in place.

For the prime coat, mix 2 parts of the N–114 neoprene with 1 part thinner and apply with a ¾″-nap roller. Once the prime coat cures (overnight is best), you can expose the panels to rain without risking a long dry-off delay (none of the Gacotred steps should be undertaken in

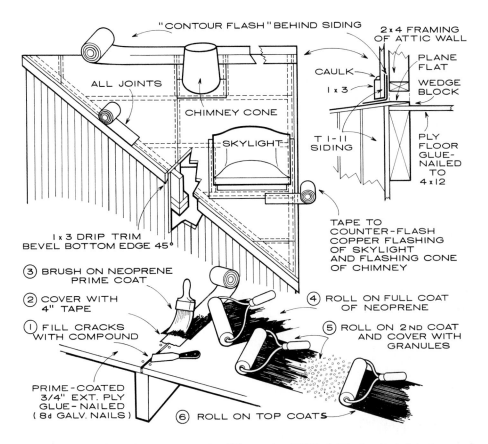

"CONTOUR FLASH" BEHIND SIDING

2 x 4 FRAMING OF ATTIC WALL

PLANE FLAT

CAULK

1 x 3

WEDGE BLOCK

ALL JOINTS

CHIMNEY CONE

SKYLIGHT

T 1-11 SIDING

PLY FLOOR GLUE- NAILED TO 4 x 12

1 x 3 DRIP TRIM BEVEL BOTTOM EDGE 45°

TAPE TO COUNTER-FLASH COPPER FLASHING OF SKYLIGHT AND FLASHING CONE OF CHIMNEY

③ BRUSH ON NEOPRENE PRIME COAT

② COVER WITH 4" TAPE

① FILL CRACKS WITH COMPOUND

④ ROLL ON FULL COAT OF NEOPRENE

⑤ ROLL ON 2ND COAT AND COVER WITH GRANULES

PRIME-COATED 3/4" EXT. PLY GLUE-NAILED (8d GALV. NAILS)

⑥ ROLL ON TOP COATS

Deck for Gacotred application must be ¾" exterior DFPA A/C plywood. Interior grades with exterior glue aren't suitable. All plywood edges must be supported on primary framing or blocking (dotted lines) with sheets in moderate contact. Since damp plywood impedes adhesion of rubber coating, it's best to prime top surface and edges before nailing fitted panels in place as shown.

wet weather; a shaded clear day is best). Before thinning, the N–114 neoprene is the color and consistency of Hershey syrup. The N–74 compound, on the other hand, is a troweling paste, resembling standard roofing cement in everything but smell. After filling all joint cracks, let the compound set thoroughly before applying the tape.

Press the tape firmly to attain full contact (we rolled the edges with a wooden wallpaper seam roller). When taping is complete, brush-coat all strips.

Since you'll be working from the attic floor, as shown in photos, page 234, you'll be able to install only the sole plate of this side wall, as shown in our section. Once this was in place, we cut an 18"-dia. hole and bracketed a trial section of fireplace chimney through it so we could install the flashing halves and cone that come with the Heatilator fireplace (see Chapter 9).

Prime-coat plywood panels and beveled drip trim (strips at left) before assembly. You can get entry's floor and roof both from three 4-by-8 sheets, but triangular piece is needed at both 45-degree corners. View here is from attic floor, under rafters.

Fill all cracks at joints between panels and nailed-on drip trim with compound that comes in kit; apply with putty knife and strike off flush with surface. Let dry before covering with tape.

Sprinkle granules generously over last base coat while still wet. Granules are light beige to help you get thorough coverage of dark base coat. Shaker is can with holes punched in bottom (as seen in center of photo, below). Excess is swept off when coat dries.

After applying Contourflash with contact cement along joint between deck and sole for attic wall, base coat is rolled over it and granules are seeded on. At right is the chimney cone. Nelson works from within unclosed attic.

Space between cone base and sole plate was tight, so we bent up the top edge of the upper flashing half to set against the sole (this option is omitted from our section). Next we ran masking tape across the roof 6″ from the sole and parallel to it. Then we brushed on two coats of N–7 adhesive (a contact cement for neoprene), coating the 6″ strip of roof and the sole edge. After wiping the back of the Contourflash strip with thinner, we applied a coat of N–7 to it and, when all coats were tack-free, made the bond, using a slip sheet (as when applying plastic laminate to a countertop).

You're now ready to coat, sprinkle, and top-coat the roof (diagram, page 233) rounding out your weekend's work. The two top coats (Step 6 in our diagram) will be H–10 Hypalon (your choice of a wide range of colors). Next week you'll erect your sidewall studs and (using the Gacotred roof as a work-deck) apply your siding, sandwiching your flashing between framing and siding. Then you'll set a trim strip in a bed of N–74 compound and tack it to the siding. A caulking bead of construction sealant (we used GE's 1300, black) completes the job. You'll now have walled yourself off from the attic, so (hopefully) you'll have removed the double-layer dome from the skylight (second photo, left) to provide an escape route.

Since our application in early '72 shown here, certain improvements in the system have been made, and we've incorporated these in the above description. Gaco originally supplied a cotton joint tape (now replaced with the polyester for better durability) and the old three-coat system has now been upgraded to four coats—two of neoprene

and two of Hypalon—for improved resistance to ultraviolet and ozone degradation.

These changes should prevent the joint cracks and minor blistering which developed five years after the application shown here. Since we were getting some leakage in our walls one autumn, we made an emergency repair by troweling on a plastic roofing cement, which sealed the voids through a severe winter. The following spring, we contacted Gaco for recommendations about recoating. Here are quotes from their reply:

"Your roof cement would have to be completely removed before any recoating because our coatings are not compatible with asphalt-based products. We suggest the following recoating procedure: 1) Apply prime coat of 50% N–110 black neoprene and 50% N–450–13 to entire surface of roof. 2) Scrape all blisters to remove material that is not fully adhered. Apply second prime coat to these blistered areas. 3) Apply two coats of liquid neoprene to these areas, letting the first coat dry to a tack-free surface before applying the second. 4) Broadcast granules into second coat while still wet; when dry, sweep off excess granules. 5) Apply two coats of Hypalon to entire surface, allowing first coat to dry tack-free before application of second."

We'd have been happy to try this fix had it not been impractical to remove our asphalt roofing cement patches. (Instead, we've resurfaced this entry triangle with roll roofing, as described in the text and photo series that follow.) But we still recommend the Gacotred system, especially with the new improvements; it will provide many years of waterproof protection.

Materials needed for applying roll roofing are (l-r): the asphalt roll itself, 36" wide; plastic roof cement and tools to spread it (trowel, putty knife); tools to cut it (linoleum and utility knives); hammer, and galvanized roofing nails with ⅜" heads.

For tricky fits, cut a full-size pattern from taped-together newspaper, the same width as roofing. Here, strip must notch around chimney cone, top left, and skylight in foreground.

ROOFING THAT COMES IN A ROLL

Roll roofing is similar in thickness and pliability to asphalt strip shingles, but it comes in an uncut roll, 36" wide, and long enough to provide the traditional "square" of coverage (100 sq. ft. of roof area). One roll was plenty for the Lockbox entry. I chose Owens-Corning's Autumn Brown as the best match for the Decramastic tile on the main roof.

The application shown in the photos is a combination of a simple exposed-nail and the more complex concealed-nail techniques. Nails should be 12-gauge, ¾" long, with heads at least ⅜" in diameter.

Cut strips from the roll enough in advance to let them "settle flat" before application. If you must work at temperatures below 50°, be sure to stack the cut sheets indoors, bringing them out one at a time to install.

Cut each strip enough overlength so it will project ¼" to ⅜" beyond both edges of the roof deck. Spread a wide band (3" minimum) of roofing cement along these edges and roll out the first (lowest) strip of roofing over the cement, nailing every 4" along the roof edges.

Next, nail every 4" along the strip's uncemented top edge, at least ¾" from the edge. (There's a margin of bare asphalt, a couple inches wide, along this edge—as shown in the first photo. The coating of mineral granules is omitted here because this edge will always be overlapped by the next-higher strip of roofing.)

Transfer pattern to back of roofing with chalk, then cut with shears or linoleum knife with metal straightedge. Note hardboard scrap at left. Positioned under knife-cut, it protects surface below.

To prepare roof/wall joint for cove treatment, triangular strips were cut from scrap wood and tacked along top and at base of wall cleat (seated in roofing cement).

Now, extend the edge bands of applied cement upward and place the second strip, lapping it over the top edge of the first a minimum of 3″. Nail as before, but before anchoring the lower half of the edges, lift the strip back and spread a full-width band of cement along the overlap—that is, along that nailed upper edge of the lower strip. Drop the upper strip and weight it overnight while the cement sets. (Ideally, you'll just see a tiny bead of cement ooze out to seal the edge.)

This procedure lets you avoid ugly exposed nailing except at the edges of the roof. Repeat these steps on up the roof. Note in the photos that I coved the roofing against the wall joint and the skylight flashing. This discourages standing water—especially snow-melt. Just be sure to seal the turned-up edge of roofing with a bead of quality caulk. Also caulk around the cut-out for the chimney cone, even though you've bedded the roofing, here, in a band of cement.

Finished job (right) isn't quite as neat as liquid surfacing, since butt-lines of strips show, as do nailheads along edges. But this reroofing should last ten years. Note vinyl gutter (with run-off flange above it, lapped by roofing) and downspout; these were added to prevent wetting of this wall, which receives no direct sun.

After coating all cleats with roofing cement, cove the pre-cut roofing by nailing along top edge and shaping it down in an S-curve (above). Then, before edge nailing, lift bottom lip and spread cement underneath. For best seal, roofing is coved up side of skylight (after coating base of side with cement). Then top edge is sealed with a bead of caulk (below). Slit corners should be filled and sealed with caulk.

4. Closing the Lockbox

The Lockbox is a showcase—and test case—in many ways. We framed all exterior walls 24″ o.c., believing that conventional 16″-o.c. studs are wastefully obsolete. So we shouldn't—technically—have used Texture 1–11 plywood for our single-layer siding (no sheathing). T 1–11 is a ⅝″ panel grooved ¼″ deep every 4″ (you can get wider groove spacings, but 4″ is the best module for the Lockbox); these grooves reduce effective strength to that of a ⅜″-thick panel, so recommended stud spacing is 16″ maximum. Both American Plywood Assn. and NAHB (the homebuilders group) have undertaken test programs aimed at changing this restriction, but neither is ready to approve T 1–11 for 24″ spans. We are—at least for the Lockbox, where the siding is less for structure than for weather closure. We've experienced no bowing of panels, even after prolonged storm exposure (the Lockbox has ridden above a couple of floods). And we applied it without any mid-height ("fire-stop") blocking or let-in corner bracing. Feel free.

Long edges of T 1–11 panels come rabbeted for invisible shiplap joints, but the 4′ ends have conventional square edges. To provide a continuous *height* of wall, without horizontal battens or Z-flashing cutting across the vertical groove pattern, we asked APA to recommend a bevel system (see section sketch labeled Siding Joint Detail, next page). With patience and practice, it's not hard to cut these bevels freehand, using a portable circular saw.

As APA suggests, we applied a water repellent to all cut edges. If I were doing it over, I'd seal them with a good exterior primer, instead, since they're concealed. After a drenching rain, it takes hours—even days—for our siding to dry evenly along some of the joints.

We chose a rough-sawn redwood for our T 1–11, to avoid any finish coating. Then we had the panels pressure-treated with Non-Com Exterior—a newly developed Koppers process where fire-retarding chemicals, impregnated into the wood cells, are unaffected by weather exposure. Our friends at the California Redwood Assn. termed this an overkill since redwood is naturally a flame-resistant wood. But a house in the midst of a forest can use all the safeguards it can get. We

toss scraps of the stuff into the roaring flames of our fireplace and note approvingly that it takes forever to burn, first coating itself with a protective char, and extinguishing itself if removed from the flames.

This Non-Com process darkens any wood—and its effect on redwood is especially spotty. Most of our panels reached us with surface stains that looked like minor scorching. Some were worse than others, so by judicious selection we were able to distribute the stains, disposing of the bad ones in waste areas, such as window cutouts. About eighteen months after we applied the siding, the stains had largely weathered away. So I'd say the advantages outweigh the risk. If you choose a plywood other than redwood—especially one you plan to stain dark (or paint)—there's no problem; and Non-Com salts offer bonus protection against decay and termites.

We also treated the ¾″ MDO plywood for our shutters. The Non-Com process turned that tan medium-density overlay a dark chocolate, but didn't affect its paintability. Treatment may raise your plywood costs about a third—assuming you're fairly close to a processing plant. Have your lumber yard arrange for it through Koppers Company (address in Chapter 1).

The Lockbox was designed just before energy conservation became so critical. If I were building it today—for the same mountain site (where winter temperatures of 20° below are not uncommon) and for radiant electric heating (as described in Chapter 13)—I'd seriously consider beefing up its thermal envelope by framing all external walls with 2x6s so I could pack the stud cavities with R-19 fiberglass.

The Lockbox closes from the top down. A boon of pole-and-beam construction is that you get a roof overhead before exposing finish flooring and wall framing to weather. In fact, since we built this 32'-tall house without scaffolding, we closed in attic first by framing and siding walls flat on attic's plywood floor, then tipping them in place under front purlin and side rafters (below). With circular saw set at 45 deg., butting ends of siding were beveled (bottom) for no-batten joint (sketch). For more on plastic-sheet weather closure (right) and attic vents (below right), see text.

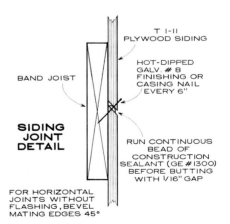

SIDING
JOINT
DETAIL

BAND JOIST

T 1-11
PLYWOOD SIDING

HOT-DIPPED
GALV. # 8
FINISHING OR
CASING NAIL
EVERY 6"

RUN CONTINUOUS
BEAD OF
CONSTRUCTION
SEALANT (GE #1300)
BEFORE BUTTING
WITH 1/16" GAP

FOR HORIZONTAL
JOINTS WITHOUT
FLASHING, BEVEL
MATING EDGES 45°

Then I'd sheathe the outside with Styrofoam TG before nailing on the T 1-11.

But all this would require an alteration of the construction plans that would violate the 16'-cube module. Interior space is already so tight I can't recommend robbing room perimeters of the extra 2", but if you expand the overall dimensions to accommodate the thicker walls, you'll end up having to patch out the corners with partial panels of siding. A compromise beef-up would be to use inch-thick Styrofoam over the 2x4 framing called for in our plans. This would "inflate" exterior dimensions only 2" per wall—leaving gaps you could cover with 1x3 corner boards.

While the siding was being cut and applied—and for the several months before we were ready to install our windows—we provided both weather closure and good interior light by means of huge sheets of a reinforced plastic called Griffolyn (see photo; address in Chapter 1). We chose Type 55 Clear—high-quality polyethylene with a mesh of tough fibers inside the film. It comes off a 100' roll and unfolds to a full 16' width—ideal for the basic 16' cube of the Lockbox. The stuff is remarkably strong, and weathered a fierce winter after being stapled up.

SPECTACULAR GLAZING

Pole-and-beam construction simplifies our spectacular glazing—as does the use of stock sliding doors of ponderosa pine. Since the massive beams bear directly on the support poles at the cube's corners, you needn't fret about header spans across wide areas of glass. The front window that opens onto our deck (and is shuttered by two sections of it that winch up) is 12' wide—a critical span for conventional framing. But in the Lockbox, the 6x12 beam above it serves as the header

Whether insulation comes in cut batts (4', left) or coiled blankets (40', right) usually depends on thickness. Both types were chosen for PS Lockbox leisure house: R-19 batts for ceilings/floors, R-11 blankets for walls, as in background.

Staple batts between joists. Despite appearance, this application isn't under house (if it were, foil vapor baprier would be up, toward heated side of floor). Foil is down, here, facing air space above second-floor ceiling to be installed after glass walls are up.

Four sliding "patio" doors glaze the front corner, the glory of the house that prows into the view. It's easier to assemble—and less wasteful of heating energy—than it looks, below: All windows are commercial ponderosa pine units, double-glazed for insulation. One panel of each slides for ventilation and access to outside shutters. Each heavy panel is handled separately. Four for upstairs are hoisted through open front well (bottom left) via block-and-tackle hung from attic joist (right). After frames are assembled and placed in rough openings (center right), panels are tipped into tracks. In last photo we're working from temporary plywood platforms tacked over well, later removed. Note exterior shutter rolled in place to prevent fall-through.

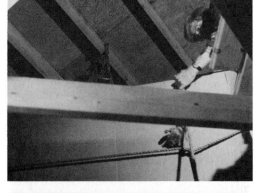

(and also supports the 8' window above). You need only short filler studs below such beams to create the rough-opening sizes the window needs. Opening dimensions were clearly spelled out in the instruction folder (with step-by-step photos) that came with our Caradco units.

These are top-quality window-doors, so they're not cheap (our three two-panel eight-footers and one three-panel 12-footer would total over $2000 in our area, today, complete with tempered insulating glass and a 4'-by-8' screen panel for each). But a major point of building your own leisure house is that your vast savings on labor can be put toward materials.

We don't recommend do-it-yourself glazing, here. Wrestling big unframed panes of glass down our mountainside to hoist into these lofty openings would have been both impractical and hazardous. And double-glazing for insulation (essential if you plan to heat the house for winter or retirement use) is a factory process that involves sealing the edges of two panes around a dead-air core.

After seven winters' experience with our glass corner, we're glad we didn't skimp. And we're glad we chose wood sash rather than metal: We were able to stain it to match our siding, and it's a more effective heat-saver. We've had no condensation, and minimal freeze-up of the sliding panels (some metal doors ice shut all winter). We *have* had some dry-rot problems, however (see text at end of chapter headed "Fighting Rot and Rust.")

On the side of the house with the stacked pair of 8' windows, no stops are needed for the shutters: Their travel is confined within the beam cage. In fact, track ends *butt* beams, providing closure

Shutters go up before windows go in; steps must be in proper sequence. Above, assembled shutter panel, with hangers installed, is hoisted through rough opening with block-and-tackle. Note that only right half of track has been installed, its open end ready to receive wheels of right hanger. Once both hangers are fed into track, shutter is pushed all the way right and second 8' length of track is mounted (as at second-story opening above).

against snow and birds. Since this shutter installation is forever, make it right!

The three photos on page 245 of our only *interior* shutter (for a casement above the stairway, where an outside shutter would be inaccessible) show one way to turn security closure into a design feature. This shutter's central panel is a decorative insert of translucent acrylic. The track is blocked out from the wall to let the shutter roll in front of a wall-mounted Circline fixture; the colorful insert is thus illuminated whether open or closed, day or night.

Three casements (we chose Caradco's C200's, 28"x40") plus the attic's circular sash and two louvered vents (matching 2'-dia. units from Webb) added around $500 to costs.

Two-story shutter (left) must be moved from outside, since casement windows must be locked before shutter will close. Closing is controlled by chain connecting this shutter with its upstairs neighbor (center). When big shutter is rolled closed from inside—and locked— smaller one tags after, seating against stop block. To open, just roll big shutter back so chain goes slack, then tug on rope attached to smaller shutter's opposite edge and dropping through a pulley to within reach of ground (third photo). Both this shutter and interior one for stairway window hang from exposed wheels on a simpler track. Inside shutter must be spaced away from casement crank (and light fixture it rolls in front of) with second stay roller, as shown in photo at far right, next page.

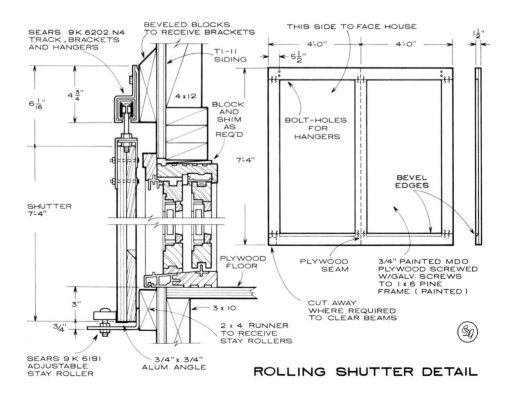

SEARS 9K 6202 N4
TRACK, BRACKETS
AND HANGERS

BEVELED BLOCKS
TO RECEIVE BRACKETS

THIS SIDE TO FACE HOUSE

T1-11
SIDING

4 x 12

BLOCK
AND
SHIM
AS
REQ'D

4 3/4"

6 1/8"

7'-4"

SHUTTER
7'-4"

4'-0"   4'-0"

5 1/2"

1 1/2"

BOLT-HOLES
FOR
HANGERS

BEVEL
EDGES

PLYWOOD
FLOOR

PLYWOOD
SEAM

3/4" PAINTED MDO
PLYWOOD SCREWED
W/GALV. SCREWS
TO 1 x 6 PINE
FRAME (PAINTED)

3"

3/4"

3 x 10

2 x 4 RUNNER
TO RECEIVE
STAY ROLLERS

CUT AWAY
WHERE REQUIRED
TO CLEAR BEAMS

SEARS 9K 6181
ADJUSTABLE
STAY ROLLER

3/4" x 3/4"
ALUM. ANGLE

ROLLING SHUTTER DETAIL

The casements and round window are factory weather-stripped; all come pre-servative-treated (for either staining or painting—we stained inside, painted out). You just nail them into rough openings and add inside trim. They're double-glazed, too, eliminating any fuss with storm windows for most climates. (But see text "Should you triple-glaze.") Removable inside screens are extra—but a must for the majority of country-home locations.

The circular units are as practical as they are decorative. Half of the window spins in its frame for air; and the pair of screened louvers provide cross ventilation below our metal-tile roof, keeping the attic storage area fresh and cool. You merely insert these wooden sash units in a snug hole cut through the siding, as shown in a photo.

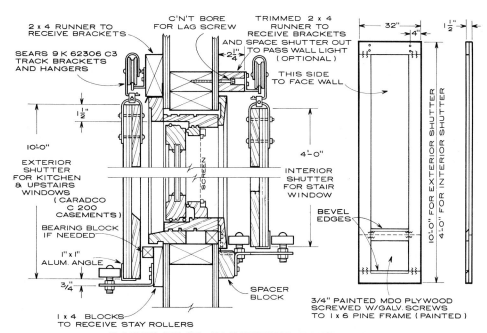

CASEMENT SHUTTER DETAILS
TWO-STORY EXTERIOR & HALL INTERIOR

WINDOW AND VENT UNITS—all ponderosa pine

Key No.	Amt.	Description	Unit Dimensions	Mfg.
1	1	2-panel sliding door XO-8 IG	6'10¾"x7'10⅜"	Caradco Dubuque, Iowa 52001
2	1	3-panel sliding door OXO-12 IG	6'10¾"x11'10⅜"	
3	2	2-panel sliding door OX-8 IG	6'10¾"x7'10⅜"	
4	3	C200' casement 2335 (two hinged left, one hinged right)	28"x40"	
5	2	192 screened louver	2'4" dia.	Webb Conneaut, Ohio 44030
6	1	112 Roundvent modern trim	2'4" dia.	

Entry door: Mediterranean-styled molded skin of Fiberglas-Reinforced-Plastic over urethane foam core (see Chapter 5).
Interior doors: hung on Stanley's Pocket Frame sets (2822); bathroom panel 26" wide; bedroom panels 30". Heights to suit.
Skylight: Ventarama P2230, clear, w/box; 4' pole operator.

SLIDING SHUTTER HARDWARE
(from Sears, Roebuck & Co.)

Amt.	Cat. No.	Description	Location
1 set	9K62306C3	Standard single door, 6 ft. wide	Kitchen wing's 2-window shutter. Use extra 6' section of flat track for interior mounting at stairwell
1 pr	9K6230	Flat-track hangers	For stairwell track
3 sets	9K6202N4	Heavy-duty single door, 8 ft. (16-ft. track)	For "patio" doors
19	9K6181	Stay rollers	4 per outdoor shutter, 3 per indoor shutter

Catalog numbers at time of construction subject to change.

Should you triple glaze?

Window heat loss is inversely proportional to the number of glazing layers (and those resulting dead-air pockets), so if you add what the industry terms a "storm panel" to a double-glazed window, you'll improve thermal performance. You'll be reducing the chill factor on the weather side of the glazing. Your added pane will be optically clear and free of condensation clouding.

Most quality double-glazed windows now offer the triple-glaze option. Your window dealer can order the storm panel designed for your window. It usually fits into a rabbet that's already in the sash. In the case of my wood casements (left photo, below) installation was a simple matter of screwing on six nylon turn buttons, supplied with the pane to hold it snugly in place (and permit easy removal next spring to relieve pivot and crank mechanism of extra weight). The pane comes framed in weather strip that compresses against the rabbet for an air seal. This pane won't impede window operation—it won't guard against infiltration either, but all quality windows already have proper weather stripping.

Check our map to see whether you should invest in this added pane. If your area has more than 6000 degree days, triple-glazing will pay off in fuel savings.

Winter Degree Days

Cut-away of modern casement shows how storm panel is clipped into exterior rabbet of double-glazed window.

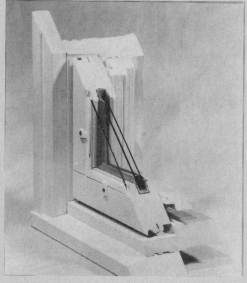

Reflective draperies for that glass corner

Though construction of the Lockbox had begun before energy considerations became crucial, the house was properly sited (the all-glass prow faces south; the north wall is windowless), and all those sliding patio doors are double-glazed in factory-weather-stripped wood frames. Even so, heat loss through the window-wall on a 20-below night more than offsets the sunny-day solar gain.

So during recent winters, we've been covering the windows with reflective thermal draperies each night (photo right) and whenever the house is shuttered between visits.

Guess what we're using for draperies? Thermos sportsman's blankets. These blankets come with a sturdy grommet in each corner that's easy to hook over L-screws in the door frames. The lightweight material is a tough, nonporous laminate (56″ by 84″) of fiber scrim and aluminized plastic film. Just be sure to place the reflective face *in*, where it can bounce back the room heat.

Blankets also prevent convection loss by keeping air from washing up the glass. For the most effective air seal, apply Velcro strips to overlaps and window frames.

The thermal improvement when that naked black glass is masked with reflective draperies is remarkable. You could also make rigid insulating shutters of Styrofoam, but you'd have a problem storing them inside such a compact house.

CLOSING UNDER FLOORS

For the suspended floor of a pole house, where insulation is called for, weather-closure is a must.

Mineral panels are ideal for closing homes in wooded areas, where under-floor fire is a hazard. Nothing could be less combustible than asbestos fibers embedded in cement. These sheets are also impervious to rot, termites, and vermin.

Gold Bond (the brand we chose) seems confused about its own products: We asked for Permaboard, with a prefinished pebbled texture on the exposed face. The 4′x8′ sheets that were delivered had that finish, but were only ⅛″ thick (with no identifying stamp or label). The thinnest Permaboard is 3/16″, so I assume we got Plia-F-Lex instead—Gold Bond's premium mineral-fiber sheet. Either grade will do.

The stuff can be exasperating to work with; it's eggshell brittle. Pick up a sheet carelessly, and the corners may snap off in your hands. Wrestling a full sheet of it up into suspension beneath floor joists is a job for three or four people, though two of us managed part of the chore by first rigging special support cradles (a 2x4 nailed along the bottom of a central joist with spacer blocks to create a gap you

All plywood floors of house (applied via APA's glued t&g system on 24"-o.c. joists) need insulation and underfacing. With radiant electric heat, we chose foil-faced batts of J-M 6½" Super-Thik fiberglass. But vapor barrier must face up, so you can't staple flanges. Instead, bow sharp-ended wires between joists (as shown beneath entry-wing floor in photos above). One brand of these wires is Tiger Teeth (write address in manufacturer's list at end of Chapter 1 for price). Sheets of asbestos-cement are then nailed across bottom of joists, as shown in two photos at left. (Lower photo demonstrates use of temporary 2x4 support, with sheet slipped between it and joists.) Photo directly below shows author lifting trimmed asbestos-cement panel in place between twin beams where kitchen wing joins main cube. All long edges of panels rest on small ledgers (quarter-round molding will do) tacked to faces of beams.

can slip the sheet through). *Don't* attempt to tack-nail one edge with scattered fasteners while you lift the bow out of the rest of the sheet. We had a sheet break out around a half-dozen such nails and drop, with a rent down its middle.

Though the manufacturer says predrilling isn't necessary, I'd advise it. Best fasteners: 1½" galvanized barbed roofing nails; head diameter must be ⅜". Locate nails 8" o.c., ½" from all edges; interior nailing can be 16" o.c. Butt sheets tight over framing members, centering short-edge joints over a joist. Since all edges must be supported, add blocking between joists.

Around the periphery of the floor, where sheets butt against joist ledgers, you can skip blocking and edge-nailing by fastening a strip of ⅝" quarter-round ⅜" below the joists. Just slip the cement board into this gap and nail other edges. Check the pair of photos on page 249 for such molding strips along a ledger and the opposite face of the same floor beam. Here, where beams flank the support poles, strips of insulation and cement board must be fitted between them. To cut latter to size, score deeply with an awl drawn repeatedly along a straightedge. Clamp a 2x4 along the "good" side and bend the scrap side up until the sheet breaks along the score.

FIGHTING ROT AND RUST

Our Lockbox has proved an ideal "test house" for home-maintenance products. We've tried out several new weapons for the battle against rot and corrosion, and our results should prove of value to any owner of a leisure home.

Our exposure is especially severe, which makes for an accelerated test situation. The house has weathered seven winters in deep woods, and the very nature of its security-shuttering system makes it susceptible to dampness damage. Since all its glazing is covered most of the time (part of the deck hinges up to secure the three-section patio door; all other glazing tucks behind rolling shutters), window frames seldom dry out thoroughly. I found that several of them harbored dry rot—surface patches of damp white scale, plus areas that were spongy under finger pressure. If I were building any shutterable house in damp woods in the future, I'd be sure to buy vinyl-clad or aluminum-clad wooden windows, and I'd take greater pains with my flashing to prevent any seepage behind the frames. I tried to plug all joints with beads of modern construction sealant. It's good, but a weather seal has to be perfect.

At the same time I discovered the rot, I found that much of the exposed hardware (nuts and washers on the threaded rods that bolt beams to poles; latches; winches) was rusted. The search for solutions was on.

And they both turned out to be just that: *solutions*—liquid applications that do everything their labels claim. The one for rot was harder to come by (and harder to use) than the one for rust, so let's tackle rust first.

Trustan 7 is a commercial treatment that actually converts rust—by chemical reaction—into a protective shield. The remarkable thing is that it spares you the chore of rust *removal*. You just scrub it into the rusted surface with a stiff brush (I used an old toothbrush) and let it react for 24 hours (you can see it work; it turns the rusted surface blue-black).

I tried it first as a solo treatment, leaving the blue-black surface exposed to weather. A few heavy summer rains washed away the treatment and the rust returned. So then I did it right with a new application; after it set, I rinsed the surface with water and let it dry before applying a metal primer and top coat.

For the latter, I've tried both an enamel formulated for metal, and a standard exterior paint. So far, they've performed equally well; it doesn't really matter what type of paint you apply over the treated, rinsed surface, but a sealing coat is essential for continued weather protection.

You can find Trustan 7 in hardware stores and home centers. A seven-oz. plastic bottle runs around $5. For larger quantities (quarts, gallons, five gallons) write Trustan Inc., Box 5204, Ironbound Stn., Newark, N.J. 07105.

The company will refund your purchase price if rust breaks out within two years on rusted ferrous metal properly treated with Trustan 7, primed, and painted.

Now our solution for dry rot. First of all, the term's a misnomer: Dry rot only occurs where wood remains wet, either through trapped water or constant high humidity. Soaking such damp spots with acetone helps dry them out; so does directing a heat lamp or hair dryer at them.

To reconstitute rotted areas, I searched marine-supply stores for a two-part formula of epoxy resin that permeates disintegrated wood cells, making rotted wood tougher and harder than new. I found several brands, all packaged in yoked containers, big one for resin, small one for hardener. The brand I chose is Git Rot. It's made by Boatlife, Inc., 65 Bloomingdale Rd., Hicksville, N.Y. 11801; and the price keeps rising. My check at press time showed a blister-pack "sample" selling for $5.50; a pint's $14.50, a quart's $26.50. That's too costly for a major job like a rotting beam, but bearable where the fix will save a major expense such as replacing a wood-framed patio door.

Mix only as much as you expect to use within a half hour, following a simple 3:1 formula. To get the solution into the wood, bore ¼- or ⅜-in. holes into rotted area, insert the applicator nozzle, and squeeze—but gently; the mix is very fluid, and drips and runs are inevitable. So it's best to mask areas below the spots you're treating. This is especially true of vertical members, which are harder to flow the liquid into (even when you angle your holes downward). It takes patience and frequent reapplication as the stuff soaks in. You can tell when the area is saturated, because the surface goes slick. The slow-setting resin spreads through the rotted area until it's stopped by the surrounding (less absorbent) sound wood. It stays tacky for several days (at 70 degrees), hardens in 10. Lower temperatures slow the process still more, as does dampness in the wood. But the resin will still cure eventually, reconstituting the wood and halting further rot. As it sinks into the wood, it will leave part of each hole unfilled. Plug these with a wood plastic.

For both the rust and the rot treatments, wear rubber gloves. With Trustan 7, I'd recommend them for both the scrubbing and wash-off stages. The label warns that it may "stain some skin," which seems equivocal since the stuff would mark the hide of an Australian bushman. It leaves purple birthmarks that no solvent removes; you have to scrub your skin with household bleach.

Both materials permit water cleanup of tools and spills—if you act quickly. But if you dribble Git Rot on raw, unsealed wood, it'll seep into surface pores and be there forever.

5. Shutter Deck and Entry Door Complete the Closure

Leisure-home decks should be something special—especially when your site is isolated and your walls boast large (vulnerable) areas of glass. Our Lockbox house is an ideal example: Hung within poles on a remote, wooded Pennsylvania mountain, it prows into its view of cascades with an all-glass corner. To leave this house unshuttered between visits would invite storm and vandal damage. So, built-in protection was primary to our plans from the start.

Views of winter-closed house show why it's called the Lockbox. Deck-shuttering can be adapted to any remote leisure home. Each section needs its own boat winch plus cable fed through brass pulleys S-hooked to heavy-duty screweyes. Only the left winch must be blockmounted for handle clearance.

Magnificent graining of deep-carved Spanish door is caught forever, without maintenance.

This door is only access to shuttered Lockbox, at end of catwalk entry. Stair drops past pole-hung cube to deck detailed in this chapter.

When I designed our deck, I incorporated the hinged-section concept for shuttering, without compromising the recreational function a summer-home deck must fulfill: It serves as an extra room—probably your most-used room when entertaining. So I ran support posts up through the deck for a built-in perimeter bench that doubles as a railing.

A deck that soars 10 feet off the ground, like this, calls for sturdy underpinnings. For flexibility in assembly, I didn't embed deck posts (except the catwalk's light standard), choosing instead to anchor posts securely to below-frost piers, using metal bases, made by Simpson.

Our ultimate choice for the lumber was garden-grade redwood—not only for the rustic effect of knots and occasional sapwood streaks (a good match for our rough-sawn redwood Texture 1-11 siding), but for its resistance to rot and infestation.

But rounding up what we needed proved a problem. We learned the hard way that in many areas the demand for construction-grade redwood has exceeded the supply. So, if you plan to duplicate this deck, you'd do well to place a firm order with your yard well in advance. Redwood may be sold on this kind of priority basis from now on—at rising prices.

Even so, what you get may not be choice. Our boards had been badly stacked (yards often abuse redwood's weatherability by leaving it exposed); all were stained, many had blackened. Hours of sanding (coarse belts on our 3-by-21 Stanley) brought all surfaces back, but slowed construction. A water-repellent finish lessens risk of redarkening (instead, the red tone slowly lightens to an overall tan). I'd recommend a flowing brush-coat of Woodlife as you ready each piece for assembly, a second coat when construction's complete.

Even if your redwood requires such extras, it's worth it. The workability of the lumber is a delight. It's pitch-free, compliant—planing, chiseling, drilling, and nailing go faster than with other softwoods. Judicious predrilling assures you'll never split out, even close to edges.

Two hinged shutters winch down (one at a time) onto deck framing to expose wood-framed patio-door unit. Cables then unhook from surface-mounted pad eyes and are cranked back onto winch.

Deck-post footing is chipped into solid rock with cold chisel where digging's impossible. Deeper recess, star drilled, at center, takes head of short ⅜" bolt for three-piece anchor.

Three types of footing are used for deck. Excavated footing (poured in Sonotube, with anchor bolt at top) is backfilled by co-builder Ron Nelson.

Embedded post is braced erect within Sonotube set on previously poured below-frost footing. (Length from which form was sawn is at left.) Lamp will top this Cellon-treated post.

We converted two other redwood disadvantages to our purposes. In his sketch for the deck, our architect had specified 6x6 posts. California Redwood Assn. advised us such timbers are now rarely milled, and not widely available. Instead, we face-nailed three 2x6s, as shown in a sketch. I designed bench and railings to take advantage of these assemblies, trimming some of the triplers back to accept cross members. It actually strengthens the whole structure.

(Post assemblies don't quite fill the Simpson bases, so tuck a scrap of T 1-11 siding along one face.)

There were other field changes: Our architect's plans call for 2x6 decking on 2x10 framing. Yards couldn't supply the latter, but CRA rustled up 2x12s for us. We prefer the appearance; framing width now matches the house beams it ties to. (Note that the right side of the deck framing ties to the beam with a stationary 12' 2x6—see the main plans in Chapter 1). The hinged area (like the anchored decking) is assembled from 2x6s alone. For economy, all support framing and stringers can be 2x10s. Large marine-supply outlets will have an inexpensive winch with on-off ratchet and 3:1 gear that's ideal; also 25' lengths of 3/16"-dia. steel cable with scissor hooks at one end. They should also stock chromed pad eyes that are the right size to take these hooks.

Shutters are held up with two slide bolts each—an exterior one block-mounted at both outer edges (see photos), plus surface-bolts mounted on the face of the deck to either side of the joint line. The latter must be shot from inside before you close and latch the sliding center panel of the glass door and make your exit via the catwalk door, upstairs.

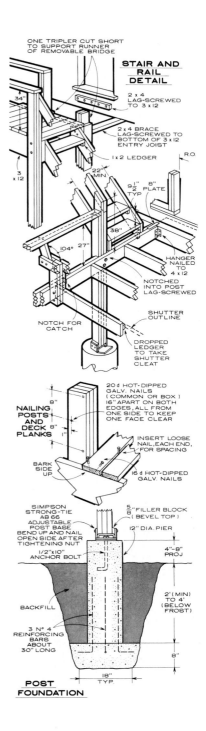

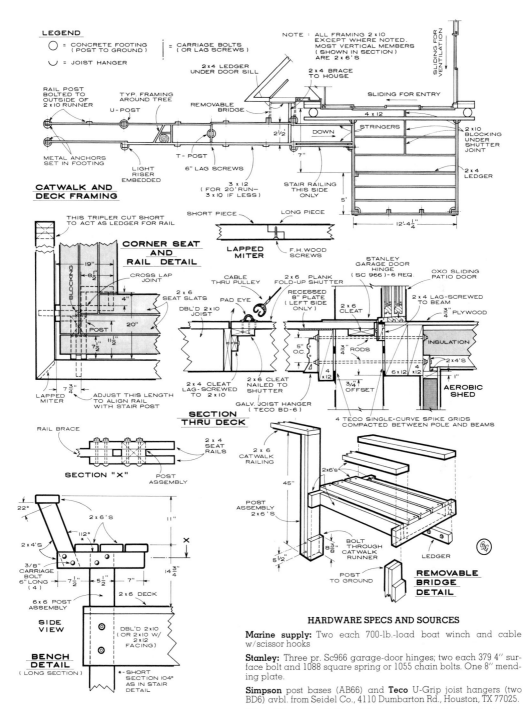

HARDWARE SPECS AND SOURCES

Marine supply: Two each 700-lb.-load boat winch and cable w/scissor hooks

Stanley: Three pr. Sc966 garage-door hinges; two each 379 4″ surface bolt and 1088 square spring or 1055 chain bolts. One 8″ mending plate.

Simpson post bases (AB66) and **Teco** U-Grip joist hangers (two BD6) avbl. from Seidel Co., 4110 Dumbarton Rd., Houston, TX 77025.

Misc.: ⅝″ carriage bolts and lag screws in assorted lengths; heavy-duty screweyes with 3″ min. shank (welded or cast eyes preferable); S-hooks; pad eyes (for boat-deck rigging) and marine or awning pulleys.

Cross-buck braces are half-lapped, applied to deck between horizontal cleats with construction adhesive and 10d nails.

Corrugated fasteners help draw crossbuck braces of hinged deck snug against top and bottom cleats. Stanley driver is under $2.

Notches are cut in deck joists to let in cross-buck so planks will rest on framing. Chisel out between saw kerfs.

Tread ledgers are predrilled redwood 1x2s glued and screwed to stair stringers (back-to-back for alignment).

Corner assembly for bench and back rail is tricky (see plan view detail, page 257). Check angle before drilling for bolts.

Short section has 2x4s for bench and rail supports set farther forward to align rail with stair post, off right.

To shelter edge of raised deck—and winches—from snow and ice, author later added shed roof of enamelled plywood strip.

Three pieces of plywood bridge four triangular brackets that are lagscrewed to structural beam behind siding.

Adding the downhill stair

Sharp-eyed readers will have noted that in our early deck photos there is no stairway *down*. This was a later addition—one that offered the structural bonus of cross-bracing the tallest deck post. And since we bolted the inner stringer to this post, we needed only one new, close-in pier (photos below).

We didn't skimp on *it*, though: We sank the footing below frost, as in our sketch. And our method of fastening the outer stringer is worthy of special note.

At the top of a pier (formed by pouring concrete into a length of Sonotube set atop a previously poured footing with projecting rebars) we embedded bolts to anchor an 8″ aluminum angle for the stringer to toe into. We kept the bolts "afloat" and positioned by passing them through the angle and turning on their nuts (if you use an anchor bolt, as

we did, you'll have to enlarge an existing hole in the angle). When the concrete has set a week, tighten the nuts and install the stringer.

As with the upper stair, our 2x12 treads are held level with 1x2 ledgers glued and screwed to the inside faces of the stringers. Then, to stabilize the assembly, we drove a ⅜″x5″ lag screw through each stringer into the ends of each tread. You now have a stair that can never twist or creep.

That sign in our last photo, incidentally, is a good idea for any stair to an unattended leisure home, and a must for the Lockbox, where the closed deck exposes open joists. The removable post that supports the outer end of the sign chain is 1″ aluminum tubing slipped through a pair of eyebolts.

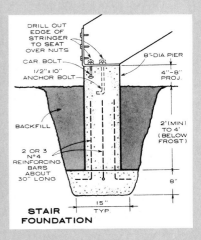

STAIR FOUNDATION

THE ENTRY DOOR

The weak link in the security chain we've built into our Lockbox leisure home is liable to be the entry door. As we've shown, other access areas—including windows—are shuttered while the house is unoccupied. So we gave special attention to design and product quality for our one unshuttered entry.

The door itself was newsworthy: our Mediterranean design is a Fiberglas panel from Owens-Corning—a one-piece panel featuring tough skins of FRP molded over a urethane foam core. Such panels stay straight and true and will take years of abuse (O-C completed tests simulating 25 years of slamming, without damage).

These panels are made in a standard 1¾"x36"x80" size. Ours came pre-hung. But it wasn't quite the package you'd expect from a manufacturer of entry doors. O-C isn't really in this business; so, although our door reached us hinged within a pine frame and an oak threshold, we had to provide our own saddle, weatherstrip, and latching hardware.

Kwikset's Protecto-Lok comes in a cleverly compartmented carton with clear pictorial instructions and a metal template for locating the four holes you drill in the door. Although instructions are for a conventional wood-frame door, they'll

And to up security still more, a removable bridge

The catwalk that soars from our mountainside path to meet the Lockbox at its second-floor level (see color photos) is spaced out from the wall of the triangular entry. This gap is bridged by a removable platform (being replaced, below) of redwood 2x6s.

We'd never claim that removing the bridge when you depart will prevent all unauthorized entry. A thief or vandal could always risk the 10-foot drop. Yet the bridge is more than a gimmick. The absence of an inviting perch from which to work on your lock will be a deterrent. A burglar is going to feel precarious, leaning across such a gap. There's an added bonus, for mountain sites: With the bridge gone, during your winter absences there'll be no banking of snow against the threshold, so no ice-ups.

Bridge construction must be tailored to individual situations. We brought our catwalk in along the entry wall at a level one step lower than the threshold. The side rails of the bridge snugly bracket the 2x4 support ledger lag-screwed under the door sill. At the opposite end, they rest on ledgers built into the catwalk posts. No fasteners are used to anchor the bridge; when you leave, you just lift it inside the door to store on edge in the hallway, then reach across the gap to lock the door.

Double protection is boast of combo-locks like Kwik-set's, above. Its inch-long brass dead-bolt has steel insert that standard hacksaw won't cut; brass cylinder is encased in steel guard and pry-proof reinforcing ring. Inside, deadlock and lockset are built into single plate (its face in left photo, its back in right photo, assembly with cylinder and knob in sketch below). Unlike many other paired units, elements are gear-linked—turning interior knob withdraws both bolt and latch from strikes.

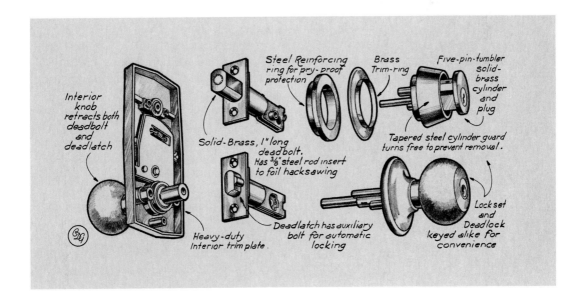

apply to a Fiberglas panel, but with exceptions:

Drilling the pair of 2⅛″ holes through the door faces for the cylinders is tougher. I ruined two hole saws cutting through the Fiberglas. Don't attempt to chisel ⅛″-deep recesses in the panel edge as directed. You'll not only wreck the tool but risk chipping the Fiberglas. Also, since the door stile is narrow for the trim plates, you'll have to carve away a bit of the adjacent panel design. Use a small router, wearing goggles.

Protecto-Lok's gear-linkage feature is vital to quick emergency exits—important for vulnerable vacation homes. You can double-lock the door when you retire, confident that if you want out in a hurry, just turning the inside knob will open the door—no panic-fumble with a separate deadbolt turnbutton.

Ingenious manufacturers have zeroed in on the security problem, and entry-door locks are much improved over those of ten years ago. Panic-proof lockset-deadbolt combinations—mechanically linked so the inside handle opens both—are now widely available.

But Pease Ever-Strait Doors now build a latch and *three* widely-spaced deadbolts into their prehung door panels. The bolts lock into rugged steel plates, yet all three retract with a twist of the indoor knob.

To frame door simply, we chose 2″ molding used in its drip-cap position only across top; for opening we flipped it to cover joint of framing and jambs.

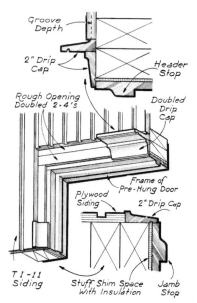

There's really only one problem with our Fiberglas door—as I explained at the end of Chapter 1, in prefacing comments to a Materials Suppliers list: Owens-Corning never *did* get into the door business, as they intended, and our beautiful entry remains a one-of-a-kind artifact.

Fortunately, other manufacturers have been less timid. If you want to stick with fiberglass (the capitalization and single "s" apply only to O-C products), write Lake Shore Industries, 2806 N. Reynolds Rd., Toledo, Ohio 43615, for a brochure on their wood-panel simulations. Their Style 102 is the closest equivalent to our O-C beauty we've seen.

And, of course, there are several manufacturers of insulating steel doors in various styles—including Lake Shore and Pease (top photo).

Customizing a threshold seal

When winter temperatures dove to 20 below at the Lockbox, icy air flowed under that entry door and spread to chill much of the home's floor area. I'd tried a number of standard doorstrips, including the channel type that fits over the bottom of the door. None stayed airtight for a full winter.

A United Industries steel-and-vinyl threshold sealer looked good in its package but proved a pain to install. It assumes that your door bottom is absolutely parallel to your existing threshold—with a very specific and consistent gap between. There's no provision for adjustability.

After trimming and renotching the metal threshold cover to fit my door width (using a hacksaw and file), I installed the unit on my oak threshold as shown in the large photo below (the vinyl insert pulls free to reveal mounting holes). But the hinge side of the door (to the right) wouldn't even pivot across the metal—though clearance was adequate on the latch side. When I replaced the vinyl insert, I couldn't close the door at all; the panel pinched the vinyl and stopped.

I filed the bottom of the door, slipped a metal shim under the jamb plate of the bottom hinge, planed and belt-sanded the oak threshold, and—after several hours' work—evened up the clearance so the full width of the door would close over the vinyl, compressing it for an air seal, as indicated in the section photo.

That (at last) stopped infiltration—and it gave good service all winter. But it was still a narrow barrier against the cold itself; some heat was being lost through conduction. So I chose to add a seal strip to the inside edge of the door. The one in the third photo is a current type from Stanley: It combines polypropylene pile with an inner plastic fin for a seal against irregular surfaces such as shag rugs. But mine is a raised threshold, so I chose a flexible vinyl sweep that would seal against my new metal threshold, as shown in the section. It's a Frost-King strip that cost only $2, installed easily, and gives me an insulating pocket of dead air. Sometimes you have to combine commercial products to get the performance you want.

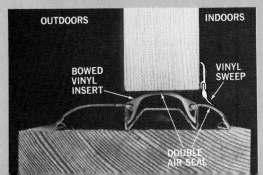

OUTDOORS   INDOORS

BOWED VINYL INSERT

VINYL SWEEP

DOUBLE AIR SEAL

6. Tie a Spiral Stair to Exposed-Joist Flooring

Three views of our installation show how stair column ties into open framing of second floor. Note that underside of flooring creates ceiling between the joists. Skewed joist hangers (for 45° joints) are by Simpson.

A spiral was the natural choice for the interior stair of our Lockbox. Since the house is basically a 16′ cube, there's no space to spare for a conventional stairway. Our second floor is open at both front and rear corners, for a "floating bridge" effect; the back opening—tightly designed into a hall that runs from second-floor entry to bathroom—offers minimal stair passage. And since we wanted to leave the underside of our t&g flooring exposed to create a beamed ceiling for the first story, we needed a stair we could use structurally, running the flooring out over it as a landing.

We ran up and down a dozen demonstration models before choosing. Three things tipped the balance to this cast-aluminum kit from Columns, Inc. (for address, see end of chapter):

- No hassle to get it down the mountain to our remote site. It arrived in two lightweight cartons (100 lbs. each) and it assembles via short lengths of pipe, so there was no full-height center column to wrestle with.
- The tread castings are shrewdly engineered to stack into an attractive sculptured column. We liked the open spoke look at the center—also shrewd, since it forces you to step on the wider part of the tread.
- The top bracket adapted well to our scheme for dispensing with the usual platform by tying the column into our floor framing. This gave us an "instant" utility stair between floors, letting us dispense with hazardous ladders. The stair served for nearly two years before we finished it off with railings and paint for these

Kit parts include (clockwise from left): balusters, pipe couplings and nipples, sample rail post, center post, railing units, tread castings, handrail sections. Angled up across center, from left: post bases and lag screws, two-part column base, top cap that lag-screws to platform frame.

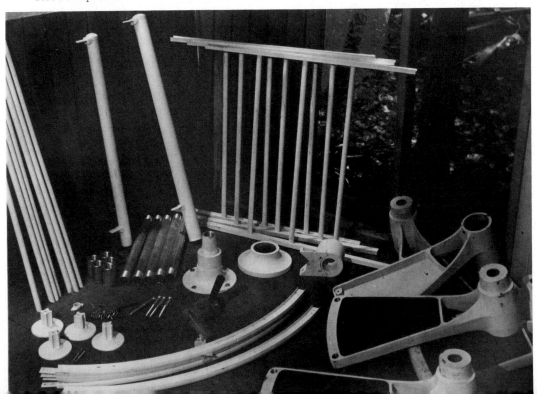

photos, and it's been in use for seven years since, so we can endorse the unit as durably sturdy.

The stair went up slick as a rocket. I've worked with few KD kits so well designed for goof-proof assembly. In addition to a portable drill and a screwdriver, you'll need a pair of good-size pipe wrenches to tighten threaded couplings that snug the whole column assembly into one unit.

Both ordering and installation are made easy by clear instructions from the

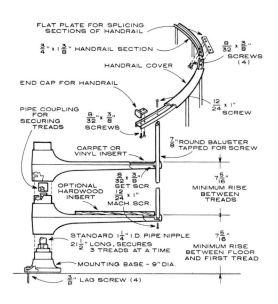

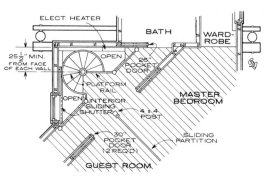

Common stair heights

	MINIMUM	MAXIMUM
9 Treads	73⅛″	77⅜″
10 Treads	80½″	85⅛″
11 Treads	87¾″	92⅞″
12 Treads	95⅛″	100¾″
13 Treads*	102⅜″	108½″
14 Treads	109¾″	116¼″
15 Treads	117″	124″

*This stairway is made with 27¾° treads and it takes thirteen of them to a full circle.

Stack tread units and—unlike other metal kits—position them as you go by slipping balusters into tread sockets.

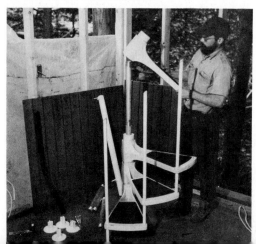

Stair ties in via V-notched column cap that bolts to 2x4 frame nailed to doubled header joists in foreground.

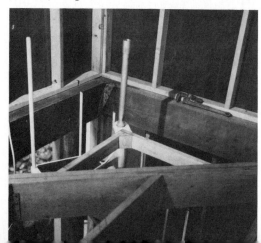

manufacturer. You'll note from our chart that *total* heights are determined not only by the number of treads (12 is average; 13 complete a circle), but by spacer rings set within tread castings. Ours came with three rings per casting, which brought our column's top cap above the floor line. So we unstacked the treads and pried one ring out of each.

Balusters are tapped top and bottom to take machine screws that pass *up* through the tread socket and *down* through the H-shaped aluminum rail, which you drill after assembly, but before you snap on the neoprene cover supplied with the kit. This cover is best applied after you've painted the stair. All parts come factory primed, so any good enamel can be used. Soak the U-shaped neoprene strip in hot water for five minutes to make it pliable; it cools in place, tightening its grip.

Details are what customize an installa-tion like this. Note that we tied the hand-rail to the top post with a gooseneck cast-ing—available as an option (right- or left-handed). Note, too, that to snug the stair into our corner, we tucked it in under but-ting beams. So an upper baluster had to *pierce* a beam (we just drilled straight down toward the tread socket, using a 1″-diameter spade bit in an extension). Our top rail turns a 135° corner; fortu-nately, Columns, Inc., offers a cast post cap with flanges at that angle.

Total cost: Just over $1000 for this 12-tread 4′-diameter stair; $16 per linear ft. for balcony railings, plus freight from Houston. (The same company recently in-troduced an all-steel stair of similar de-sign—at about one-third less cost. It, how-ever, is designed around a one-piece center column.)

As for that flooring, our 2x10 joists are 24″ o.c.; this framing unites into a sturdy bridge when 2x6 t&g floor planks are nailed diagonally across it.

Railing posts are added after flooring is laid. For snug fit inside center post, wrap top coupling with duct tape.

Posts for balcony rails are driven onto their bases; connecting rail assemblies bolt between flanges on post and cap.

Starting at one corner, t&g planks are laid diagonally across framing and nailed at each joist by angling nail through tongue (pre-drilling optional).

To minimize squeaks, you may want to run a bead of adhesive along tops of joists. Each plank is driven in place by striking a grooved block (foreground), then nailed through tongue.

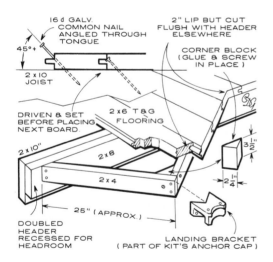

At the lumber yard, select from one of their two top grades of flooring (check grade stamps). It'll probably be Douglas fir or "hem/fir"—hardest of the WWPA grades. Spruce is okay, but it's softer.

All top edges are beveled, and we had the bright idea of laying the planks with these bevels down to give the beamed ceiling of the room below a finished appearance. What we failed to anticipate was how much even kiln-dried boards shrink after they're laid. Tight joints may widen into ¼″ cracks, and those face bevels are meant to minimize this, visually. So: Our ceiling looks great, but the floor above required extensive patching with wood plastic.

To minimize shrinkage, be sure your flooring is delivered dry, and stack it loosely, under cover, at your building site for several weeks before installation. Be certain that your boards are straight-grained and without bow or warp. At best, it takes some muscle to seat a long plank's tongue into a mating groove. Best method: Use a scrap block of the flooring, sliding its grooved edge along the tongue of the plank while striking the block's

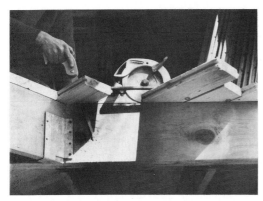

Trim projecting ends after entire floor is laid. Portable saw set to depth of flooring is fast, but to finish corners use a keyhole saw, with blade kept vertical.

Exposed-joist ceilings can take recessed fixtures; just box them in leaving air circulation around concealed housing. Here ceiling flange was drilled for three matching oval-head screws.

outer edge with your hammer. Angle a 16d nail through the tongue into each joist as you go.

To order full lengths, we carefully laid out our floor area on graph paper and computed the number of boards we'd need of each rough length (12', 10', 8' and 6'). You can't butt boards end-to-end in a diagonal installation.

Once all the planks are laid, smooth with a belt sander (with the grain), working down from a coarse grit.

One of the greatest floor finishes you can apply to softwood planks is poly-urethane varnish for durable, low-maintenance protection *and* good looks. We applied three coats of Sherwin-Williams Marvethane, sanding lightly between. The prime coat must be gloss, but our finish coats are satin. The effect—with nothing done to the final coat—is of a deep buffing with low-sheen wax. A finish for the bottom (ceiling) side? It's not a wear surface, so just brush a preservative on it and on the exposed joists. We used Woodlife.

WHO MAKES SPIRAL STAIR KITS?
ALUMINUM or STEEL: Columns, Inc., Box 895, Pearland, Tex. 77581; dias.—4' to 6'. STEEL: Studio Stair by American General Prod., 1735 Holmes Rd. Ypsilanti, Mich. 48197; diameters—3½', 4', 4½', 5', 6'. CAST IRON, STEEL, or ALUMINUM: Duvinage Corp., Box 828, Hagerstown, Md. 21740; dias.—3½' to 8' in 6" increments. Iron Craft, 1000 90th Ave., Oakland, Calif. 92603; dias.—3' to 7'. Mylen Industries, 650 Washington St., Peekskill, N.Y. 10566; dias.—3½' to 8½'. WOOD: Stair-Pak Products Co., Route 22, Union, N.J. 07083; dias.—4', 4½', 5'.

7. Ceilings Float in Invisible Grids

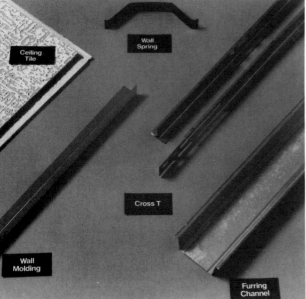

Here's the hardware—developed by Armstrong Cork—to install tiles shown at left, and (top photo) installed as our kitchen ceiling.

They named this novel ceiling system Integrid, because the suspending grid is integral with the acoustical panels. But they might well have called it Indigent, since it has no visible means of support. On second thought, the pun isn't appropriate; the ceiling is one of the most luxurious in Armstrong's famed Chandelier line.

The suspension system is unusual for acoustical ceilings. To demonstrate the installation, Armstrong sent John Shenk from their installation school to install our ceiling. Later, another installer from the school appeared to put up the angled, insulated ceiling in the alcove off the master bedroom. The step-by-step photos, here, are shots I took of those installations combined with other Armstrong demonstrations.

We finally ended up installing Integrid ceilings throughout the complex, many-angled second story of the Lockbox and found it a real problem solver.

We'd have been at a loss without the early demonstrations, however, since the procedure owes little to familiar methods of putting up acoustical ceilings. There are no hanger wires, no main runners, no furring strips—so the panels go up in half the time it used to take. Also, there's minimal ceiling drop, so the system rates high for areas where headroom is at premium. This proved ideal for our Lockbox kitchen, where we'd kept our joists low enough to butt our wall cabinets against them (no grease-catching waste space above);

Apply molding around perimeter of room, 2″ below bottom of joists. Note metal wall angle already nailed to face of cabinets, right. Corners can be butted or mitered.

Nail up metal furring channels, either across joists, as here, or along bottom of joists. Keep them 4′ apart. To anchor, just drive nail every 48″ along channel.

only a very short homemaker will find top shelves out of reach.

Those cabinets seen in the first photo came prefinished, ready to clip together and screw to the framing through their backs and tops. We simply tacked Armstrong's wall angle across their top rails for the quickest, neatest cabinet-ceiling joint imaginable.

Some sort of molding—for perimeter support—is the initial step in the Integrid system. Armstrong offers metal (in several colors, metal tones or woodgrain) in 10′ lengths you trim with tin snips. Nailing holes are made with a punch awl. Or you can substitute any wood molding that offers ⅝″ support. Whichever, your supporting surface should be 2″ below the lowest joist—and level around the room.

One of the cleverest aspects of the system: When you come to the end of your first row and trim a standard 1′x4′ tile to

Snap in Integrid cross tees—which in turn support the ceiling tile. To attach, squeeze sides of channel slightly, clip on tee. Tee should slide easily along channel.

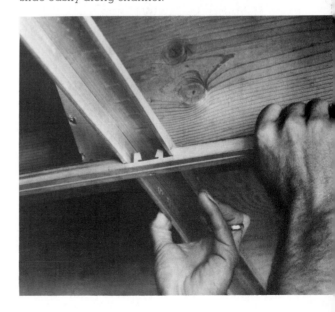

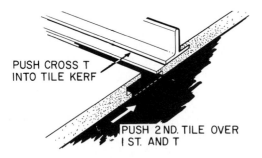

Begin installing tile in corner of room, laying it on molding, then move the cross tee along the channel and into the concealed slot in edge of tile (see sketch).

First row of tile was trimmed narrower here to match jog at corner. (You'll want to narrow your starter row, too, if final row would otherwise be less than 4″ wide.)

Fitting around ceiling-fixture boxes is a simple matter of notching with sharp knife. Here Shenk is about to slip first tile of third row onto cross T already concealed.

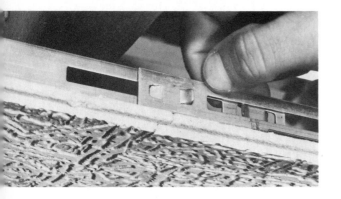

Self-leveling Ts have slotted and tabbed ends that engage to provide continuous support, even at skipped-channel location shown. Ts come in 4′ lengths, but can be cut.

Metal channel runs along bottom of exposed rafter in Lockbox alcove. Metal angle will support ends of tile at Peg-Board walls.

Cross T snaps into channel by pinching flanges together, then slips along it to seat in groove in edge of first tile.

Channel is nailed every 4' through 1" increment grooves. Exposed face of angle is 2" below rafter along all walls.

Completed alcove ceiling shows how neatly all joint lines disappear when spring clips are inserted along two edges.

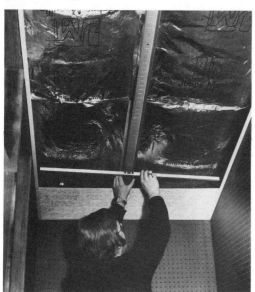

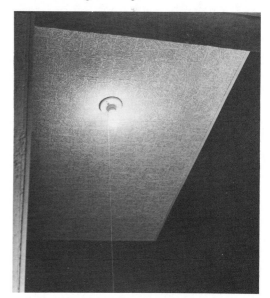

To keep moldings level around room, fill transparent tubing with water. Raise one end till water column tops out at 2″ mark on wall, then mark at other end of column (it's easier with a helper). Metal molding cuts easily with Channel-lock aviation snip.

fit, you use the cut-off piece to begin your *next* row (back at the wall you started from). This not only eliminates waste; it staggers joint lines so you'll never notice them. Even the long-edge lines disappear into the textured pattern.

Armstrong offers several patterns in 12″x12″ tile, only one (Amarillo, as we go to press) in the 1′x4′ size I worked with.

When trimming tiles to fit at the "working" end and (finally) along the "working" side of your ceiling area—the walls you're working *toward*—always trim tile ⅜″ short to leave a gap for a tension spring. These are compression clips you tuck between wall and tile edge to exert a joint-closing tension across the ceiling. Using the furring channels, the run is usually *parallel* to the joists. But—as our second Lockbox installation shows—you have the option of nailing the channels *along* the bottom edge of joists or rafters if this makes for an easier installation in your situation.

8. How We Laid the Vinyl Floor Coverings

Sheet vinyl can be a glamour floor—don't limit it to utility areas. It's ideal for low-maintenance leisure homes like the Lockbox.

Everything required—materials, from left: 12' vinyl roll, cleaner and wax, shellac to seal subfloor, adhesive, filler for cracks. Tools: putty knife, chalk line, seam roller, notched trowel, square, knife with notched blades.

Subfloor—glued t&g plywood—was exposed to abuse as house was built, needed patching, sanding, sealing.

Ease of maintenance is a prime consideration in the choice of any material for a leisure home. That's why we chose a sheet vinyl floor covering for the first story of the Lockbox. This floor borders our deck and, winter or summer, debris is constantly tracked in. Nothing cleans up easier than sheet vinyl—there aren't any joints to catch dirt, no corners to lift.

Many homeowners have shied away from laying big-sheet floor coverings—and the top-of-the-line stuff was often available through flooring contractors only.

Now there are sheet materials that can be wet-laid (in troweled-on cement) or dry-laid (stapled around the edges, with the staples then concealed by shoe molding). Either installation is fine for the plywood floor of the Lockbox—except that you're dealing with a room 16' square, and no sheet goods come *that* wide. (Most sheets come in 12' and 6' widths; a few in 9'.) You'll end up with at least one seam, and seams are still a problem with dry-laid sheet.

Armstrong offers clear, concise instruction brochures outlining their recommendations for both methods. A dimensioned floor plan is of major importance. In a kitchen, be certain to indicate the positions of all cabinets; the fit *along* them isn't quite as critical if you're planning to cover the toe-space with vinyl cove base.

Armstrong recommends you do all layout and cutting in a room larger than the one you're fitting—a floorspace that lets you roll the sheet flat and mark it with a chalk line. (That's tough with the Lockbox, but if you can manage it, slip thick cardboard scraps under the lines to keep your knife sharp and prevent damage to the floor below.) Sheet floorings come in

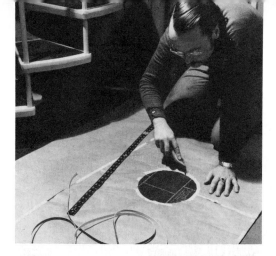

Full-size pattern was made for filler strip after 12' sheet was laid. Stair-base hole was cut with access slit to strip's nearest edge on pattern's grout line (above right).

other, nongrid patterns, of course, but where you've a seam to make, stick with a grout-line grid: It makes an ideal edge to trim along, and the seam will be invisible.

To keep a vinyl floor covering clean, sweep regularly and sponge mop with detergent. Some surfaces never need waxing. Others should be cleaned thoroughly a few days after the cement bond is set, then waxed.

If you prefer not to work with big sheets (and wet-laying a complex fit like ours is no picnic), you can always go the peel-and-stick route. We opted for this in our compact entry hall upstairs, using Armstrong's Place 'n Press Excelon tile in the olive Omega pattern. These small pre-glued pieces (12"x12") are easy to cut into the odd shapes you're stuck with here. The only preparation for the plywood floor shown: sand smooth, sweep clean, apply sealer coat of shellac.

Not only does cove base installation call for different adhesive than flooring: Armstrong offers one type for straight runs, another for those preformed inside and outside corners. S-285 (right) is a paste, not unlike the adhesive used for the sheet; you apply it with a notched trowel. S-1200 (left) is thick liquid-contact cement you brush on back of corners and on rear of toespace.

Cut peel-and-stick 12-by-12's to fit odd shapes before removing the backing sheet. Cut with shears or sharp knife along straightedge.

9. A Fireplace for the Lockbox

Platform installation let us tuck big woodbin under the metal firebox. Raised hearth makes fire tending and grill cookery handier, too. Total security theme of Lockbox is preserved by two husky drawbolts to fasten removable panel, barring break-in from rear. Stone hearth hadn't been laid at time of left photo.

The delights of an open fire are so evident that few of us demand a practical contribution from a fireplace, as well. For leisure homes, especially, we're likely to settle for a free-standing unit that's little more than a pleasant accessory.

This wasn't good enough for our Lockbox pole house. We wanted both winter-weekend and year-round retirement options built in—which meant built-in heat sources. Our major heaters are radiant-glass panels recessed into various walls, upstairs and down (see Chapter 13). But, efficient as these are, electric rates are steep—and climbing—so we wanted our fireplace to offer more than delight: It had to help heat.

That meant a heat circulator. We gritted our teeth as we went in search, expecting the cumbersome metal inserts of the past, with their clearance requirements, their masonry foundations and brick or stone facings. The Lockbox is a tight house, engineered for total space utilization. Would we have room?

And since the entire Lockbox floats above its steep site within a pole-and-beam cage, any foundation to support a conventional fireplace was impractical.

So we grabbed one of the first Heatilator Mark 123C models off the assembly line. It was a breakthrough in heat-circulating fireplaces, since it was the first to offer *zero clearance*. This means you can mount the metal unit directly on a wood floor or platform and frame it with studs snugged against the firebox—no space lost, no fuss with masonry. Yet it's one of the most efficient open-fire heaters we've seen.

There are two separate heat chambers and each has its own outlet duct. As the labeled photo and our sketches indicate,

Fireplace hangs outside the cube in a chase, with a firewood pass-through built in. Exterior views show how tapered shape matches triangular wing from which the chase hangs.

we brought the right-hand duct back into the living room, above the fireplace opening, and angled the left-hand duct up to the second-floor bedrooms. The fireplace is designed to suck cold air from near the floor, waft it through hot metal chambers around the firebox, and expel it, either back into the room (through grilles near the ceiling) or into an upstairs room.

PARTS YOU'LL NEED FOR LOCKBOX

1 Mark 123C fireplace (Heatilator catalog #3138); includes 2' chimney starter section, fire screen, two outlet assemblies including duct sections (two each #606, #612, and #690)

1 12" duct section, additional (#612)
1 Adjustable duct elbow, additional (#690)
1 Fan-powered inlet kit—two units (#600)
1 30-deg. chimney offset/return (#3930)
2 2' chimney sections, 9" dia. (#912)
4 3' chimney sections, 9" dia. (#913)
1 Contemporary cap (#921) for pitches from flat up; includes one chimney bracket; flashing halves; cone, collar, and cover
1 Chimney bracket, additional (#923)
2 Joint bands, 9" dia. (#922)
1 Grate (#26)
1 Barbecue grill (#6260)
1 Fire-stop spacer, oval (#3931)

Misc. (not supplied by Heatilator): 2 6"-dia. adjustable elbows (single-wall) and 2 6"-dia. 1' duct sections (single-wall) for inlets; 3 11-oz. cartridges 3M adhesive for tile; 28 5½"x11" tile or equivalent; noncombustible hearth; 4 2x6s 10' long; 6 2x4s 8' long; 1 4'x8' sheet ¾" exterior plywood; 3 4'x8' sheets plywood siding (T1-11); 1 roll each of 15" and 23" fiberglass wall insulation; 12 ½"x4" lag bolts; 6 ½"x5" carriage bolts; continuous hinge (Stanley STS 311¼), padlock hasp, screw hook, 2 interior drawbolts for removable panel.

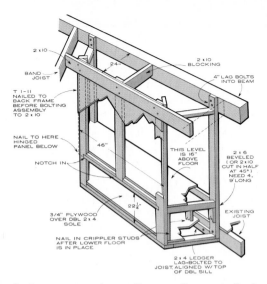

A chase moves the wall out so liner sets flush with interior surface of cube.

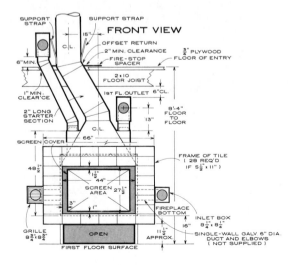

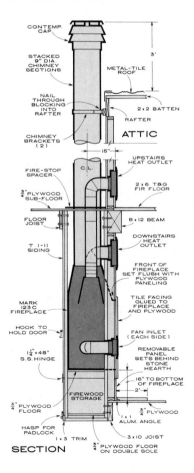

We angled the chimney, too, to move the fireplace a comfortable distance from the corner and still tuck the stack alongside our upstairs hall.

To further customize this fireplace to our house, the Heatilator design engineer sketched us up a compact, tapered chase to hang from our entry joists—an installation that doesn't rob an inch of space from the living room—and contributes a firewood storage and pass-through bin. Since our installation, several makes of heat-circulators have introduced models vented for outside combusion air. Our chase would make such a provision easy to include.

All Heatilator parts are designed for foolproof assembly, and the instructions

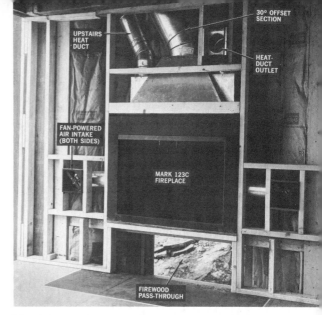

Metal liner slips between studs that frame opening; 2x4 header is added, on edge, resting on spacer tabs welded to unit; then vents are framed.

Chase is part of wall, so must be fully insulated if house is to be winterized. One roll each of 15″ and 23″ fiberglass does it.

Same siding used on house encloses chase. It's Texture 1-11 plywood, Non-Com-treated by Koppers, Pittsburgh, to be fire-resistant.

Metal firebox slips into place on platform. Note pre-scored side hole for inlet duct has been punched out at both sides.

Underside of chase and inside of woodbin door are best insulated with glued-on rigid 1½″ Styrofoam. Scrap from tapered bottom piece will complete the door below.

Chimney sections stack—and lock with twist—to extend upward from offset/return, which has support straps for nailing to adjacent studding. Smaller pipe to left is double-wall duct for upstairs heat outlet.

Author applies beads of 3M's EC959 before pressing tile firmly across joint between firebox and wall panel. Bottom row has scrapwood props to support tile while glue sets.

packaged with various units are clearly written and illustrated. We got the optional fan-driven inlet kit (without it, heat circulation depends on natural airflow through firebox slots). The kit complicates installation: You must duct, frame, and wire the two inlet boxes.

Whether to raise a fireplace hearth is mostly a matter of personal taste, but it does have a couple of advantages. It eases fire-tending for people whose backs may be a bit creaky; removal of ashes is easier, as is fireplace cookery.

Unless your wall facing is of noncombustible material, you'll need trim around the opening that won't burn. Typical requirement is 6″ at the top, 5″ minimum at the sides. Some makers of fireplace units offer masonry, tile, glass, or metal trim in kit form. The front of the firebox sets flush with the finish wall surface, so you're mainly interested in covering the gap between. For the Lockbox we wanted a bold tile design. Our search took us to a factory in Seville, but there are attractive domestic patterns, too.

We'd recommend ordering the full line of accessories. (For local-dealer addresses, write the company.) The grate is tailored to the tapered firebox, and the chromed grill sets into a socket provided at the left of the fireplace opening, to suspend food over coals. We later added glass doors by means of a retrofit kit, but suggest you order this option initially—it's an energy-saver. The Lockbox fireplace provides all the basic delights—and helps heat the house as a bonus.

It's easy to lay a real masonry hearth

You'll need a nonflammable hearth extension (that part of the fireplace floor that sticks out into the room) for safety. Local codes may require this to be at least 16″ wide, and extend 8″ on each side of the opening. More is neater and safer, especially with a raised fireplace.

Job shown was laid in a couple of hours. Two 40-lb. bags of Sakrete Mortar Mix were plenty for both bed and joints. After bottom of form was covered about 1″ deep, stone slabs (soaked in a bucket) were pressed in, duplicating pattern established by dry trial. Where ooze-up around edges didn't fill joint gaps flush, mortar was added with fingers, taking care to keep faces of stones clean. Completed hearth was covered with damp newspapers, kept moist for three days; form wasn't removed until a week later. Door to wood bin sets in place behind aluminum angle that defines rear of hearth.

10. Action Built-ins for Compact Bedrooms

During the three years we ran our Lock-box series in *Popular Science*, the most persistent questions from readers who studied our floorplans were "How do you fit beds in those angled upstairs rooms?" And, "Where are the clothes closets?"

This is an innovative house where you shouldn't expect conventional solutions. The entire upstairs of the Lockbox is a complex of built-ins that offers multiple use of each square foot. Even walls and doors roll back to convert the space into one uniquely shaped floating bridge over the living area below.

The most important—and *least* important—rooms in a leisure home are the bedrooms. A lifestyle at a country place differs drastically from that at home— that's the point of a second home: to break with routine. Back home you may be able to justify the luxury of entire rooms whose only function is to house a bed, but you don't have that kind of space to spare in an up-country house.

To snug into its rustic site, a leisure home should be as compact as possible. That often means a limited area to be devoted to so static a pursuit as sleep. That's why the bedrooms of our Lockbox are shrewdly designed to pack bed space into a minimal area, without sacrificing either comfort or privacy. And when the space isn't needed for sleeping, every-thing tucks up to make way for other activities.

The many guests who've overnighted at the Lockbox invariably comment on the ingenuity of the sleeping accommodations. Most of them readily endorse the special philosophy behind our design: Limited floorspace is best utilized for day-time activities and evening socializing. Convertible bedding folds quickly away and other units, such as desks and iron-ing boards, drop down to transform the space for house chores or leisure crafts.

Open-shelf wall niches replace con-ventional storage. The guest room has no closet since its transient occupants won't bring more clothes than can be hung from wall pegs or the end rungs of an attic-access ladder.

Even our two-story window well, which the bedrooms share through dramatic shuttered openings, isn't for esthetics alone: You can adjust air flow to match the seasons. Close the movable slats of those ponderosa-pine shutters in winter and you discourage convection of room air past the colder glass of the sliding doors that glaze this corner. (Close the pocket doors as well and you keep circu-lation cozily within the "sleep bridge"; for ventilation, just crack the casement in the wardrobe alcove.) On a warm summer night, you can swirl as much air around

Upstairs built-ins provide maximum use of space. Everything's self-storing—even the partition wall. Murphy bed is concealed behind folding wood-slat door, hung from a ceiling track. Sleep cells are transformed into single spacious room for daytime activities by pushing plywood partition through slot in the front wall (top right), so it hangs in corner light well (center). Metal shoes on bottom corners of partition nest in a pair of brackets at both ends of travel to hold ceiling-hung panel firm. Drop desk (right), hinged to wall (raised in photo above), has compartments and drawers for stationery and home records.

Small upstairs rooms allow for dramatic two-story window corner.

the bridge as you want by swinging the shutter panels back and pushing the sliding glass wide open. Privacy is still maintained by viewing-angle limits.

The solid partition gives a greater sense of privacy *between* rooms than an accordion door would (we've utilized the folding concept elsewhere when only visual closure is required). But the assembled panel is heavy, and since it hangs in space when not in use, make certain the track is securely anchored to ceiling or joists.

The panel can be highly decorative. I hand-painted the guest-room face with a supergraphic blowup of the Moorish tile pattern that dominates my fireplace and dining bar. The other face became a mirror and corkboard through application of commercial tile (cork and mirror pack-

ages cost around $6 each, for a total expenditure of $12). This rolling partition should even give you a tax advantage, should an appraiser drop by: The Lockbox legally qualifies as a single-bedroom house.

The unique shapes of the upstairs areas offer a challenge where wall paneling is concerned. Though we ran our rough-sawed redwood T1–11 exterior siding down the entry hall, for the interiors of the sleep cells we chose prefinished Masonite, using both "natural" and off-white tones of the cork-like Valencia texture. This two-tone effect—the white used on reflective walls, the dark on adjacent, shadowed walls—is a much-admired feature.

The panels mount quick and easy on open framing. Standard recommenda-

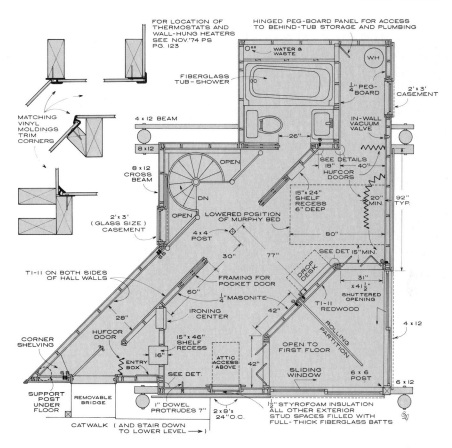

FOR LOCATION OF
THERMOSTATS AND
WALL-HUNG HEATERS
SEE NOV.'74 PS
PG. 123

HINGED PEG-BOARD PANEL FOR ACCESS
TO BEHIND-TUB STORAGE AND PLUMBING

WATER &
WASTE

WH

FIBERGLASS
TUB-SHOWER

¼" PEG-
BOARD

2'x 3'
CASEMENT

MATCHING
VINYL
MOLDINGS
TRIM
CORNERS

4 x 12 BEAM

8 x 12

IN-WALL
VACUUM
VALVE

8 x 12
CROSS
BEAM

OPEN

26"

SEE DETAILS
18"   40"
HUFCOR
DOORS

20"
MIN.

92"
TYP.

DN

15"x 24"
SHELF
RECESS
6" DEEP

2'x 3'
(GLASS SIZE)
CASEMENT

OPEN

LOWERED POSITION
OF MURPHY BED

80"

4 x 4
POST

30"   77"

SEE DET. 15" MIN.

DROP
DESK

31"
x 4½"

TI-11 ON BOTH SIDES
OF HALL WALLS

FRAMING FOR
POCKET DOOR

¼"MASONITE

SHUTTERED
OPENING

60"

42"

TI-11
REDWOOD

4 x 12

28"

IRONING
CENTER

ROLLING
PARTITION

CORNER
SHELVING

HUFCOR
DOOR

15"x 46"
SHELF
RECESS

OPEN TO
FIRST FLOOR

16"

ATTIC
ACCESS
ABOVE

42"

ENTRY
BOX

SLIDING
WINDOW

6 x 6
POST

6 x 12

SUPPORT
POST
UNDER
FLOOR

REMOVABLE
BRIDGE

SEE DET.

1" DOWEL
PROTRUDES 7"

2 x 8's
24"O.C.

1½" STYROFOAM INSULATION
ALL OTHER EXTERIOR
STUD SPACES FILLED WITH
FULL-THICK FIBERGLASS BATTS

CATWALK (AND STAIR DOWN
TO LOWER LEVEL ──→)

UPSTAIRS FLOORPLAN

tions for ¼" hardboard call for studs 16"
o.c., but our 24"-o.c. framing gave no
problems. By running a bead of panel
adhesive down the face of each stud, you
can get by with minimal nailing (though
Masonite's colored threaded nails don't
show on the deeply textured face). You
simply butt the prefinished vertical edges
of your panels, trimming them to correct
width only at corners, where the cut will
be masked by a matching vinyl molding
(check details on floorplan to see how we
utilized standard extrusions for our
unusual corners). A prefinished wood
shoe molding covers the floor joint.

You'll note we cut all our recess holes
(for shelf niches and ironing center) after
full panels were up. That's much simpler
than trying to match prefitted panels to
framed openings. Jigsaw these cutouts
carefully so the scraps can be used for
the backs of niches and facing of the sewing center. Since the desk mounts on the
wall surface, no cutout is needed; the prefinished facing, here, to match the wall
was a scrap from elsewhere.

For full storage flexibility, we lined the
wardrobe area off the main bedroom with
¼" Peg-Board. Clothing is stored in see-
through plastic drawer boxes, stacked on

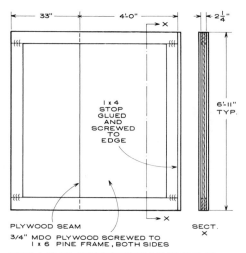

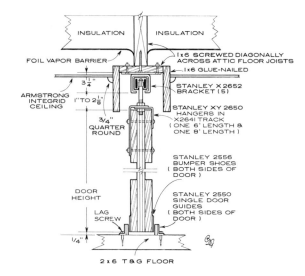

ROLLING PARTITION DETAILS

Two snug sleep cells can be opened into an upstairs area of intriguing shape. Heart of the convertibility is where three tracks butt against the 4x4 post (top right photo) that separates two pocket doors and serves as stop for rolling partition. Latter consists of one and a half 4'-by-8' sheets of ¾" ply framed in 1x6's. A 1x4 screwed across inner edge closes against post and prevents open panel from rolling through wall slot. Face of partition seen here was covered with one strip of mirror tile plus ½" cork—ideal for thumbtacking a poster display.

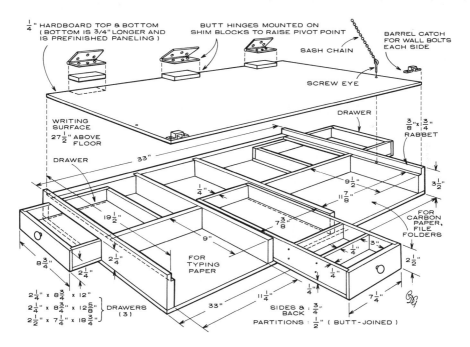

Compartmented desk is scaled to miss bed when both are lowered (right photo). Open slots are sized for typing paper (left) and file folders (right). Three small drawers store pencils, envelopes, and stamps. Drive screws through hinges and top link of support chains into studs for solid support. Bottom panel is prefinished hardboard to match wall when unit is held vertical by bolts.

Handy ironing center tucks through partition between guest room and entry closet. To plan for unit, space studs 14½" apart and provide sill at proper height. Run wiring before paneling the partition framing. Self-supporting board pivots out of recess that stores the iron.

Shelf niches—deep or shallow—also put stud spaces to work for you. Deep niche for bedding was cut after paneling. Mark limits by drilling blade holes at each corner of framing, from rear. Shelves for shallow niche were inserted from rear, nailed to studs.

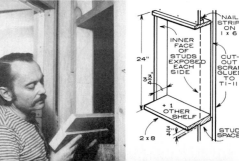

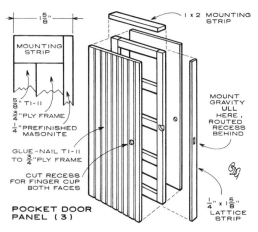

MOUNTING STRIP

1 x 2 MOUNTING STRIP

MOUNTING STRIP

$\frac{5}{8}$" TI-11
$\frac{3}{4}$" PLY FRAME
$\frac{1}{4}$" PREFINISHED MASONITE

MOUNT GRAVITY ULL HERE, ROUTED RECESS BEHIND

GLUE-NAIL TI-11 TO $\frac{3}{4}$" PLY FRAME

CUT RECESS FOR FINGER CUP BOTH FACES

$\frac{1}{4}$" x 1$\frac{5}{8}$" LATTICE STRIP

POCKET DOOR PANEL (3)

In tight rooms and halls, hinged doors are a luxury; their swing can eat up seven times the floor-space an accordion-fold door requires. A pocket door takes none at all, since it rolls into the stud space of a partition wall. As bonus, custom-made pocket doors can match the walls they tuck into. Our bedroom doors are hollow-core (top photo): frame strips are faced on both sides with wall paneling—T1-11 on the hall face, prefinished Masonite on the inside. Photo below shows them installed from inside the bedroom area, with rolling partition moved forward.

Photos show installation of three folding doors. Top, adding curved wood track section for bed closure. Center, hooking nylon hangers into track at entry closet. Below, anchoring wardrobe track to bottom of construction beam. Here, track is cut to exact length to butt between walls, hangers are fed into it before anchoring.

shelves mounted on Stanley brackets that also take a clothespole for conventional hanging.

Only after all paneling was in place did we apply our Armstrong Integrid ceiling—panels that float in a concealed metal grid fastened directly to overhead joists. Since the ceiling hangs below the tops of all wall panels, no molding is needed here: Prefinished metal wall angles for installing the Integrid are tacked directly to the face of the paneling.

In the photo below, I'm removing ceiling panels to climb the built-in ladder to the attic; note that these tilt-out panels rest on a flange created by clamshell molding mitered around the hole. (Hidden above my head is a hinged section of the attic's plywood floor.) There are two tilt-out panels to permit a snug fit not pos-

Attic access "door" is self-storing. It's a split panel of 1½" Styrofoam with ceiling tile cemented to one face.

sible with a single panel. They're faced with pieces of the Armstrong tile used for the adjacent Integrid ceiling. But they aren't just for looks—they complete ceiling insulation. Behind the tile facing, they're Styrofoam. To prevent wear of the facing, all edges are capped with metal angle—I glued on scraps of the enameled wall angle. Note in that same photo that a 1"-diameter dowel, glued into a socket drilled at an angle into a stud, serves as a hanging peg.

The hangers that come with Stanley's pocket door-frame sets are top-mounting. Since it's impractical to screw into plywood edges, you must glue a sturdy mounting strip across the top of the panel. Use the drilling template that Stanley supplies with the mounting hardware. Before assembling each panel, be sure to rout a recess for the gravity edge pull.

We waited until all our door openings were finished with trim before ordering our Hufcor accordion-fold doors, so we could specify actual widths and heights. We installed Style 20 wood-slat units for closure of the entry closet and Murphy bed. A Style 90 vinyl panel closes the wardrobe alcove. Both styles fold compactly into a 5"-wide stack. You can't, of course, mount the track on a suspended ceiling like the Integrid. For the path of the track, you must provide a header—or a solid ceiling panel such as the plywood above our bed. Hanging the doors couldn't be simpler, whether the track that comes with them is wooden or metal (see photos). Hufcor is only one of several folding-door brands. You may prefer Pella or Panelfold.

The pivoting bed frame shown in our photos is Murphy's 4'6" coil-spring recess (CR-54). You supply the mattress, so you

Murphy's coil-spring kit is easy to install. You anchor base assembly with longest screws practical for your floor. Add U-shape mattress brackets to head of frame, then lift frame's pivot pins into slots in base uprights. With mattress in place, hook balance springs, one by one into drilled rails of base and frame.

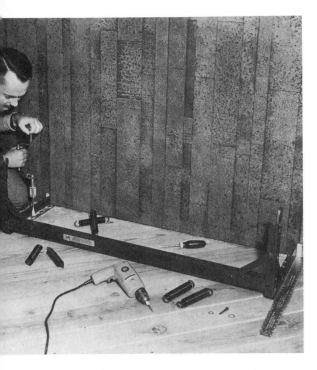

determine the degree of sleeping luxury. I've slept years of weekends on the bed shown and can attest to its comfort. The mattress is held (when bed's vertical) by U-shape brackets at the head end and a buckled strap across the foot. This strap holds the bedding in place (you can even cinch pillows under it) so the bed comes down fully made. As it descends, a rod linkage automatically extends the leg. The lowered bed is sturdier than a standard box spring and mattress since it's anchored at its pivot point.

The only disadvantage to a fold-down bed is that, when the mattress pivots away from the wall, it leaves a gap that prevents your propping a pillow behind you to sit up in bed. We solved this by designing a hinged headboard to mount on the wall just above mattress height. When you lift its free lower edge, a hinged leg drops in back to the limit of its restraint chain and props the upholstered headboard from the wall at an angle that covers the gap and provides comfortable back support.

One caution: Mount the bed's steel-angle base far enough from the wall to leave space behind the pivots for mattress thickness plus folded headboard. Otherwise, the bed can't pivot fully vertical. Use only enough of the balance springs provided in the kit to ease raising and lowering. Hook on too many and the bed's own weight won't keep it seated on the floor.

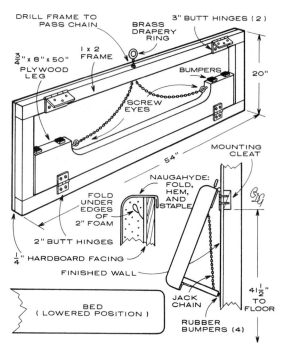

Double-hinged headboard unit consists of ¼″ tempered Masonite on a frame of 1x2s, into which the folding leg unit recesses, controlled by a chain through the frame's top rail. Ring at chain's end limits the leg drop, as in section sketch at right, and also serves as a handle for raising leg to fold the backrest flat against wall (photo above). Padding is 2″ foam cut oversized so long edges can be butt-cemented to face panel (below). Staple on upholstery cover, add hinges.

PRODUCT SOURCES

Armstrong Cork Co., Lancaster, Pa. 17604 (Integrid ceiling and Place 'n Press tile); Hough Mfg., Janesville, Wis. 53545 (Hufcor folding doors); Iron-A-Way Inc., 220 W. Jackson, Morton, Ill. 61550 (recessed ironing center); Masonite Corp., 29 N. Wacker Dr., Chicago, Ill. 60606 (Peg-Board and Valencia pre-finished paneling); Murphy Door Bed Co. Inc., 40 E. 34 St., New York, N.Y. 10016 (upright coil-spring bed frame CR-54); Stanley Works, New Britain, Conn. 06050 (door and partition hardware). Also: Dow Chemical (1½″ Styrofoam for ceiling access panels); Gerber (½″ cork for partition); Uniroyal Coated Fabrics (Naugahyde cover for foam-padded headboard).

11. The Open Kitchen: Ideal for a Leisure Home

You're never isolated from activities while preparing meals; dining counter has fourth stool on work side. Compact 7'x10' plan keeps all within reach, offers floorspace for two standing or one seated. Folding door, left, masks plumbing and stored cleaning gear; it closes against fridge with magnetic catch.

Your home away from home demands a whole new lifestyle, and the last thing you want to do is close the kitchen off from social activities.

We devoted more time to planning this open kitchen for our Lockbox leisure home than any other aspect of the house—and why not? It's the room in which you'll invest the most cash and spend the most time. And since KP's no fun activity, you'll want the kitchen open so that whoever's on duty keeps a piece of the action.

The heart of this scheme is our tiled work counter—at a height to screen the messier tasks from guests seated in the living room, yet a height that permits easy conversation across it. And should guests

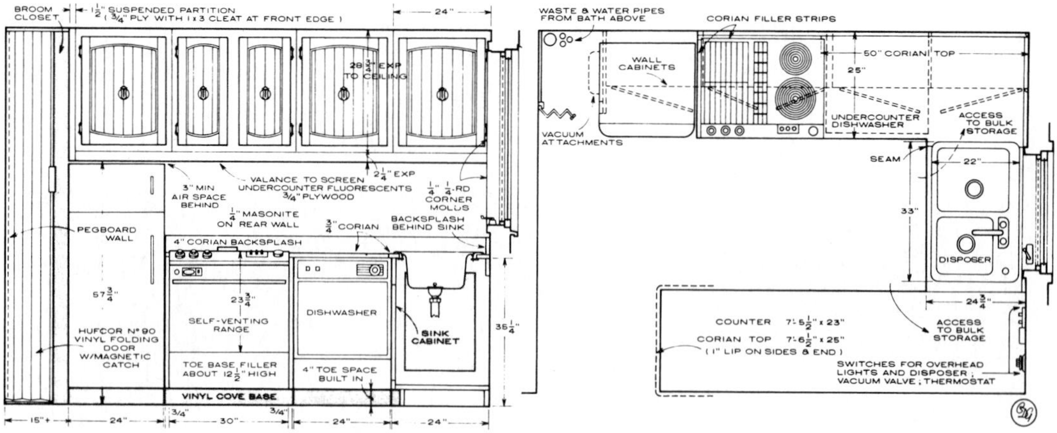
BROOM CLOSET
1½" SUSPENDED PARTITION
(¾" PLY WITH 1 x 3 CLEAT AT FRONT EDGE)
24"
28¾" EXP TO CEILING
2¼" EXP
VALANCE TO SCREEN
UNDERCOUNTER FLUORESCENTS
¾" PLYWOOD
3" MIN AIR SPACE BEHIND
¼" MASONITE ON REAR WALL
¾" CORIAN
¼" ¼-RD CORNER MOLDS
BACKSPLASH BEHIND SINK
PEGBOARD WALL
4" CORIAN BACKSPLASH
57¾"
23¾"
SELF-VENTING RANGE
DISHWASHER
SINK CABINET
35¼"
HUFCOR Nº 90 VINYL FOLDING DOOR W/MAGNETIC CATCH
TOE BASE FILLER ABOUT 12½" HIGH
4" TOE SPACE BUILT IN
VINYL COVE BASE
15"+
24"
¾"
30"
¾"
24"
24"
WASTE & WATER PIPES FROM BATH ABOVE
CORIAN FILLER STRIPS
WALL CABINETS
50" CORIAN TOP
25"
VACUUM ATTACHMENTS
UNDERCOUNTER DISHWASHER
ACCESS TO BULK STORAGE
SEAM
22"
33"
DISPOSER
24¾"
COUNTER 7'-5½" x 23"
CORIAN TOP 7'-6½" x 25"
(1" LIP ON SIDES & END)
ACCESS TO BULK STORAGE
SWITCHES FOR OVERHEAD LIGHTS AND DISPOSER ; VACUUM VALVE ; THERMOSTAT

volunteer to help with dinner, just invite them to pull up a stool. There are so many custom features built into our counter (which doubles as a dining bar) that it's a project all its own. We'll detail it in the next chapter.

For now, let's consider other features that make up an "ideal country kitchen." Concepts of leisure-home living have vastly altered from the days when getting away from it all meant leaving creature comforts behind. The point of owning country property is having time to enjoy it, so you make your home there maintenance-free.

You'll want to include as many labor-saving devices as possible, since they contribute to the leisure time you've built your home to enjoy. A built-in dishwasher is a must (there's no space to store a portable).

It only makes sense to rid yourself of time-consuming cleanups like dishwashing and sweeping. The built-in vacuum system (next page) makes special sense for the Lockbox because you can tuck the power unit under the house in the shed for the aerobic tank. That makes cleaning not only quick but quiet—and free of recirculated dust, since the power unit and its exhaust are out of the house. And there's no heavy machine to lug up and down that spiral stair.

Disposing of garbage is a special problem at remote sites—you usually have to tote out the remains of whatever you carry in. So a sink disposer that lets you feed organic wastes right into your aerobic system (see Chapter 15) will lighten your end-of-weekend load.

Recessed lighting is a feature of our kitchen. Fluorescent fixture set between structural beams over counter (left) has diffuser of W-2447 (⅛") Plexiglas tipped onto ¼-round ledgers (trial fit shown here, before stripping protective paper mask).

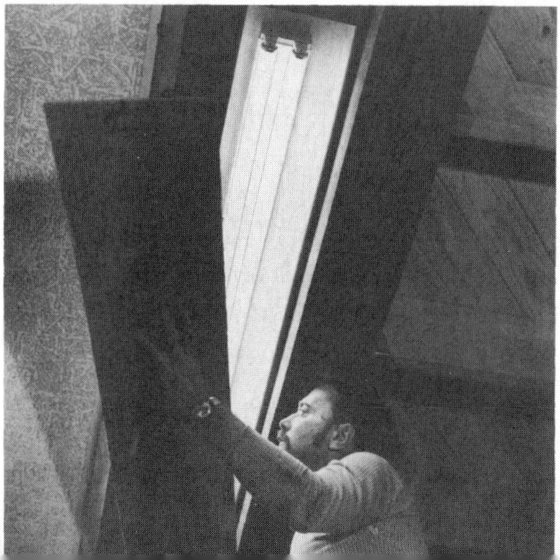

Building a second home from scratch, it's easy to tuck a vacuum system into stud walls before you insulate and close them. System shown here assembles like plumbing from rigid vinyl tubing, elbows, and branch fittings. Wand hose reaches over 25', so we needed only two wall outlets: over kitchen counter (above) and on second floor, in Peg-Board wall of bedroom alcove. Connecting pipe drops through lighting recess between beams, continues on to shed below. Low-voltage wires taped to side turn on power unit when hose is inserted in wall valve (being installed below).

Power unit mounts on wall of shed under house. Bottom part is half-bushel canister that unclips for emptying. Unit exhausts through wall vent (exterior photo).

Accessories for built-in vac include 25' hose and rack for broom closet.

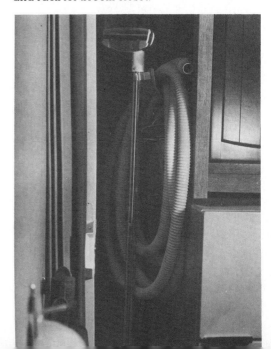

Counter assembly involves only one purchased cabinet—a backless, two-door sink
unit, 36″ wide. To mask gap between it and
dishwasher, order 3″ filler to extend left stile.
Hardboard wall surface above range/dish-
washer counter can be wallpapered horizontally from standard roll (above). Note Corian
backsplash strips at right. Toe filler that closes
gap below range is seen in bottom photo prior
to assembly—as is disposer. Dishwasher hose
connects to latter with kit.

CABINETS

While *assembling* a kitchen, nothing
will lighten your load better than ready-
made cabinets. Expensive, yes—the best
wooden ones qualify as fine furniture,
featuring much hand finishing. But to
construct equivalents at a country site
would be a long chore, and you can't
settle for mere utility in an open kitchen,
with wall cabinets on constant display.

You may prefer to go the knock-down
route, however—both for cost saving and
for easier delivery to a remote site. We
chose to buy Sears top-of-the-line assembled units, as itemized in the chart. They
come with hardboard backs, ready to butt
together with a simple clip system. We
screwed them directly to exposed studs
and joists, then closed in the wall beneath
with ¼″ tempered Masonite. The adjacent
wall was also faced with Masonite, then
all exposed surfaces were papered with
textured vinyl. (Sears no longer catalogs
the exact cabinets or appliances shown,
but equivalents are available.)

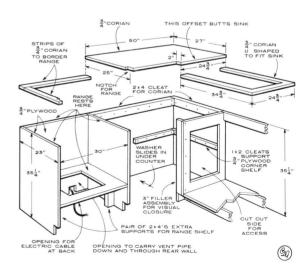

We discarded some old notions about wall-cabinet mounting—for example, that cabinet tops can't be more than 7' from the floor. Butting our cabinets against overhead joists put their tops at about 7'6", but let us tack our ceiling molding right across their top rail, for the neatest closure imaginable; this technique also eliminates any dirt trap above suspended cabinets, without fussing with soffit closure. And, it provides more generous work height between cabinets and countertop: Conventionally, this is 10"; our space is twice that. As our helpful guest demonstrates in a photo, this wall space is wide enough to let you run a patternless wallpaper strip horizontally, eliminating vertical seams.

Careful positioning of the adjustable shelves keeps contents of these lifted cabinets within normal reach. As a final

After countertop slabs and sink are installed, set 4"-wide backsplash strips into beads of epoxy run along wall. Areas of wallcovering have been removed for better adhesion.

touch, we attached a valance strip of ¾" plywood (covered with matching wallpaper) beneath the cabinets to mask the fluorescent fixtures we'd mounted on their recessed bottoms.

To match raw moldings and the frame of the 2'x3' wood casement window to the prefinished cabinets, try two coats of Minwax's No. 224 plus a buff coat of their Antique Oil Finish.

Appliance (or cabinet)	Source
Convertible-cooktop drop-in range/grill/oven with accessories (rotisserie, shish kebab, deep-fat frier, griddle) + 5" wall cap	Jenn-Air Corp., 3035 Shadeland, Indianapolis, Ind. 46226
2-basin steel sink w/dual-control faucet and rinser ½-hp disposer Undercounter dishwasher 12-cu.-ft. refrigerator-freezer 30-gal. dual upright water heater† Brass relief valve Built-in vacuum cleaner Attachments + 25-ft. hose* Cabinets: 24" wall, right-hinged door ⎫ 24" wall, left-hinged door (2) ⎬ 30" tall 30" wall, two-door ⎭ 36" sink-base, two-door 3" base filler 30" toe filler	Sears, Roebuck & Co. (retail stores or catalog)

Stools are bentwood imports,
upholstered to order,
from Tip Top Equipment, Inc.,
220 Bowery, New York, N.Y. 10012.
Folding closet door from Hough Mfg. Corp.,
Janesville, Wis. 53545.
† Located next to upstairs bathroom.
* Wall valve assemblies and vinyl tubing extra

A final note on the neat effect of our cabinet assembly: Since we chose a self-venting range and a "shorty" refrigerator, we could use full-height cabinets above them. We didn't have to "notch up" for an exhaust hood or freezer bonnet.

We ignored the triangular floorplan rule which places stove, sink, and fridge at the points of a fat triangle, usually putting stove and fridge on opposite walls. Since this isn't practical in our open plan, we snugged them side-by-side. This unorthodox proximity calls for a heat guard when you use the grill for elevated cooking (see photos).

THE RANGE

Ron Nelson, co-builder of the Lockbox, and a gourmet cook by avocation—tells why we chose the Jenn-Air range. "Being used to gas, I was wary of an electric range, though it's the only practical choice for remote sites. The Jenn-Air over-came my doubts. It heats up rapidly and adjusts quickly. Surface venting, with nine times the capture velocity of an overhead hood, is a special boon to an open-plan kitchen, where cooking odors, grease, and heat would otherwise spread through the house. The countertop elements, with 12 heat settings, let you run the gamut from instant omelette to slow-simmering stew. The oven, large enough for a standard roasting pan, is reliable in temperature. But it's the Char-Flavor Grill and its four easily installed accessories that adapt the range to flexible country dining; two of the units provide year-round outdoor-cooking fun inside, while the effective venting system keeps the house free of odors, smoke, and heat. The grill produces delicious steaks—but be sure to trim off excess fat (the venting once proved inadequate with untrimmed steaks; drippings produced flash flame and clouds of smoke). Fowl and roasts on the rotisseries are crisp outside, juicy in.

Surface vent eliminates need for hood and is easier to install: Just duct blower to Jenn-Air's wall cap (photo next page)—sabersaw hole through siding to pass sleeve. Photo and diagram show how steam and smoke are sucked out before they can spread moisture, grease throughout house.

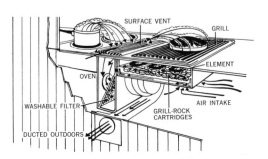

The shish kebab unit, which clips into the same spit motor, tends to dry out meats, so marination is advisable. The no-stick griddle is ideal for a Lockbox breakfast; the cook just pivots on the counter stool to flip a flapjack. The deep-fryer makes a handy spaghetti pot (you drop in the pasta full-length). As a fryer it's effective but requires at least 1½ qts. of oil, and you must watch the temperature. The range is easy to clean (don't use abrasive cleansers): Grill's flavor cartridges and metal-mesh filter go in dishwasher; a disposable jar collects grease that drains from grill; the continuous-clean oven does most of that chore itself. Unorthodox proximity of range and fridge calls for reflective-asbestos heat guard when you use the left-side grill unit for elevated cooking."

Later models of this range offer a plug-in cartridge to convert the grill side into another pair of conventional burners.

THE COUNTERTOP

The countertop isn't marble, but Corian must still be rated a luxury; it's consistent with the Lockbox philosophy that low maintenance is worth paying extra for in a leisure home. Corian resists food stains and scorching, wipes clean with a damp cloth, and—since it's a solid panel, with the subtle pattern running clear through—lets you polish scratches with an abrasive cleanser or fine sandpaper.

One 30"x98" sheet, the smallest size offered at most building supply houses, is enough for our L-shaped counter and backsplash pieces. (Corian requirements for the dining divider are detailed in the next chapter. The subtle veining is often available in a choice of several colors.) Since our spans are unsupported, we used the ¾" thickness throughout.*

Attaching a Corian countertop is a simple matter of laying the panel into beads of adhesive run along the top edges of the cabinet sides and wall cleats (most construction or panel adhesives will do). The best way to treat edge joints is to fill the cracks with a white epoxy after all pieces are anchored in place. For a neat job, flank crack with strips of masking tape.

To avoid multiple joints, we cut a U-shaped surround for our stainless steel sink. We did our cutting with a portable circular saw equipped with a carbide blade. To avoid chipout, support the Corian on a scrap panel, with the blade set to cut about ⅛" into the scrap. Finish corner cuts with a metal-cutting blade in a saber saw.

---

* A less expensive ½" thickness can be substituted, but we'd recommend center braces across the spans. For further saving, you could buy ¼"-thick Corian, laminate it to ½" ply or particleboard, and glue on edge strips.

If Corian suppliers aren't listed in your Yellow Pages, write Du Pont's Corian Division, Wilmington, Del. 19898, for local dealers.

12. Build a Dining Divider for the Open Kitchen

Corian-topped dining counter divides the open kitchen from the living room. Three pull-out shelves provide additional surface space. Wine-and-liquor rack tucks into kneewell where hostess is seated. You pull it forward (top right) for access to bar service, then roll it back into recess for comfortable stool perch, as in lower photo.

Any resemblance between our dining counter and a snack bar is coincidental. With this ingenious storage built-in dividing your open kitchen from the living room, you'll need no dining table.

Our notion in designing this unit for leisure homes is that many of your meals will be served outdoors on deck or patio (using stack snackers like those for which we give plans at the end of this chapter). And any *indoor* meals should be kept as convenient to the kitchen as possible to minimize the serving and cleanup fuss.

This elegant counter boasts three pull-out dining shelves of Corian—to match the spacious top. Add four comfortable stools, and it's an ideal solution for informal breakfasts, cocktail snacks, and full dinners for two couples.

There's even more action on the kitchen side of the counter. Five drawers organize utensil storage, and a sliding rack puts everything for bar service at your fingertips. Forming a U with the sink and range counters, the divider's an ideal ''workbench'' to perch behind for preparing food without missing any social activity.

Though our counter is faced with glazed tile from Seville and topped with ¾'' Corian, a man-made marble from Du Pont, these are luxuries for which there are economical alternatives: Plastic laminate could be substituted for both, or the facing could be patterned vinyl floor tile.

If you go the ceramic-tile route, choose a square-edge pattern (no grouting) and apply to the MDO face with Scotchgrip Mastic adhesive—about $3 per caulking-gun cartridge. (Actually, I used 3M's EC-959 industrial adhesive, but 3M tells me their Scotchgrip is the general-market equivalent.)

We strongly recommend ready-made drawers. They have four big advantages for a leisure-home project: They simplify (and speed up) construction; they discourage those rodent invaders you're likely to encounter at a country site; they're designed for fast, easy cleanup; and they won't give you the swell-and-stick or mildew problems that can plague an often-closed-up leisure house.

This counter is designed to serve for the life of the house. For the ¾'' plywood, we recommend MDO two-sides (medium-density overlaid on both faces). Not only do the resin-impregnated cellulose fibers fused to the plywood provide a superior paint base, eliminating problems with wild grain and checking, but MDO is made with higher grade core material, so you avoid some common plywood's problem of large voids and poorly bonded

Ready-made drawers of molded plastic simplify construction, offer varied storage with other three compartments.

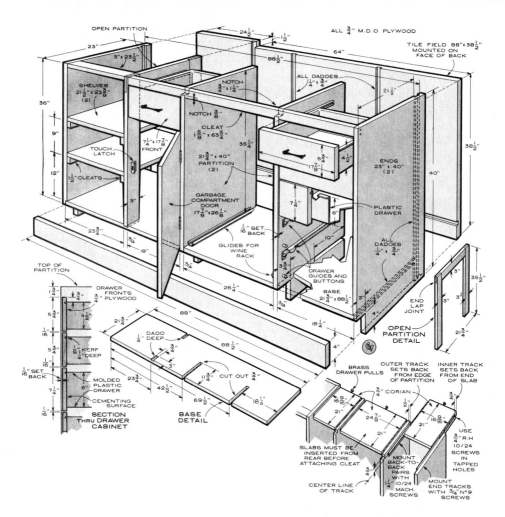

OPEN PARTITION
23"
3" x 23½"
ALL ¾" M.D.O. PLYWOOD
24½"
1½"
88½"
64"
TILE FIELD 88" x 38½"
MOUNTED ON
FACE OF BACK
SHELVES
21½" x 23⅜"
(2)
36"
9"
TOUCH
LATCH
12"
1½" CLEATS
NOTCH
¾" x 1¼"
ALL DADOES
¼" x ¾"
21½"
NOTCH ⅜"
CLEAT
1⅝" x 63¾"
7¼" x 17⅞"
FRONT
35¼"
5¾"
4½"
17⅞"
21¾" x 40"
PARTITION
(2)
38½"
ENDS
23" x 40"
(2)
40"
GARBAGE
COMPARTMENT
DOOR
17⅝" x 26⅞"
3"
7¼"
6"
PLASTIC
DRAWER
23¾"
3¾"
1¹⁄₁₆" SET
BACK
GLIDES FOR
WINE
RACK
18"
3¾"
ALL
DADOES
¼" x ¾"
26¼"
3¾"
3¾"
10"
DRAWER
GUIDES AND
BUTTONS
BASE
21½" x 88½"
3"
35½"
3"
3¾"
18¼"
4"
END
LAP
JOINT
21¾"
3"
3"
OPEN
PARTITION
DETAIL

TOP OF
PARTITION
1¾"
¾"
5¾"
¹⁄₁₆"
4½"
5¾"
¹⁄₁₆"
¹⁄₁₆" SET
BACK
7¼"
¹⁄₁₆"
DRAWER
FRONTS
¾"
PLYWOOD
⅛" KERF
¾" DEEP
MOLDED
PLASTIC
DRAWER
6"
CEMENTING
SURFACE
SECTION
THRU DRAWER
CABINET
88"
21¾"
DADO
¼"
DEEP
¾"
3"
88½"
23¾"
42½"
3"
11¾"
69½"
CUT OUT ¾"
18¼"
BASE
DETAIL

BRASS
DRAWER PULLS
OUTER TRACK
SETS BACK
FROM EDGE
OF PARTITION
INNER TRACK
SETS BACK
FROM END
OF SLAB
⁹⁄₁₆"
¾" CORIAN
2¼"
24⅞"
21"
21"
¾"
1½"
2¼"
2⁹⁄₁₆"
21"
USE
¾" R.H
10/24
SCREWS
IN
TAPPED
HOLES
SLABS MUST BE
INSERTED FROM
REAR BEFORE
ATTACHING CLEAT
CENTER LINE
OF TRACK
MOUNT
BACK-TO-
BACK
PAIRS
WITH
1¼" 10/24
MACH.
SCREWS
¾"
MOUNT
END TRACKS
WITH ¾" N°9
SCREWS

Dining slides—three Corian slabs of sizes given in detail sketch, above right—are suspended between metal tracks.

plies. We didn't have to give any special treatment to our cut edges before priming.

Because of the sizes of the panels involved, this is a project for portable power tools. Use a fine-tooth plywood blade in your circular saw and take time to position all clamped saw guides for accurate cuts. This project has many moving parts; it must be square.

Rather than start right off with a router to cut the dadoes, outline them first with saw kerfs. This avoids splintering or raised edges.

You'll note we recessed the plastic drawer guides by routing their outlines

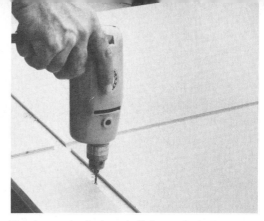

To align pilot holes, drill through dadoes; assemble parts, then drill into mating edges from other side.

Border cuts—parallel kerfs ¼″ deep—assure clean dadoes, top. Clamped guides keep router within these kerfs, lower photo.

Trial-fit two identical partitions into base slots and back dadoes. Then remove to mount drawer guides.

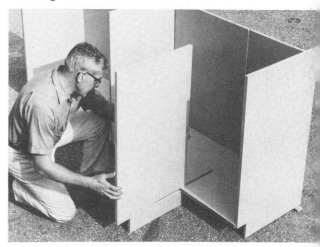

into the inner faces of the partitions. This is optional, since the guides are intended for flush mounting. Note *all* recesses—including sockets for dowels and drawer buttons—are ¼″ deep.

That pair of plastic buttons near the front of each drawer adds correct tension and prevents racking. If you recess the side guides, you must drill sockets to recess these buttons to match. If you *don't* recess, increase the width of both drawer bays to 18½″—which adds an inch to the overall counter length. As shown, the assembly will measure 23″x89½″; the Corian top, with a 1″ lip on sides and end, must be 25″x90½″.

Note button dimensions are all from top edge. Buttons and guides needn't be recessed, as here; they can mount flush.

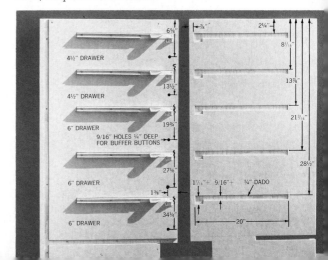

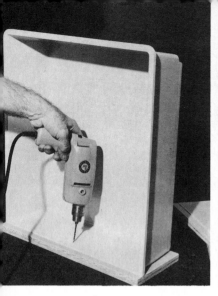

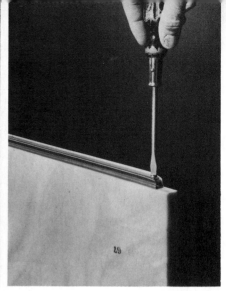

One-piece molded drawers need plywood faces, attached by screws (as here) or with contact cement.

Slice through center of seven 2″ holes to form pair of strips to cradle wine bottles, as seen in layout of rack parts, right.

Drill and tap holes in edge of Corian slabs (center photo) for mounting inner track with RH screws (above).

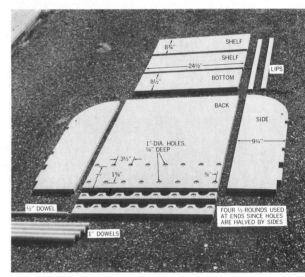

Butt-assemble bar rack with glue and nails. Sides, shelves, and lips are identical pairs. Drill cut-apart strips and back panel for dowel sockets, spacing as shown. Since end holes are halved by sides, glue half-rounds in place, here. Strips and lips set into notches in edges of sides. Set-in bottom could be omitted; assembly is sturdy without it.

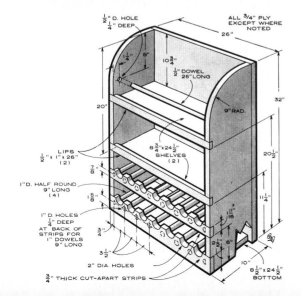

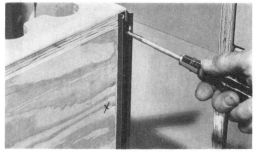

Same type of track used for dining slabs moves wine rack in and out. But inner slide must be shortened as pointed out in top photo, to match 10″ rack depth before it's attached to base (lower photo) with limit-stop nicks to rear.

RETRACTABLE DINING SLABS

These are best cut from a Corian panel with a guided saber saw, using a 10- to 14-tooth metal-cutting blade. Sand the edges starting with 80 grit and working to 220.

Both these slabs and the wine rack call for sliding hardware that looks neat when exposed. We chose HDI Model 703 slides, which consist of a U-shaped inner track riding on four ball bearings contained in a stationary outer section. These outer tracks are marked to indicate the front. Mount them on the counter partitions with front ends toward the tile face.

Anchor the countertop by setting the Corian slab into a bead of paneling adhesive applied to all top edges of the assembly.

Track-mounting the wine rack is tricky: Install the "front" of each outer section toward the rear of the bay. After cutting each inner track back to 10″, mount with its nicked end to the rear of the rack.

Ends of counter project to create recessed field for tile facing. Here, bead of 3M adhesive is quickly run around edge of rear face with air gun, but same cartridges fit standard caulking gun. Start with bottom row, press each tile in place against counter face.

Door has garbage rack on back. Corner storage shelves are fine for range accessories like this deep-fry unit.

MATERIALS LIST
3½ panels ¾″ MDO plywood (4′x8′)
½″ and 1″ dowels, 1″ half-round
1 pc. ¾″ Corian, 21″x60″ (for slides)
1 pc. ¾″ Corian, 25″x7′6½″ (for top)
2 molded drawers (4½″) w/side guides
4 molded drawers (6″) w/side guides from Amos
Molded Plastics, 600 S. Kyle St., Edinburg, Ind. 46124
4 pr. HDI drawer slides (20″) from Hardware
Designers Inc., Mt. Kisco, N.Y. 10549
Other hardware: 1 pr. hinges, 1 touch latch, 6 brass
drawer pulls, 3 brass knobs (slides)
Screws: 1½″ #10 FH for counter assembly; ¾″-10/24
to attach track to Corian; ¾″ #9 and 1¼″-10/24 for
track, as shown in detail
56 tiles, ½″ thick, 5½″x11″ (or equivalent)
Glue, paint

13. Radiant Panel: Versatile Install-Yourself Heat

Only electric-panel heat offers this kind of flexibility: During winter, heaters valance-mount on beams between windows (via easily-built frames detailed next page); but during summer (inset) they're unplugged, stored for uncluttered view.

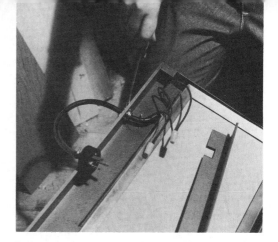

Galvanized, painted-steel backpan is bolted right through frame assembly; heat panel is face-down, foreground.

Special 240v plug is attached through knock-out and connector. Two screws detach race-way cover for wiring access.

Whether you're building from scratch or winterizing an existing leisure home, a relatively unfamiliar type of electric heat can keep you cozy when the snows fall.

Radiant panel—also called infrared, long-wave, or glass heat—has been around some for years, but has never received the promotion it deserves—and has recently shared the stigma attached to electric heat in general. Yet where leisure homes are concerned it has several advantages.

For a do-it-yourself installation (where codes permit) it's about as simple as you can get. Panel heaters are wired for 240 volts with ordinary No. 12 three-wire romex. As shown in color on our floorplans, up to three heaters can be wired to one thermostat, located across the room.

The choice of any electric heat system depends on a couple of factors. Full in-

sulation is essential*—as is double or triple glazing, preferably in wood frames. Electric heat is most efficient where rooms are stacked under a relatively limited roof area, rather than sprawled out in one-story ranch or split-level designs. So our cube-shaped Lockbox (with a second-floor area floating above the first) was a prime candidate. Like most leisure homes, it's snugly designed, with no space to spare for ductwork—or a furnace, for that matter. Furnace-fed heat systems (whether distribution is by air or water) are expensive and cumbersome to install at remote sites.

* A good review of insulation requirements is included in "Home Heating and Cooling with Electricity," a 12-page booklet published by Small Homes Council, University of Illinois, One East Saint Mary's Rd., Champaign, Ill. 61820. Send 25¢ for Tech. Note 10. Typically, it doesn't include radiant panel in its discussion of electric heating systems.

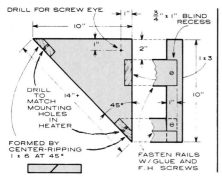

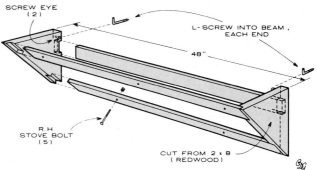

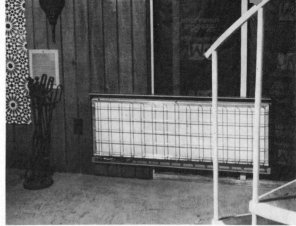

Mounting options are many: since backpans can screw directly to wall surface, heaters can lap pocket of sliding door (top left and floorplan, next page). Or, screw pan to studs and cut in thicker wall paneling around it (T1-11 has been partially installed, top right). Under window is ideal mount (bottom left). Final photo: pumphouse heater, set at 45 degrees to prevent storage tank freeze-up.

So we went the electric route. But we wanted something other than conventional resistance heaters, such as baseboard units. And ceiling cable wasn't feasible, since our downstairs ceiling is really the exposed joists and underside of the flooring above.

When we made our decision, energy conservation wasn't yet a major issue. But shortly after we got our 240-volt line run to our entry box, the local power company abandoned the special rate offered to new homes to encourage electric heating. We qualified, but you're unlikely, these days, to find a special rate still offered; so you've got a decision to make.

Personally, I doubt it can be made on the basis of conservation. Your alternate heat sources—oil and natural gas—will be in increasingly short supply, with no guarantees that new customers (particularly those in remote areas) can get prompt delivery. Conversely, there can be little doubt that this nation *must* continue to satisfy its electrical needs, whatever new generating methods must be employed. The fossil-fuel crunch is here to stay, but a U.S. with a chronic shortage of electricity is unthinkable: we'd grind to a halt.

And the advantages of electric heat are undeniable—it's:

- Maintenance-free (set, forget).
- Clean, safe (no combustion).
- Zone-controlled (independent thermostat in each room).
- Draft-free, noiseless (no fan).
- Free of fuel delivery and storage problems.

The additional claim is often made that electric heat is 100% efficient—despite the equally familiar (and valid) rejoinder that *generating* it at the power plant is often neither efficient nor clean. Practically speaking, at a country site, you're concerned with *local* pollution. The plant is far away and better able than a homeowner to deal with the problem of increasing fuel efficiency—and doing it cleanly.

In short, I can think of only two *dis*advantages to electric heat: You don't have the option of central air conditioning that a ductwork heating system offers (but few leisure homes are in climate areas that need artificial cooling; those that are should be small enough for window units to handle). And, of course, there's the cost factor.

Initial installation costs are comparable with other heating systems—will even run you *less* if you do your own wiring. And with flame-fuel costs soaring, your end-of-winter electric heat bill shouldn't look bad by comparison—especially if your local utility still offers any special rate.

A point could be made that power companies with long-range vision should dis-

A dozen radiant panels heat the Lockbox

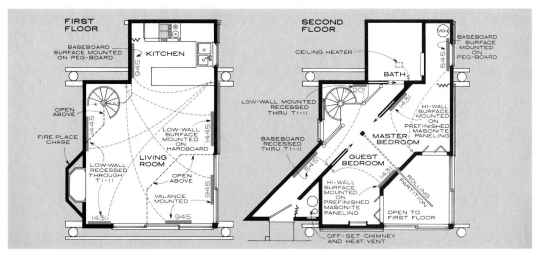

GLASSHEAT ELECTRIC UNITS (ALL 240-volt)
(from Continental Radiant Glass Heating Corp.,
215 B Central Ave., East Farmingdale, N.Y. 11735)

Model	Wattage	BTU	Quantity	Location	Size and type	Price per unit
1445	1500	5150	2	Living room	18¾¾¾″ x 47½″ wall	$179.16
1431	1000	3414	3	Living room, bedrooms	18⅞″ x 33½″ wall	$147.05
945	1000	3414	3	Kitchen, plus pair angled over windows of living room	13¾″ x 47½″ wall	$147.05
1520	625	2140	2*	Upper stairwell, aerobic shed	19¾″ x 22½″ wall	$134.80
545	650	2217	2	Entry hall, wardrobe	6¾″ x 48″ baseboard	$104.35

plus six double-line-break thermostats @ $21.13
*A third 1520 (but with built-in thermostat) was wall-mounted in pumphouse; not shown on floorplans—see photo.

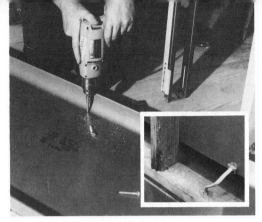

Heavy-gauge backpan is best drilled with stepped Unibit for lagscrew mounting to studs. Wiring (inset) is simple.

Double-pole thermostat has four screw terminals for wiring. Note outlet boxes face opposite sides of this partition.

courage central air conditioning before electric heat. Power-drain statistics indicate that any electrical facility that beefs up its capacity to handle summer load should have more than ample power for customers' electric-heating needs. It often takes double the amount of energy to cool a house, since air conditioners—unlike heaters—run continuously.

Manufacturers of radiant-heat units claim 20% to 40% lower kilowatt-hour usage than more familiar types of resistance heaters. I've seen documentation from utility companies who've metered identical houses equipped with alternate systems; the figures are persuasive.

Radiant panels—since they stay relatively cool—offer considerable versatility in mounting. They can be screwed directly to studs, with the finish wall fitted around them, or simply surface-mounted. We installed ours both ways—recessed into our ⅝" T1–11 (rigid enough to require no framing or edge nailing around the cutout), and surface-mounted on our ¼" prefinished Masonite paneling.

A unique bonus of a panel system is demonstrated by the valance-mount between our stacked "patio" doors. Continental Glassheat's experts tried to persuade us to mount the panels at floor level below this expanse of glass, but we refused to block any of our floor-to-16' ceiling window area. Instead, we devised detachable valances for the beams *between* the windows, and wired two 240-volt outlets under the heater positions. Standing in this corner to bask in the heat is especially pleasant, since it feels like sunshine, even on a frozen gray day.

Below-window mounting is fine, but less vital than it is with other electric heaters, where a blanket of air must be heated as it moves up across the glass. Radiant panels can go above, or across the room from, windows, since they heat directly, via broadcast rays, not by convection currents. (The heat plates are either pebbled glass or porcelainized sheetmetal, with a conductor fused on back. After seven years' use, we can recommend only the glass. Quality control is apparently harder to maintain in manufacturing the sheetmetal units. We've had to replace a half-dozen of them with glass panels, over the years. They simply burned out, like a light bulb. Continental sells all its units with a five-year warranty.)

There may even be bonus health benefits from radiant-panel heat: The penetrating infra-red rays are similar to those used to treat arthritis and muscle ailments. And a draftless, non-drying heat should mean fewer winter colds.

14. Freeze-Proof Waterline You Don't Have to Bury Below Frost

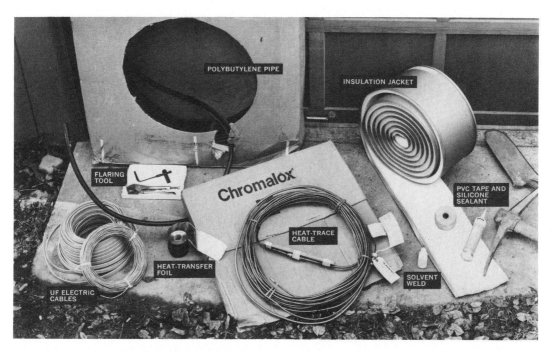

POLYBUTYLENE PIPE

INSULATION JACKET

FLARING TOOL

Chromalox

PVC TAPE AND SILICONE SEALANT

HEAT-TRACE CABLE

HEAT-TRANSFER FOIL

SOLVENT WELD

UF ELECTRIC CABLES

All ingredients—except thermostat and flare connectors—are displayed at pump house before installation. Rolls of wire, far left, are ca-bles (for a post lamp and intercom) also buried in waterline's shallow trench (code minimum: 18″ deep).

If you wrestled with an iced-up waterline last winter—or denied yourself weekend use of your leisure home because you'd drained your buried supply line and didn't dare risk reactivating it at freezing temperatures—you'll greet the title of this chapter with skepticism.

You've always heard that outdoor waterlines had to be run below frostline—and that when the mercury *really* plunges even *that's* no guarantee against freeze-ups—right?

Well, forget all that. For the Lockbox, we combined various aspects of industrial technology in a way nobody's ever proposed for residential use, and came up with a waterline that defies that hoary old gent with icicle fangs—yet spares you the

1. Working a few feet at a time, wrap pipe with heat-transfer foil, lapping edges ½". As you go, straighten cable from coil and tape it to pipe.

2. Rewrap assembly with second layer of foil— this time shiny side in—taping every 16". Cable is one continuous length, so coil moves with you.

3. Once you've completed 25', apply insulation jacket, shown rolled in photo on previous page. Uncoil it along line, and slip underneath. Here, author closes built-in snap seam by pinching with left hand, pressing with right thumb. Spot-anchor, every 16", with 2" plastic tape. Cross seam, when next length is butted against this one, is sealed with silicone, then wrapped with waterproof tape.

chore of major excavation (the just-below-surface burial is merely to protect the line from "traffic"). We developed the line for our famous home in the mountains of northern Pennsylvania, but the system is equally appropriate for any rugged leisure-home site. As demand for such sites pushes them ever farther into the wilderness, the problems of private water and waste systems become more acute. The soil of these areas usually has poor percolation, and today's sanitary requirements often state that a potable water source must be at least 100' from the leach field of your waste system. That usually means a long run across rocky, wooded terrain—especially if you've perched your house (as we did) on a site that's inaccessible to a drilling rig.

If your experience is anything like ours, you'll find local workmen are shrewd enough to give a wide berth to waterline installation—which leaves *you* to dig that long, 4'-deep trench through boulders and critical roots, disrupting a site you chose, in the first place, for a beauty you want to preserve. The problems are so extreme they defeat most homeowners before they start—and don't expect much help from manufacturers (see box: "The Fight to Find the Answer").

We've combined several fairly new products into a system that lets you snake a continuous-length flexible waterpipe around boulders and under roots, in a shallow trench. The secret is a line heat-traced with a thermostat-controlled cable to keep the water temperature just above freezing. Our system would be as effective at 40 below as it is at 30 above, and the energy drain to heat a long run isn't great because the line is wrapped in the best insulating material yet devised: polyurethane.

4. Seal snap seam with solvent weld, squeezing bottle as you run nozzle along seam. Water-thin solvent flows ahead under those tape anchors.

5. Plant the line by feeding it into shallow trench. Flexibility lets you snake it under roots and around big boulders. This is first 25' section.

6. At house end of line, riser gets same treatment—except that copper tubing needs no heat-transfer wraps. Cable is taped to one side of riser, capillary from thermostat to other (it's mounted on floor joist, off left). Wrap jacket around, solvent-weld snap seam. Entry box has hinged-door, open above for draining hot and cold house lines after winter visit.

That insulation jacket, called Thermazip, may be the one element you'll find hardest to get. It's designed for industrial plants, and the manufacturer doesn't court the consumer market. It's worth a bit of extra effort, since I know of no good alternative. We chose Thermazip 275, with an inch-thick layer of 1.5-lb.-density foam laminated to a buryable PVC hide that features a built-in snap-closure system. (Thermazip is made in other combinations, including fiberglass inside an aluminum skin.)

The heat-trace cable must be custom-ordered for your line length. We needed a 150' hot section to trace a line down from our well head and up a riser to the entry box beneath our kitchen floor. The

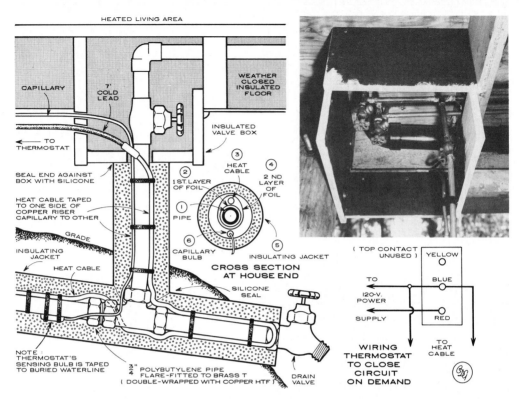

Buried joint of waterline and riser consists of brass T with flared connector at one end, other threaded for drain nipple. Photo inset shows valve box before closure and insulating. Wire thermostat as shown, set between 40° and 45°.

cable consists of twin resistance wires suspended in mineral insulation that's densely compacted within copper tubing. Brazed onto this hot length is a 7' cold lead (also copper-sheathed) that runs to the 120-volt thermostat. It's a rugged cable, but use care in its installation because if the copper sheath is punctured, the cable is ruined.

The combination of this cable and insulation is so effective that the choice of our waterpipe became critical. It had to withstand heat, yet be flexible enough to snake through our trench and to keep the entire run free of joints or connections. The cost of copper tubing is prohibitive, so we went in search of a plastic. The common waterline plastic, polyethylene,

can't be used because it goes flabby when heated. Other types—developed for indoor hot-water lines—can't be used underground; still others come only in rigid lengths.

We finally came up with the ideal water service tubing for this job: polybutylene. The manufacturer of our cable specified a pipe that could withstand 140°; polybutylene is rated to 180°. Only one hitch: It won't solvent-weld, so it must be installed with mechanical fittings. Since we had only the two end connections to make (uphill at our pumphouse and below at the entry riser) this was no drawback. We rented a cold-flaring tool.

You insert its knurled body in the square-cut end of the pipe (after inserting the pipe through your fitting's threaded collar), clamp with the special wrench provided, then just crank a handle that lowers a flaring wedge.

Once you've assembled the line as shown in our photos, just feed it into a shallow trench. Thermazip's slick PVC jacket makes it easy to slide the assembly under big roots. It may be best to work both ways from the middle of your trench, moving 25' sections.

Two cautions, though. When feeding loops of the assembly into the trench, try to avoid curving the core pipe against its natural coil. (It's not easy to gauge, once you've stiffened it with heat cable and bulked it up with insulation.)

This will spare you our disheartening experience: After a month's weekends of labor, trenching and assembling our line, when we completed the installation and opened our bottom valve, nothing came out but a gasp of air! After probing from both ends with an electrician's snake, we found an obstruction near the bottom end. When we cut it out, we discovered a minor manufacturing defect in the pipe: a small flat on one side. We'd looped the assembly back to feed it under a root, and the curve had been against the pipe's natural coil; the wall had snapped shut at this flat. Some clay in the line had washed down and packed above that kink to complete the seal. Not a drop of water could pass, despite the 40 lbs. of pump pressure (plus gravity feed) behind it. To avoid this, check your polybutylene as you wrap it; and be sure to cap the ends before you feed them into the trench.

The other caution: Our bottom valve is, of course, to drain the line when it's not in use. There's no reason to waste electricity if you close the house during the winter. But be sure to kill the thermostat circuit before you drain, so you won't be baking an empty pipe.

Backfill? Any soil is okay, as long as you remove sharp rocks that could puncture the insulation jacket. (That foam wrap protects your pipe and cable from impact even better than conventional burial.) Since soil at our site is minimal, we bought a load of sand to bed the line, and sealed it from washout with several inches of what little clay our trench yielded.

Now, about costs: My cost-analysis box reflects prices when this article was first published, in 1974. These were already considerably higher than they were when we ordered our materials six months earlier, and they've gone higher still as raw materials continue to be scarce. The cost of copper, for example, shot the price of the heat-transfer foil from $30 (quoted us in August) to $48 by February. Our heat-trace cable—catalog number MIE (R14/2C–7) (19EB2–150), 6.5 amps, 750 watts (five watts per foot)—soared from $132 to $168. They're both higher by now.

If you're planning a similar installation in the future, you'd be wise to order your materials now and store them. Plastics are going up, too, affecting both the insulation and the pipe—ironically, the cheapest element in the line, and the only one that performs all year.

And does our system work? Would we trumpet a fizzle? We've now enjoyed seven winters' use of this assembly. Even with that minimal backfill (in some spots, less than 6″ atop the line) water continues to flow on demand at 20 below—even when pipes inside the insulated walls of our heated house have frozen up!

The fight to find the answer

Since most aspects of our Lockbox leisure house were innovative, our series involved a lot of ground-breaking; yet no other area of my research was as frustrating as the months of letters, telegrams and phone calls required to bring this chapter on a freeze-proof waterline to fruition. Initially, I mailed out two dozen identical query packets, soliciting expert advice on a project for publication. To make the problem clear, I enclosed photos of our rocky, wooded site, plus the diagram below. It was evident from our scattered replies that manufacturers serving this industry have established no

dialogs with one another, so it would be pulling teeth to get a maker from one field—pipe, heat cable, insulation—to work with a company from another. More surprising was a general resistance to do-it-yourself. I wanted plastic pipe, but the big boys in that field—Cresline and Nibco—declined advice, as did the Plastics Pipe Institute. Some makers of heat tape wanted no part of the scheme; other contacts advised me flatly to bury our line well below frost, though I'd made it clear that the whole point of the project was to avoid just that. The Nat'l. Water Well Assn. could only propose a continuous flow into a dry well (running water won't freeze)—hardly the advance in waterline technology we'd hoped to inspire, and rather hard on a submersible pump.

I got neurotic enough to suspect a conspiracy: Maybe plumbers pressure manufacturers (and their associations) to discourage progressive techniques—especially by non-pros? Yet, where leisure homes are concerned, this isn't even self-serving. Pros aren't interested in (or available for) remote-site installations.

At any rate, I'd like to think my grim persistence helped open up this whole field to DIYers, because in the last few years many manufacturers have created whole lines of install-yourself plumbing components, with thorough instructions to encourage the homeowner to tackle virtually any waterline job. All this is a particular boon to the leisure home builder; with the new plastic systems, installing home plumbing is a cinch.

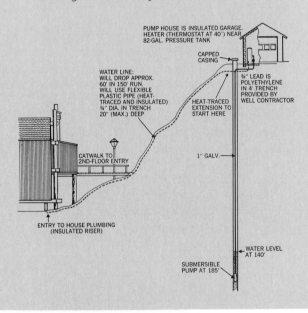

PUMP HOUSE IS INSULATED GARAGE.
HEATER (THERMOSTAT AT 40°) NEAR
82-GAL. PRESSURE TANK

CAPPED CASING

WATER LINE:
WILL DROP APPROX.
60' IN 150' RUN.
WILL USE FLEXIBLE
PLASTIC PIPE (HEAT-
TRACED AND INSULATED)
¾" DIA. IN TRENCH
20" (MAX.) DEEP

¾" LEAD IS
POLYETHYLENE
IN 4' TRENCH
PROVIDED BY
WELL CONTRACTOR

HEAT-TRACED
EXTENSION TO
START HERE

CATWALK TO
2ND-FLOOR ENTRY

1" GALV.

ENTRY TO HOUSE PLUMBING
(INSULATED RISER)

WATER LEVEL
AT 140'

SUBMERSIBLE
PUMP AT 185'

MATERIALS

Innovation doesn't come cheap—or easy. This is what materials cost in 1974. Write manufacturers for sources nearest you. **Polybutylene pipe**—Clow Corp., Box 516, Bensenville, Ill. 60106: ¾" SDR 13.5, 160 psi, 18¢ to 25¢ per ft., depending on quantity; minimum packaging is 500 ft., but dealer may offer cut length. **Heat cable and thermostat**—Chromalox Comfort Conditioning Div., Emerson Electric Co.,

8100 Florissant Ave., St. Louis, Mo. 63136: MIE cable, approx. $1.25 per ft. (proportionately higher for lengths under 50'); roll of HTF-500, $48; thermostat w/capillary bulb, $65. **Insulation jacket**—Accessible Products Co., 1350 E. 8th St., Tempe, Ariz. 85281: Thermazip 275 G 1", $32 per 25' roll; 2" tape and 12-oz. silicone sealant, $5 ea.; 2-oz. bottles solvent weld, 60¢ ea. We did our 150' line with one each of these.

Flow control vs. heat trace

When our water-line story first appeared in *Popular Science*, it elicited a heavy response from readers—many of whom shared their own solutions to a similar problem. Several voted for a system that empties the line when water isn't flowing, avoiding all need for heat. One expert—John Andrews of Lake Region Services, Penn Yan; N.Y. 14527—revised our sketch to show how he'd have solved our problem. The solenoid valve opens the lower end of the supply pipe to the atmosphere while the tank pressure's up and pump is off. All plumbing exposed to freezing is drained until pressure switch calls for water and starts pump: solenoid valve closes, providing path to tank. Cost of materials for our 150′ run? Andrews estimates around $100 *plus* sump excavation.

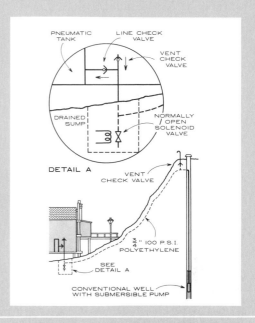

And to keep water flowing in the underfloor lines

Because of those house-line freeze-ups I mentioned at the end of the text, I sent off for 30 feet of a unique heat cable called Frostex to trace the underfloor waterlines at the Lockbox. Though the underside of this pole house is insulated and weatherclosed, the runs shown in the photo and sketch froze at −20°. They never will again.

After dropping weatherboard and fiberglass batts, I found it a simple matter to feed the cable through the joist holes, snugging it to the bare pipes every 12 inches with vinyl tape. Wrapping the valves (inset) is especially easy with this material since—unlike conventional heat cable—it can cross itself without damage. Tracing completed, I wrapped the entire run with fiberglass strips, then replaced insulation and weatherboard.

The flat cable in our photo—and the straight-line attachment in our sketch—were a prototype installation. The cable that has now been put on the market—called Frostex II—is round, and is spiraled around the pipe run. For installation tips (and where-to-buy), write Raychem Corp., Consumer Div., 2201 Bay Rd., Redwood City, Calif. 94063.

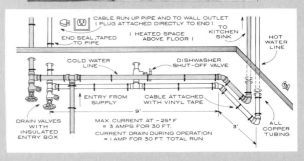

15. Aerobics: The Waste System for Leisure Homes

What's the biggest problem in siting a leisure home "away from it all"? You're away from municipal sewers, too. And as vacation parcels get scarcer, they move ever farther into areas of "unbuildable land." One of the reasons nobody's built there before is that the soil is impermeable—it just won't absorb the flow from a septic tank.

Since the last thing a leisure-home builder wants is to foul his own nest, an alternate sewage-disposal system is a prime consideration—one that provides fast, efficient, *on-site* treatment of organic wastes. That system: aerobics. This relatively new sewage-treatment principle is just the reverse of a septic system. With the latter, you seal a holding tank from air so that *anaerobic* bacteria can break down the solid wastes. But it takes a long time and isn't fully effective, so a smelly effluent must be discharged underground into a leach field large enough to avoid quick clogging of the soil with untreated particles. Solids left in the tank must be periodically pumped out and hauled away.

Our entire system arrived on car trailer: tank is 6' fiberglass sphere; note optional drain provision at rear, and plastic hose coiled around shoulder, for connecting to sand filter. After startup, top photo, author lifts lid to check turbulence within cone.

None of this was practical at the Lock-box, which stands on a mountain far below any access road, on a site consisting of boulders held together by clay. Excavation for any type of tank was impractical.

It's still possible you'll encounter some resistance to aerobics on the part of local sanitation authorities—and even remote sites, where no building permit or inspections may be required, are likely to be covered by sanitary codes. We encountered strictures against locating a waste tank under a house—intended, of course, to prevent burying a *septic* tank where it couldn't be serviced. Some local codes even state that a tank must be a specified distance from the house. To install an aerobic tank as shown here you'd have to apply for an experimental permit.

Not that aerobic tanks are intended for above-ground use; in most installations, they're buried, just like septic tanks, but fed air from a remote compressor. For that's how the system operates: You bubble the tank's contents to break up solids and, at the same time, charge the fluid with air so that a whole different set of micro-organisms—a type that thrives on oxygen—is brought to bear on the organic particles. Ironically, these bacteria—barred from septic systems—are far more efficient at consuming waste than anaerobic types.

If you decide on a freestanding tank like ours, shown here, it's best to prop it with 2x4s wedged under its center rim (one prop per pair of ribs should be plenty). The tank, when filled, weighs nearly 4000 pounds. With a buried tank, this weight is supported by the surrounding earth; but in aboveground installa-

Empty tank is light enough to wrestle to inaccessible site. Here, trailer drops it 150' to Lock-box via rope played out through bumper of car parked at top.

tions, the weight could cause the tank to squat. This would be especially critical if you ordered your tank with the bottom-drain connection shown in our photos. It's one of the bonuses of aboveground installation—you can drain the tank at any time (for winter closure of your house, for example) by opening the bottom valve. This option, ordered by your contractor, may run about 15% extra.

Prefab insulated walls of shed are erected on 8'-square slab; tank will be set in place, front wall added. Left foreground: fiberglass distribution box.

Inside shed: 2x4 props, through-slab drain, and compressor with air hoses.

Another aboveground bonus: You can control the heat of a tank for winter usage. We do this with a wall-mounted electric heater, thermostated at 60°—optimum temperature for aerobic bacterial action. The heater also warms the shed air the compressor sucks on.

To avoid or minimize any external heat requirement, you could wrap the tank snugly in 4″- to 6″-thick fiberglass insulation. The bacterial process within the tank generates its own heat, so if you can retain this heat, an external source becomes unnecessary. If you *do* install a heater (as we did), you'll want to insulate

FRP sphere of Cromaglass Model CA-450—for small-home use, ideal for tucking under front corner of our pole house—is compartmented for various stages of treatment. Wastes flow into central cone (A) where turbulence—created by bottom air outlet—breaks up and partially oxidizes solids. Only reduced-size particles pass into secondary treatment chamber (B). Filter bag is coated with activated bacterial sludge that consumes solids. Only liquids with tiny dissolved particles pass through (into C) for discharge into drain field.

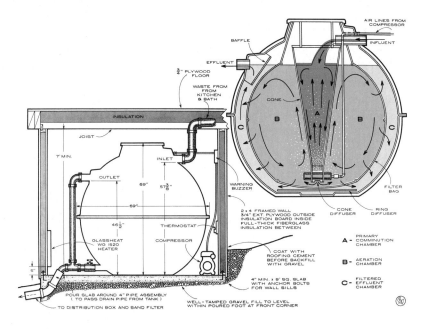

the concrete slab (as we did not) before placing the tank. Though the walls and ceiling of our compact enclosure are insulated, the ground temperature plunged enough, one winter, to form ice inside the bottom of the tank.

We rigged our compressor to a timer for controlled operation. The manufacturer of our system—Cromaglass Corp., Box 3215, Williamsport, Pa. 17701—doesn't recommend this, preferring the compressor to run constantly while the house is in use, though they claim there's no need to run it when you leave the house for more than a day; you just unplug it. Even if you try it our way, it's a good idea to put a manual override switch into the circuit so that at

Sketches show subsurface drain designed for our installation by Cromaglass engineer to meet local requirements on discharge of effluent near brook. Field was laid by novice crew with minimal excavation for walled trough (see section) which was then half filled with sand (lower photo). Next, stone for drainpipe layer was brought down mountain in sheet-metal chute held between logs (upper photo). Backfill was mounded on top. Job was done entirely by hand in one day at cost of $300.

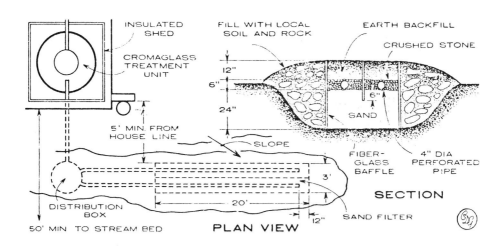

INSULATED SHED

CROMAGLASS TREATMENT UNIT

5' MIN. FROM HOUSE LINE

DISTRIBUTION BOX

50' MIN. TO STREAM BED

PLAN VIEW

SLOPE

3'

20'

12"

FILL WITH LOCAL SOIL AND ROCK

EARTH BACKFILL

CRUSHED STONE

12"

6"

24"

6"

SAND

FIBER-GLASS BAFFLE

4" DIA PERFORATED PIPE

SECTION

SAND FILTER

times of heavy sewage you have the constant-aeration option. Our rule of thumb for timed operation: Never run the compressor less than 12 hours in each 24 that the system's in use. We have our timer set to run it from 9 a.m. to noon, 4 to 7 p.m., and midnight to 6 a.m. But when we leave the house we set those on-times back further, for a total of about 8 hours. We've never tried the total shut-off—even for extended absences—because we feared the system would go septic and the aerobic culture would perish.

Before you go aerobic, either be sure you can service your own system, or that the manufacturer has a servicing contractor within a reasonable distance. Cromaglass' N.S.F. Seal of Approval depends on provision for prompt servicing by their growing national network of dealers, and there's a warning alert built in.

Costs for an aerobic installation (using Cromaglass' Model CA-450) should run around $2000 to $2500, depending on local conditions—and the degree of enlightenment of local sanitation codes. Since the aerobic process is demonstrably more effective than the septic, disposal-field requirements should be far lower. Aerobic decomposition of organic solids takes about four hours—against 70 *days* required by anaerobic bacteria. Some enthusiasts claim that aerobics reduce soil-absorption requirements to one-third of a septic system's! Which saves cash on a drain-field installation—if you can convince local authorities to approve it. They should be more knowledgeable now than when we built, since the passage of a new Clean Water Act, at the end of 1977, specified federal grants for certain installations of on-site aeration systems.

Our model CA-450 will process 200 gallons of influent per day—ideal for a small leisure home like the Lockbox. But for a house that's regularly used by a family of four or more, that frequently overflows with guests and has full laundry facilities, you'll want a unit with greater capacity. Cromaglass' Model CA-5 (a horizontal cylinder rather than a sphere—about 6' high, 8½' long) will handle the largest year-round home. There's an added advantage for winter use: Submerged pumps help keep the water warm, for best bacterial action. They're quieter than an exposed compressor, too. The CA-5 utilizes a settling tank in place of the filter bag. Solids that settle here are voided back to the big aeration chamber for reprocessing; at the same time, clarified effluent is pumped from the system (50 to 75 gals. per batch, so this is termed a batch-treatment process in contrast to the more-or-less continuous flow of the CA-450 system). In some areas, effluent may be surface-discharged, and used for irrigation.

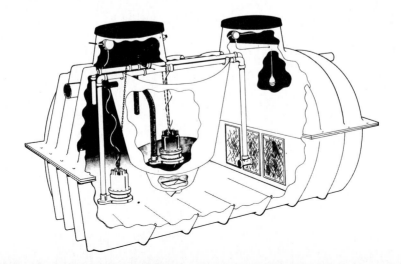

16. Security Electronics for Leisure Homes

A remote second home—especially one set in deep woods like our Lockbox—is vulnerable to damage from natural forces, as well as unnatural ones like thieves and vandals. Even with all the security concepts we've designed into the house—such as closure shuttering that leaves no glass exposed (Chapter 4) and the removable bridge that puts a gap between the 10'-high catwalk and the entry door (Chapter 5)—we've availed ourselves of current technology to add three types of *electronic* protection. Take your pick:

MOVIE-CAMERA SENTRY

Activated by the weight of any intruder who pauses at the front door, it captures on film all attempts at unauthorized entry. If you find something amiss on your next visit, you'll have a record of any callers during your absence.

Surveillance camera records visits while you're away. Mounted in attic, special movie camera spies through tiny window at home's only entry. At right, I'm loading camera with standard super-8 cartridge prior to screwing down pivot mount (comes with camera) as shown in lower photo. Cover (below mount) can be added for protection and soundproofing. I've applied tape stripe as gauge for repositioning camera after future reloads: When aligned with stud, angle is right for field of view at far right, showing culprit attempting entry. This shot was made through spy window. Can you spot it in top photo?

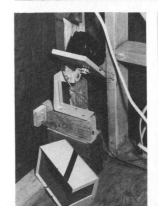

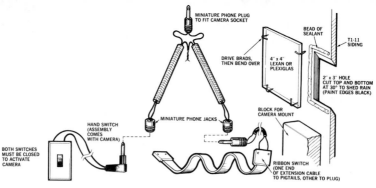

Two aspects of the installation you must work out yourself: mounting the camera and attaching dual-control switches. One male and two female connectors (to match those on camera and hand-switch supplied) are wired as shown to make up a series circuit. This yoke then plugs into camera socket.

The hookup is simple, and the only modification of the equipment I bought from Kodak is the series circuit sketched above. Ordinarily, the on-off switch Kodak supplies plugs into the camera for remote control. To make the system automatic, I added an exterior ribbon switch in series with this hand switch, running extensions from the Y at the camera to both controls. (There's no polarity to the circuit, so it doesn't matter which switch plugs into which socket of the Y.)

Keep the hand switch near the entry door: Flicking it off when you arrive deactivates the system until you switch it on, when departing.

To mount the waterproof ribbon switch along the top edge of a catwalk stringer, we nailed the spaced 2x6 crossplanks to the *opposite* stringer only, letting the free ends rest on the switch. To anchor these ends, yet allow the essential up-and-down movement, I drilled out holes larger than the body of the galvanized 16d nails, then drove these nails flush after inserting a spacer shim temporarily beneath each plank.

The weight of the planks alone is insufficient to activate the switch, but the added weight of a person turns on the attic camera. It's run by four AA-size alkaline batteries; to avoid the nuisance of

changing them, Kodak offers a handy voltage converter as an accessory. It slips into the battery cavity and plugs into any household outlet.

Ribbon switches come in lengths from 2 to 5 feet. The length needed for our catwalk depended on how many planks we wished to activate; we decided five was plenty to cover the limited field of view of our setup, so we ordered a custom 30-in. length. If you'll settle for less, a standard 2' length is still cheaper. Specify "waterproof" to assure that your switch will have a solid-conductor lead (18" long) to seal out moisture. And use outdoor two-wire cable for your connection back into the house.

The camera comes with a mounting tray and multipivot bracket that lets you aim it accurately. The tiny window our lens peeks through can be spotted in one of our photos—if you search—and is detailed in a sketch. It's inconspicuous and weathertight, but don't locate a window in so inaccessible a spot that you can't wipe it clean occasionally.

The soundproof cover that comes with the camera isn't essential for our installation, but it keeps the camera cleaner.

All standard super-8 film cartridges fit this camera. I've tried both Kodachrome 40 and Ektachrome 160. The latter—outdoor ASA 100—extends exposure latitude into dusk. If you want to go even faster, you can buy super-8 black-and-white film—but you may have to process it yourself. (The camera is, alas, a sleeping watchdog at night—but most unauthorized entries of remote leisure homes are attempted in daylight. If you want to add a spotlight to the system, see the next chapter.)

Kodak tells me that their super-8 security cameras will soon be phased out, because of a shrinking market for them (see "You're on your own" box that follows). One of the major sources for sales—banks—has largely turned to 16mm cameras because many courts now require evidence to be in this larger format. This development is too bad, since it pretty much removes photographic security from the home market. If you have to go to a security-systems dealer for your camera, you'll probably have to spend in the $500 range—a dubious investment for second-home protection.

REMOTE INTERCOM

Since a leisure home is for getting away from it all, you may not welcome abrupt surprise visits. For a small investment you can equip your site with a security intercom that invites *all* callers to announce themselves from a weatherproof remote station, giving you a chance to compose yourself—or your house—before they're on your doorstep.

The system shown used to be available from Sears for $30; it included a master station, outdoor remote and 50' of wire; an extra 100' roll was $5. The master is powered from any 110-volt outlet; plug it in when you arrive at the house, but leave its switch in the off position (the call sig-

Intercom identifies caller from remote station. Unexpected guest—my niece Pat—announces arrival from remote station mounted on jamb of garage door, some distance from house; my reply from master (just inside entry) gains me few minutes to towel off from shower. Note master plugs into wall outlet.

nal from the remote is inoperable if the master is switched on).

When the buzzer sounds, you flick the switch and press a big talk button to answer. Conversational flow is then controlled from the master: push to speak, release to listen. The tone over our 150' buried line—we ran it in our waterline trench (Chapter 14)—is of surprising quality, far better than a telephone.

I've found only one disadvantage to the system: Since it's designed to replace a conventional doorbell, it's equipped with a one-way signal only. The master has no "call" button; so in our setup, to alert someone we think may be near the remote station (at the garage), we have to shout over the line.

The lightweight plastic case of the remote unit has holes at the back that clip over mounting screws, so it's easy to detach and store inside the garage when I'm not in residence.

Sears hasn't cataloged this fine little unit for several years now, so you'd have to hunt up an equivalent at local electronics outlets. As with the security camera, if you must go to an elaborate $350 or $400 intercom system, the leisure home application probably no longer makes sense.

SMOKE DETECTOR

Another device for your security *while in residence* is a smoke detector. Fatal fires usually start small and sneaky, while you're asleep; an early-warning alarm gives you those extra minutes that make a life-or-death difference.

Old-style thermal detectors are of limited value as house alarms, since they sound only when the fire is well established. Sleeping occupants may already have succumbed to smoke inhalation, or will find themselves trapped by flames.

The alarm we chose—Guardion model R-1X—was the first on the market to feature dual-chamber ionization. Each chamber has two charged plates and an alpha source that ionizes air molecules, causing a constant flow of current between plates. When combustion products reach the outer sensing chamber, they impede the flow of ions; the voltage shift triggers the alarm. (The sealed inner chamber compensates for atmospheric changes, stabilizing the detector at all temperature/humidity levels.)

The alarm is triggered before there's visible smoke or noticeable heat—and it sounds as long as combustion products are present. When the air clears, the alarm stops; there's no resetting needed to ready it for duty again.

The unit requires no maintenance beyond an occasional whisk with a vacuum-cleaner brush. Its remote transformer plugs into any wall outlet, offering flexibility of installation, since its low-voltage cord can be stapled along a baseboard (20 feet are supplied; you cut it to the length you need).

You can test the unit with a puff of tobacco smoke. It's so sensitive it has sounded several times, over the years—while we were grilling chicken downstairs. Since the house features an open kitchen plan, we elected to mount our detector over the head of the bed, upstairs (see photo, page 336), rather than in the hallway *outside* the bedroom, as the manufacturer suggests. The latter would give an earlier warning and assure an escape route, but it would also be more vulnerable to false alarms since the hall is up an open stair from the kitchen.

That tiny red indicator lamp is the last thing I see as I drop off each night. And since I'm a heavy sleeper, it's comforting to know—here in the middle of my forest—that a guard remains alert for the first sign of fire, indoors or out.

MATERIALS

Monitor security camera: around $310
Eastman Kodak Co., Customer Relations, Graphic Data Market, 343 State St., Rochester, N.Y. 14650, can tell you which dealers still handle the camera

Ribbon switch, 131-AMT
Tapeswitch Corp. of America, 320 Broad Hollow Rd., Farmingdale, N.Y. 11735

Wire-type intercom system
Sears, Roebuck & Co. (see text)

Smoke and fire detector
Many makes at hardware or houseware stores

Burglary protection for a leisure home? You're on your own

For over seven years, now I've done much to promote the concept of "second home" construction. Thousands of *Popular Science* readers have built from our plans, on typically remote sites.

So it's with a sense of responsibility that I face up here (and in the following chapter) to the unhappy truth that the bouquet of delights to be found in leisure-home ownership may include a few thorns.

You may, alas, have already found this out for yourself—as I have. The most painful thorn for any leisure-home owner is the appalling rise in burglaries nationwide—up more than 30 percent in the last five years. An isolated, part-time home is especially vulnerable, and statistics indicate that if yours has not yet been attacked, your odds are swiftly narrowing. An estimate from a new U.S. Dept. of Justice publication indicates that, if the trend continues, one out of every four homes will be burglarized within the next three years. Burglary is the most frequent crime in the U.S.: A house is smashed into every 12 seconds.

"It's no longer a question of *whether* you'll become a victim," says the booklet,* "but only a matter of *when*."

So there's some urgency about choosing the hardware that will offer the most effective protection. Good locks are relatively inexpensive, but electronic gear comes high. As an example, let's evaluate two wholly different approaches to security that involve similar investments:

● There's a story behind the filmstrip at the right. It's from a Kodak super-8 security camera set up to monitor a leisure-home entry. The camera is triggered by someone pausing at the door as described in this chapter—an effective means of recording visits while the house (at an isolated site) is shuttered. The full reel shows repeated visits by the culprit to try this securely locked door.

* *Home Security, Book One: Basic Techniques of Home Guardianship* is first in a series. *Book Two: The Burglary Game* shows how to assess the vulnerability of your home. *Three: Choose a Good Lock* completes the series. For copies, write Law Enforcement Assistance Adm., Washington, D.C. 20531.

The owners of this monitored home, arriving as usual the following weekend, routinely checked the camera and made a note that the film had advanced. The weekend after that, they arrived to find the door battered in, the house stripped of over $3,500 worth of equipment and furnishings.

The Pennsylvania State Police officer summoned to the scene urged the owners to rush the film to a lab and file it with the local barracks. *File* was the right term: The police never made any use of the film, or blow-ups from it later provided at the owners' considerable expense.

Although this investment in a surveillance system proved worthless (despite the camera's good performance) your own situation may be different. Perhaps you are lucky enough to have bought your site in an area where law-enforcement officers take their jobs seriously and will make proper use of sophisticated tools.

● An intrusion-alarm system, complete, can be purchased for about the same price. (The Midex we tested for the following chapter is $200, plus $80 for two blast horns; if you add perimeter switches, you've matched the camera cost).

With intrusion-detection gear, however, your purpose is quite different: You're less

concerned with apprehension than with prevention. You're hoping that the jolting discovery that they've been detected will send burglars packing. There can be another important advantage to these alarm systems. Assuming you have resident neighbors within the reach of the siren, it pays you to cultivate them in an effort to set up a community security network. Tell them how your system works, encourage them to install one of their own so you can return the monitoring favor.

One result may be to *force* a response from local police, who otherwise (in our experience) often regard "summer people" as a nuisance burden. When a law-enforcement officer receives an emergency call from an alerted neighbor, he knows there's a "witness"—a citizen he has to answer to in addition to the victim. This is often enough extra pressure to make him perform at least a token investigation—and even this can act as a local deterrent to further crime.

Whatever the hardware you choose, don't expect too much from state police or the county sheriff. Burglary arrests in recreational areas have plunged below 10 percent, largely because local authorities too often treat leisure-home owners as second-class citizens, at the bottom of local priorities.

In researching the chapter that follows, I've often had State Police or County Sheriff shrug and say: "You gotta expect this if you're not there all the time." When I ask if someone's in *their* home every hour of day and night, their eyes glaze over. It's just not the same: They're *citizens*, after all, and their houses are *home*. It matters not at all that your sweat-equity investment in your retreat doubtless makes it more precious to you than where they hang their hat is to them. It matters even less that your property taxes support the schools their kids attend. They're not impressed that you probably spend more waking hours in and around your retreat than they devote to their homes, or that you most likely plan to retire there and thus are—potentially—a member of their community. The years of sweat and savings you've lavished on your labor of love can be jeopardized by a slack-jawed punk cutting a midweek high school class, and the "law" probably won't care. Where mounting crime

statistics are concerned, many local law officers are no longer part of the *solution*—they've become part of the *problem*. Whether through indifference or ineptitude, they encourage criminal activity by their inaction.

Since becoming a victim myself (see next chapter), I find two clichés about home security especially repellent. Some people tell you they make it deliberately easy for housebreakers to gain entry—espcially at a frequently unoccupied "summer place." The theory (which they can usually back up with case histories of how it's worked for them) is that if you don't frustrate the robbers by barring their way, they'll spare you their worst offenses. Thus these homeowners put only the flimsiest lockset on the door and prop a welcoming note in a conspicuous place, asking only that the intruder respect the property and leave it as he found it. I wince at such recitations of craven irresponsibility and the climate of permissiveness to which they contribute.

The other bit of advice that raises my homeowner hackles—and this is consistently heard from police: "If you approach your home and find evidence of a break-in, run away to avoid confrontation." Such advice is both well-meaning and supercilious: The assumption is that only a trained law officer can deal with a miscreant caught in the act. Yet I find the cowardice that's being recommended wholly unpalatable.

Such mincing attitudes toward property and toward the inviolable rights of any man to enjoy control of his own home are contributing factors to our soaring burglary rate. Unless homeowners are willing to stand firm and defend those rights—and demand that local law-enforcement agencies back them up in that defense—burglary will reach a level where civilized living is no longer possible in this country—and especially in this country's *country*. My own experience suggess that we homeowners may have to break a few heads before we get this point across to crook and cop and court alike.

Meanwhile, with a leisure home you're on your own. So roll up your sleeves and start beefing up your built-in security. The time is already upon us when a man's home is not his castle but his fortress.

17. Beefing Up Your Burglary Protection

Guarding your leisure home from theft presents special problems that don't apply to conventional homes. First off: Forget the advice we've all heard for years about burglary protection. Very few of those hoary old cautions apply to leisure homes. Most of them come from neighborhood police: Leave lights on when you're absent, preferably on an automatic timer. . . . Leave windows and doors locked so burglars will pass you by rather than risk the racket necessary to break in. . . . Stop newspaper and milk deliveries while you're gone, to avoid giving the house an unoccupied look. . . . Avoid a privacy-wall or shrubbery screen at windows and doors so any activity there will be exposed to passersby. . . . Avail yourself of the best alarm system: a large watchdog.

All such advice assumes that the home in question is only rarely vacant, is in a peopled neighborhood, and is subject to at least an occasional visual check by police patrol. But none of these hints is of the slightest use to a leisure home in a secluded or remote area. There, the home-owner's efforts must be devoted to *securing*—literally—the house against attack. The task is much more difficult, and the techniques are usually quite different.

In most cases, you're not dealing with professional burglars—those crooks who pride themselves on their skill at circumventing locks and alarms. Here your enemies are more likely to be brutal house-*breakers*, who needn't concern themselves about alerting close neighbors, and who are likely to have the op-portunity and time to force their way in. Now, let's admit at once that *no* structure, short of a concrete vault with a steel door, can keep out a musclebound moron determined to break in. But you can make it as risky and effortful and unnerving a job as possible; and since most of the criminals who prey on leisure homes will be after the laziest pickin's, you stand a good chance of being spared.

In what follows, we're dealing only with *vacated* homes. It's rare for a leisure home in a remote area to be attacked while occupied, so we won't concern ourselves with panic alarms, protective weapons, or guard dogs—none of which are operable while you're absent, whether for a few days, a few weeks, or over the winter. Everything we propose stands guard while you're gone.

As we've said, "Make the home look occupied!" is standard advice for primary dwellings, but this can be ludicrous with a vacation retreat. Such a house is usually shuttered while vacant to protect it from storms and casual vandalism. And at any rate, in isolated areas, local thieves may have a pretty fair reading on your comings and goings. What could be more laughable to them than a house standing in lonely grandeur in the midst of an untracked, week-old snowfield with carefully programmed lights marching from room to room?

In facing the question of leisure-home security, there's one decision you don't have to make, and that's *whether* to beef it up. Unless your retreat is that vault I spoke of, you'd better. Crimes against lei-sure homes are already epidemic and bound to get worse for the next few years, until the percentage of our population between the ages of 14 and 25 drops back to normal. Crime statistics agree that this age group commits 85 percent of all home burglaries.

Also, the "take" is more tempting than it used to be. Until our post-war affluence, relatively few families had much worth stealing. And only in recent years have leisure homes become more than rustic retreats. Finally, the soaring statistics re-flect a steady decline in the quality of lo-cal law enforcement (see box at end of previous chapter).

Burglary and vandalism are no longer peculiarly urban crimes. They've spread across the countryside like the plague, and many tranquil country towns where nobody used to lock a door now sport higher crime rates than most cities.

These are all reasons why there's better than a 50–50 chance your leisure home will be ripped off this year or next—unless you take steps now to prevent this mis-fortune.

I speak from bitter experience, since—irony of ironies—the Lockbox itself has been the victim of an attack that left it stripped of everything that could be car-ried away, including all the power tools we'd used in construction! The irony here is that the Lockbox was designed around the idea of security against break-in, as we've stressed throughout this book.

While most of our systems functioned, a security chain is only as strong as its weakest link. This proved to be our entry door, which also turns out to be the prime entry point for burglaries by the 18-or-younger age group. The ease with which

our burglars smashed through demon-strates my first major point: the myth of the 1″ deadbolt.

DOOR LOCKS

At the time I was choosing the windows and doors for the Lockbox, major door-lock makers were launching a cam-paign—endorsed by law-enforcement agencies—to promote installation, on all entry doors, of deadbolts with a full-inch throw. Crime statistics bear out that most burglars look for entries that have only key-in-knob locksets. Even when such a lock resists the old plastic charge-card ploy, the short, tapered latch tongue is easily popped free of the strike plate by springing the jamb with a crowbar. This shortcoming also applies to stubby dead-bolts that enter their strike plates only a half-inch or so.*

"Much safer," went the promotion, "to install a deadbolt that extends a full inch into the jamb." This is perfectly true, *if* your jamb is sturdy enough. In the case of the Lockbox (and, I'd guess, of most other leisure homes) the entry door came pre-hung in a softwood frame. I secured this finish frame solidly within the rough opening, but the "high-security" com-bination lockset I bought came with a conventional surface-mounted strike plate. Even though I replaced the absurdly short mounting screws with ones that would pass through the finish frame and on into the doubled stud behind, it proved a simple matter for the thugs to

* The difference between a latchlock and a deadbolt: A tapered, spring-loaded latch closes and locks into a strike automatically when door is closed; a deadbolt must be turned into its strike by means of a key (from the outside) or knob (from inside).

pry and kick the door until the wood frame and studs splintered. The combo lockset stood up to this impact beautifully and is still performing—a credit to the lock maker, but not much compensation to me. Latch and bolt simply carried the strike-plate—still attached to the splintered jamb—inside with them.

So your full-inch deadbolt isn't much protection unless it passes into a heavy metal frame, or unless you reinforce your wooden jamb with steel mending plates. Or unless you apply one of the newer strike plates that wraps around the jamb and mounts with extra-long screws driven from two directions.

Even so, clustering a latch and dead-bolt puts an immense strain on one small, central area of the strike jamb when tension or impact is applied to the panel. The panel, too, may give at its unattached corners since its opening edge is only held at a small midpoint (the separation between a clustered lockset and deadbolt is often only 3 to 3½ inches). Wider separation spreads the stress. You can achieve this by installing new (and separately keyed) deadbolts toward the top and bottom corners of the door panel—as far apart as family members find handy.

Even more effective—especially if you suspect an easily splintered jamb—is a floor-brace device such as that made by Fox Police Lock and shown in our photos. It's quick to install but somewhat clumsy to use, especially in our dead-end entry hall, where you must climb over the bar after setting it in place. As you open the door to exit, the bar rides up within a hoop. It drops back down into lockable position when you close the door from outside. The brace lifts out for easy storage on re-entry.

A pry and a kick, and the punk is in (top photo)—or is he? Inside this leisure-home entry, surprises await him: A slant-bar lock has been added above the key-knob/deadbolt combo (below), to prevent easy break-in. And a reed switch will trigger an ear-splitting alarm if he does succeed in forcing this massive door. If he enters elsewhere, a microwave detector will sound the same alarm.

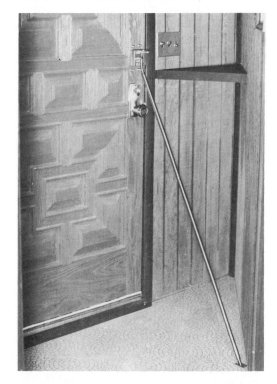

It's easier to install a brace lock than a strike-plate lock. After measuring 30″ at right angle from base of door, counter-sink floor socket. Place bar in socket and set base of lock plate against tip as shown. Mark socket for cylinder hole and drill through door with 1¼″ bit. Insert cylinder from outside, securing it to base of block with bolts through door. Note that tip of bar bears against cast lug on base. Key will move it into this position from outside. Jimmy-proof cylinder cover (exterior photo at right) is recommended.

We haven't even considered, here, that the entry door of your leisure home might have only a key-in-knob lockset. In tests, these have been forced in under ten seconds. If you have such a lock, replace it.

We've also assumed that your entry has a solid panel door. In a remote location, you should never install an entry with glass panels—either in the door or as a sidelight. If you're stuck with such an arrangement, you'll need a deadbolt that's keyed on both sides, so that if a burglar smashes a pane he can't reach through and release it.

INTRUSION ALARMS

As I said, a determined hood can smash through virtually anything. Assuming he's dumb enough to persist, even after learning you've made it tough for him, it's best to have a backup alarm. Unless he can locate and silence it quickly, it's likely to drive him off. For top psychological impact, you need a siren or blast horn inside, and one mounted at the highest point of the roof, or weather-protected inside an attic vent. No burglar is going to stay long with all that commotion.

There are several types of intrusion alarms—each of which assumes that the burglar makes it past a locked window or door. Some depend on an elaborately wired system of perimeter switches to trigger an alarm if a door or window is forced. (There are also similar systems with battery-powered *wireless* switches that beam a radio signal to a central receiver.) A surface-mounted switch is fine for a solid door, since it can't be spotted from the outside. For windows, plunger-type switches, recessed into the frame (and thus invisible) are best.

There's a bonus for the leisure-home owner in a perimeter switch installation. You often close up such a home in the dark, or in the confusion of departing house guests, and you may miss closing and locking a vulnerable window or door. If it's equipped with a switch, once you arm your alarm, it alerts you, loud and clear, to your oversight.

Install a perimeter alarm to guard windows and doors and back it up with tear gas.

Perimeter system consists of magnetic reed switches mounted on entry doors and accessible windows and wired in series (with standard speaker wire) through a keyswitch, transformer, and relay to an alarm. Our installation uses mechanical siren shown above (its long-range howl is ideal for remote sites). Mount it at the highest point of the house, as in our photo of a peak installation: Siren sets on shelf inside hole screened with hardware cloth; hood keeps out snow and rain. Reed switches (those shown are from Universal) are installed in pairs: Magnetic half attaches to movable part—door panel or window sash—and powered half screws to frame. When door is shut, switch keeps siren unpowered.

BurglarMist unit can be mounted near any entry door so that trip cord pulls out lever in its side, discharging canister of CN gas. If direct connections shown in the sketches don't work, pass trip cord through screweye or (as in photo) nearby hardware.

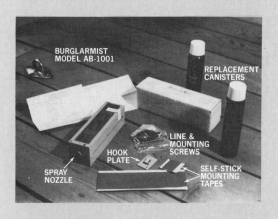

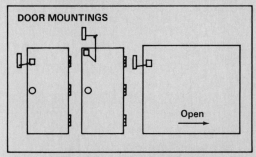

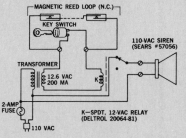

Microwave intrusion detector sounds alarm indoors and out

It looks like a hi-fi shelf component—the Midex 55 on the lower step, below. But when set to beam across a critical path inside your home, and armed by one of the magnetic keys in the foreground, it will yelp for help when an intruder steps into range. Transformer (left) plugs into any 115-V outlet. Mount a horn at highest point of house (on Lockbox, that's atop pole extending above the roof, lower right). Second horn goes indoors to blast intruders out. We ceiling-mounted it next to our smoke detector (below right).

A bonus advantage of the Midex is its capability of tying into existing or additional security systems. Note extra rear-panel connections in photo. If you have (or want) reed switches on doors and windows, just wire this loop to first pair of posts. (Other posts are for panic-button loop, speakers in parallel, transformer input.) *Popular Science* Electronics Editor Bill Hawkins created circuit diagram shown for add-on control box that customizes the Midex to the Lockbox: It feeds our previous system (mat switch, actuated by weight of anyone pausing at entry, starts Monitor camera) into Midex blast-horn and battery-backup circuits. Wired into our reed-switch loop, timer control adds an outdoor spotlight to capture a nighttime visit on film and also sounds alarm. (Electric-eye override avoids horn-blast greeting for daytime callers.) All components called out are available from Williams Electronic Supply, 1863 Woodbridge Ave., Edison, N.J. 08817. This add-on circuitry in no way affects the intrusion functions already built into the Midex.

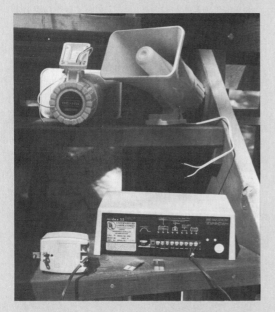

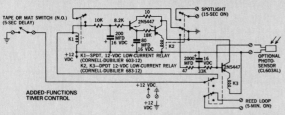

Various commercial systems detect the actual bodily presence of an intruder, either by means of a broken beam of infrared light or by filling a critical area with unseen "waves" that "read" his body mass. These can be ultrasonic sound waves or RF (radio-frequency) micro-waves.

While trying to decide which system to install at the Lockbox, I spotted an ad in *Popular Science* headlined "Burglar Alarm Breakthrough" which described the Midex 55 as "a new motion-sensing computer . . . so advanced that it doesn't require installation."

A bit of research revealed that Midex is the Consumer Products Division of Solfan Systems Inc.—the major manufacturer of microwave intrusion-detection systems for commercial applications. The 55 contains a directional transceiver of the same type used by the U.S. Treasury to protect currency. It responds only to physical motion, and its beamed pattern is adjustable from maximum range (50-ft. length, 20-ft. width, 10-ft. height) down to only several feet.

Once adjusted, the range remains stable, even in extremes of heat and cold. And since leisure homes are especially subject to power failure (and vulnerable to electric-line cutting), the Midex's battery backup makes it ideal for these locations.

Trial-and-error testing to determine best location and range for your unit is done in a disarmed mode—before you hook up the blast horns. A test light flashes on to indicate when an alarm *would* be triggered in the armed mode, so you can check out the unit's total performance without risk of a false alarm.

Most *disadvantages* of a motion-detection system don't apply to a leisure-home situation. When you close the house and arm the system, you needn't worry about the alarm being triggered by your pets or children, since you only arm it in a vacated house. And the one aspect of a microwave beam that can make range-adjustment tricky in a city or town doesn't apply to a remote site: The beam is powerful enough to penetrate windows and some walls, so in built-up areas you must be sure that a passing car or train won't trigger the alarm.

In the country, you only have to concern yourself with a windblown shrub or tree near the house, and I've found that by pulling back the range you can avoid all such hazards at no loss to indoor protection. In the several years I've armed the Midex, every time I closed the house, I've yet to have a false alarm in my absence. (I couldn't, of course, recommend the Midex for any *outdoor* coverage at a country site where the deer and the antelope play.)

The Midex has a broader capability of which I've availed myself. I wired a series of perimeter switches into its delay circuitry, through posts provided on the back of the unit (see photo). This affords a positive back-up: Even if a shrewd intruder was able to foil the perimeter electronics, the minute he steps into the invisible beam inside, he's given himself away. And the alarm continues to shriek for as long as he stays around. Shortly after he makes tracks, it shuts off and the unit resets.

I've one carp. The built-in delay after arming gives you only thirty seconds to get out. If you install a perimeter switch on your exit door, that means you not only have to be out of the microwave range, but out the door, with the reed switch closed behind you. In our installation, this requires a desperate dash.

The Midex people assure me that the delay duration was market-tested, that a half-minute is sufficient for most houses, and that a full minute compromises some homeowners' sense of security by allowing a watchful intruder to slip in while you're exiting. For this unlikely possibility, I've had to become an Olympic sprinter.

Of course, the Midex is only one of many commercial systems available, with more introduced each passing month. As we go to press with this book, two new home security systems have been announced. Although I've seen them demonstrated, I've not installed or tested either. But both seem well suited to leisure-home use.

● From Wells Fargo (8 Ridgedale Ave., Cedar Knolls, N.J. 07927) comes a battery-operated perimeter system with many unique features. The unit that goes on your most vulnerable windows is a seismic sensor that detects motion rather than sound, and reacts to any movement or vibration.

On the entry door you mount a complete-in-itself (no wiring hookups) magnetic switch that can be set to sound its built-in, 90-decibel alarm instantly, or with a delay that lets you identify yourself (or arrival home) by punching in your own three-digit code.

You buy only as much of the system as your house needs: $50 gets you the door unit and one window unit; $100 gets you a unit for both front and back doors, plus three window units. For about $150, you get the two door units and *five* window units, plus a remote unit that plugs into any wall outlet and sounds an alarm in response to the alarm of either a window or door unit. This feature is especially valuable for a remote leisure home, since an intruder could smash and silence the

alarm at the triggered unit, if he persisted in his break-in; but a distant unit sounding elsewhere, at some unknown spot in the house, would doubtless send him packing.

There's also the option of a plug-in outdoor horn that operates the same way as the remote unit. One or both of these adapt the system ideally to unoccupied leisure homes.

● From Universal (see address in the general source list) come several new electronic detection systems with programmable punch dials rather like a push-button telephone. These versatile devices are too complex to describe here; write the manufacturer for a brochure and price list.

TEAR-GAS DETERRENT

One final device for leisure-home security, which I can recommend from personal Lockbox testing, is made by a company whose name forms the shrewdest acronym I've spotted for a while: Security Control Research and Manufacturing. They make a whole family of burglary deterrents, including the BurglarMist Model AB 1001, shown in two of my photos.

It's an ABS housing 2 inches square and 7 inches tall, with a trigger lever in a slot down one face. If this lever is pivoted out, a tear-gas canister inside discharges 4 ounces of a non-toxic CN gas (chloracetophenone) that's such a severe eye-irritant it will drive any intruder from your home. I hooked the devices to the entries of my leisure home, and have been closing up each weekend with a heightened sense of security. If thieves or vandals try to smash in, they'll be greeted not only by a blast from my alarm horns but by a gas that will prevent their entry for several hours—without causing personal injury or harming any interior furnishings. The simple mechanical units I'm using sell for around $25 each and can be installed without tools if you choose the peel-and-stick mounting tape method. I used the screws that are also provided. Three sides of the housing are predrilled so you can point the lever in whichever direction gives best operation. The nozzle can be rotated 360 degrees.

One way of activating the device is by means of a simple trip cord like the one shown. More sophisticated (and costly) models are electronically triggered, some with a built-in time delay. So BurglarMist can be your *only* security device, or can be added to any existing system. Use is restricted only in California and North Carolina.

In the interests of thorough research for this book, I recently tripped the Burglar-Mist I'd installed at the Lockbox—and can attest that its effectiveness is even greater than the manufacturer claims. Unfortunately, warnings and explanations are too scant in the literature provided with the AB-1001. (These instructions are being revised and expanded, so what you receive will doubtless be adequate.) I did my test—it turned out—at a poor time, arriving at the house after dark one winter night. The trip cord pivoted the lever outward, allowing the spring-loaded canister of gas to lift within the housing, depressing its top stem (as with any aerosol dispenser) and sending its full charge of tear gas throughout the house.

Any nearby surface that the gas lights on—a wall, clothing—is marked with large white spots, so a fleeing intruder would be easy to identify—in the unlikely event of fast police response. This spotting dis-

appears within half an hour or so, without damage to the surface.

What I wish I'd realized before my test is (a) there's no way to stop the discharge once it starts and (b) it's much harder to air out affected premises in cold weather. Since the temperature at the time of my test was below freezing, and since I had to leave the door wide open for airing, I had to dash right through the discharge to turn on my heat-trace switches, to prevent waterline freeze-up. As a consequence, I got severe exposure.

If you've ever been gassed, you'll know what a painful experience it is: CN gas will cause violent eye irritation in concentrations as low as *3 parts per million* of air, so you can imagine the effect when you take the blast right in the face. The eyes well with tears in an effort to protect themselves from the contaminant, and the burning pain in eyes and on exposed skin is intense.

The stuff is obviously an ideal deterrent to burglary, because no one would stay around to expose himself to it. In fact, a would-be intruder is likely to injure himself in his haste to escape it. And the effects are not short-lived: The eyes continue to smart for several hours; I bore the evidence of superficial skin irritations for several months.

But if a discharge is painful to an intruder, it is not without inconvenience to the homeowner. BurglarMist instructions indicate that you can dissipate the effect with two hours of thorough airing. But that's at a temperature of 75° or above—fine in the summer when you can fling open every window and turn on every exhaust fan. In a warm, dry house, almost all the material evaporates as it discharges, so it can easily be vented outdoors. But at low temperatures, a much higher percentage of the active ingredient settles out as *dust*, and the evaporation rate is slow.

To return the home to livability under these conditions, you must air out for two hours, then vacuum up the dust, then reheat the house to 75° for two hours *more* and air out again—with a strong fan, if possible.

Lacking this information, I had to sleep both nights of the test weekend in a detached garage—and felt generally "wrung out" the whole time. And even when I returned to the closed house a week later, sufficient irritant was present to make occupancy uncomfortable.

That dust remains a problem. If you go back to the scene of the discharge days later and scrub any residue off walls and floor, the irritation may begin anew.

Recharging the unit with a new spring-loaded canister is relatively easy (you'll have to demount the case and open it); S.C.R.A.M. assures me that the new instructions will cover this procedure.

Considering all this, you may want to avoid any risk of an accidental discharge. If so, I'd suggest you invest a bit more in a newer, more sophisticated model (write manufacturer for price, at address in this chapter's "Sources" list). The AB-1008 virtually eliminates the chance of misfiring. It's a time-delay unit, connected to a tiny piezo buzzer that warns you when the gas is about to be released. If tripped accidentally, such a unit gives you just enough time to deactivate it—though a burglar wouldn't have time to figure out how.

Installation is more complex, of course, since you must wire this unit to a switch (any normally open type, whether magnetic, under-mat ribbon or photo-electric), to a 6-volt battery, and to a warning buzzer.

Does all this seem obsessive? Not—I guarantee—if your treasured leisure home has been violated (yes, burglary is a rape of your most cherished property). And in the two years since I installed these devices—and posted the property that I had done so—I've suffered no further intrusions. (Just as well, for when I pressed the matter of my burglary and its non-investigation right up to the Pennsylvania State Capitol, I found that the Attorney General himself had just been dismissed for improprieties. And as this book goes to press, I learn that the county sheriff I long tried to pressure into action has just been arraigned for his *own*, unrelated misdeeds. See why my lack of confidence in the law-enforcement structure prompts me to reiterate: A leisure-home owner is on his own?)

I hesitated to close this book on so extreme a cautionary note: I like happy endings as much as anyone. But to assure that *you* will have a happy ending to your leisure home adventure, I urge you to give proper consideration to security. After all, your investment of time, cash and energy in a second home may well be the biggest you'll ever make. Protect it well and your rewards will continue—and grow—all the rest of your life. Enjoy!

BIBLIOGRAPHY

Since this book makes no pretense of being a general home-building manual (construction details in Part Two are confined to one unique structure and would not apply to most of the houses shown in Part One), we list below some of the newest and best instruction guides for the owner-builder.

In order to make the listing as useful as possible, we've briefly described each title and given its price at the time this book went to press. Printing costs (like nearly everything else) are rising, and so these prices are offered for comparative use only—they give you an idea of the *range* of prices involved, so you can determine how much of an investment you wish to make.

If you can't find a title you want in local bookstores, write directly to the publisher for ordering information—such as current price and shipping charge.

How to Build Your Own Home by Robert C. Reschke (Structures, 356 pages, $7.95 paperback) is one of the "Successful" instruction manuals, with 500 photos and sketches covering everything from site selection to standard framing techniques to plumbing and electrical work, to carpet laying.

Complete Building Construction (Audel, 800 pages, $19.95) is a typically thorough Audel text that covers every skill and technique involved in erecting and finishing a house—a professional builder's guide written for the layman.

Building Construction Illustrated by Francis D. K. Ching (Van Nostrand Reinhold, 320 pages, $11.95 paperback) is aimed at home designers as well as builders, but covers all aspects from proper siting and foundation work on up.

How to Design, Build, Remodel and Maintain Your Home by Joseph Falcone, AIA (Wiley, 597 pages, $18.95) is an encyclopedia of house building, from site selection through design and construction (over 1000 illustrations).

Natural Solar Architecture by David Wright, AIA (Van Nostrand Reinhold, 244 pages, $8.95 paperback) is a comprehensive guidebook to the passive approach to solar architecture.

Kit Houses by Mail by Brad McDole and Chris Jerome (Stonesong, 206 pages, $14.95) is an excellent catalog of all the kits you can have trucked to your site, if you decide to go the kit route instead of building from scratch. *The Complete Guide to Factory-*

Made Houses by A. M. Watkins (Dutton, 184 pages $8.95, paperback) discusses manufactured alternatives to stickbuilt, site-erected housing: modular, panelized, pre-cut, notched-log and mobile homes.

Garden Way Publishing, up in Vermont, has a number of paperbacks on special construction techniques: *Low-Cost Pole Building Construction* by Doug Merrilees and Evelyn Loveday (112 pages, $5.95); *Build Your Own Low-Cost Log Home* by Roger Hard (208 pages, $7.95); *Build Your Own Stone House* by Karl and Sue Schwenke (144 pages, $5.95); *Building the House You Can Afford* by Stu Campbell (200 pages, $9.95) and *Your Energy-Efficient House* by Anthony Adams, AIA (120 pages, $4.95).

Van Nostrand Reinhold publishes text books for technical schools that are useful for self-teaching basic skills. These include: *The Use of Portable Power Tools* by Leo McDonnell and Alson Kaumeheiwa (256 pages, $8.95); *Electrical Wiring—Residential* by Ray Mullin (272 pages, $11.95); *Basic Plumbing* by Harry Slater and Lee Smith (210 pages, $10.95).

And here are five other Popular Science books (all hardcover) that contain essential information for anyone building his own home (prices subject to change): *DeCristoforo's Housebuilding Illustrated* by R. J. DeCristoforo (644 pages, $16.95); *Basic House Wiring* by Monte Burch (240 pages, $12.50); two by Max Alth: *Do-It-Yourself Plumbing* (320 pages, $12.95) and *Masonry and Concrete Work* (512 pages, $14.95); and, finally, a guide to saving and producing energy in and around your home: *Home Energy How-To* by A. J. Hand (258 pages, $10.95).

All of these titles are distributed to bookstores by Harper & Row, but if you can't find them locally, you can order them from Popular Science Books (BO8A), Box 2033, Latham, NY 12111.

OTHER PUBLISHERS ADDRESSES: **Theodore Audel,** 4300 W. 62 St., Indianapolis, IN 46206; **E. P. Dutton,** 2 Park Ave., New York, NY 10016; **Garden Way Publishing,** 9520 Ferry Rd., Charlotte, VT 05445; **Harper & Row,** 10 East 53rd St., New York, NY 10022; **Stonesong Press,** 51 Madison Ave., New York, NY 10010; **Structures Publishing,** Box 1002 Farmington, MI 48024; **Van Nostrand Reinhold Co.,** 135 W. 50 St., New York, NY 10020; **John Wiley & Sons,** 605 Third Ave., New York, NY 10016.

INFORMATION SOURCES

American Hardboard Assn., 205 West Touhy Ave., Park Ridge, IL 60068

American Plywood Assn., 7011 So. 19 St., Tacoma, WA 98411

American Wood Preservers Institute, 1651 Old Meadow Rd., McLean, VA 22101

Asphalt Institute, College Park, MD 20740 Brick Institute, 1750 Old Meadow Rd., McLean, VA 22101

California Redwood Assn., 1 Lombard St., San Francisco, CA 94111

Manufactured Housing Institute, 1745 Jefferson Davis Hwy., Arlington, VA 22202

Mineral Insulation Mfgs. Assn., 382 Springfield Ave., Summit, NJ 07901

National Burglar & Fire Alarm Assn., 1101 Connecticut Ave. NW, Washington DC 20014

National Concrete Masonry Assn. (block) Box 135, McLean, VA 22101

National Fire Protection Assn., 60 Batterymarch St., Boston MA 02110

National Paint and Coatings Assn., 1500 Rhode Island Ave NW, Washington DC 2005

National Particleboard Assn., 2306 Perkins Pl., Silver Spring MD 20910

National Solar Heating and Cooling Information Center, Box 1607, Rockville, MD 20850

National Water Well Assn., 500 W. Wilson Bridge Rd., Worthington, OH 43085

National Woodwork Mfgs. Assn., 205 W. Touhy Ave., Park Ridge, IL 60068

Portland Cement Assn., Old Orchard Rd., Skokie, IL 60076

Red Cedar Shingle and Handsplit Shake Bureau, 515 116th Ave., Bellevue, WA 98004

Small Homes Council, Univ. of Illinois, 1 E. St. Mary's Rd., Champaign, IL 61820

Tile Council of America, Box 326, Princeton, NJ 08540

Underground Space Center, 11 Mines & Metallurgy Bldg., 221 Church St., Univ. of Minnesota, Minneapolis MN 55455.

Western Wood Products Assn., 1500 Yeon Bldg., Portland, OR 97204